HOLMES:
A SERIAL KILLER'S DOWNFALL

The Holmes-Pitezel Case, updated with 21st–Century additions

FRANK P. GEYER

With Notes And Updates by Matt Lake

This Edition: Copyright © 2017 Parnilis Media

Interstitial notes and appendix: Copyright © 2017 Matt Lake

All rights reserved.

ISBN-13: 9781546759638

ISBN-10: 1546759638

The Holmes-Pitezel Case, 2017 update, written by Frank P. Geyer

Illustrations reproduced from the original HOLMES-PITEZEL CASE published by the Authority of the The District Attorney and Mayor of Philadelphia 1896

and from other sources in the public domain.

New illustrations and photographs courtesy of Matt Lake

Publisher: Alex (Sasha) Parnilis

Editor: Matt Lake
Layout: Morgan Frew
Cover: *Deep Dreams of Holmes* by Ed Garpo

Parnilis Media
P.O. Box 1461
Media, PA 19063

DISCLAIMER BY ALEX (SASHA) PARNILIS
Owner and Publisher of Parnilis Media

H.H. Holmes gives me the creeps. I loathe how slickly he tells his lies. I hate the idea that someone can come across so sympathetically, and yet be so hateful a criminal. That's why I'm glad that my editor Matt Lake decided to publish this book, in which his contemporaries uncovered how vile he was. This book serves as a companion and antidote to to the book he insisted I should publish last year, HOLMES –A SERIAL KILLER IN HIS OWN WORDS.

Of course, I shall never entirely forgive him for forcing my hand to publish that original book in the Parnilis history series, but this is a reasonable cure for the poison of Holmes's unchallenged words. So read on. And if you don't like what you read, blame H. H. Holmes and my editor Matt Lake.

I wash my hands of this whole sordid business.

Sasha (Alex) Parnilis
June 2017

EDITOR'S PREFACE

Last year, I made a bet with Sasha Parnilis, owner and publisher of Parnilis Media, that the public would find some interest in the autobiographical writings of the notorious serial killer H. H. Holmes, ending in his dramatic recanting of all his confessions directly before his death by hanging in 1896.

Mr. Parnilis was blunt in his appraisal. "Nonsense. But if you're convinced of it, I shall give you enough rope to hang yourself. Publish the thing, and I bet you nobody reads it."

A year later, I found myself no fewer than four times in front of NBC-10 news cameras explaining the finer points of H. H. Holmes's confessions, trial, and strange burial. Somehow, 121 years after his execution, 2017 became the year of H. H. Holmes. It was as if he rose from the grave to grab the public attention one more time. In fact, he literally rose from the grave—but you'll have to read the final appendix to this book to learn those details.

This collection of writings about Holmes is a companion to Parnilis Media's 2016 book HOLMES—A SERIAL KILLER IN HIS OWN WORDS. Most of it is drawn from the book *The Holmes-Pitezel Case*, written by Frank Geyer, the detective who brought Holmes to justice. It was inevitable that Geyer would publish his field notes along with the confessions and court documents surrounding the trial. It was necessary too: The only book about the case that existed at the beginning of 1896 was *Holmes's Own Story*, the self-serving memoir by Holmes himself which formed the core of our book HOLMES-A SERIAL KILLER IN HIS OWN WORDS.

For the sake of completeness in this edition, we've added a few details to this book. Frank Geyer's original book is an excellent resource with court documents and first-hand detective work. But like all detectives, he felt his work was done when the conviction was made.

We know that a lot happened in the few months that followed. For one thing, Holmes was executed. We include an eyewitness narrative of that event here.

A few years later, newspapers began circulating a bizarre urban legend that Holmes had faked his death.

And 121 years later, Holmes's descendents petitioned the courts to exhume his body so they could use DNA testing to ensure that their great-grandfather was indeed buried there.

You'll find that information in this edition alone, mostly in contemporary eyewitness accounts. And that includes the 2017 additions about exhuming Holmes's body, because although I wasn't actually in the vault, I did visit the site while he was being dug up, and saw them fill his grave back up again afterwards.

Matt Lake
crash@crashreboot.com
July 2017

The Holmes-Pitezel Case

A

HISTORY

OF THE

Greatest Crime of the Century

AND OF THE

SEARCH FOR THE MISSING PITEZEL CHILDREN

BY

DETECTIVE FRANK P. GEYER

OF THE BUREAU OF POLICE, DEPARTMENT OF PUBLIC SAFETY, OF THE CITY OF PHILADELPHIA

A TRUE DETECTIVE STORY

By permission of the District Attorney and Mayor of the City of Philadelphia

FULLY ILLUSTRATED

PUBLISHERS' UNION
1896

Frontispiece to Frank P. Geyer's original "true detective story," published in part to correct the the fabricated narrative that his nemesis put out in the memoir, *Holmes' Own Story*, published the year before.

District Attorney's Office,
PHILADELPHIA

GEORGE S. GRAHAM,
DISTRICT ATTORNEY.

Feby 4th 1896.

Mr. Frank P. Geyer

My dear Sir:

I cheerfully consent to the publication by you of your proposed book giving a full and complete history of the Holmes-Pitezel case and including that portion of the evidence excluded in Court. The latter part of the history will in itself constitute one of the most marvellous stories of modern times.

Yours Sincerely

George S. Graham
District Attorney of Philadelphia

Endorsement for Frank P. Geyer's narrative from the DA's office. "

> **Office of the Mayor**
> **PHILADELPHIA**
>
> February 7th 1896
>
> Mr. Frank P Geyer
>
> Dear sir :—
>
> I do not object to the publication of your book giving a complete history of the Holmes case one of the most remarkable in the annals of crime.
>
> Yours very respy.
> Chas F. Warwick
> Mayor of Philadelphia

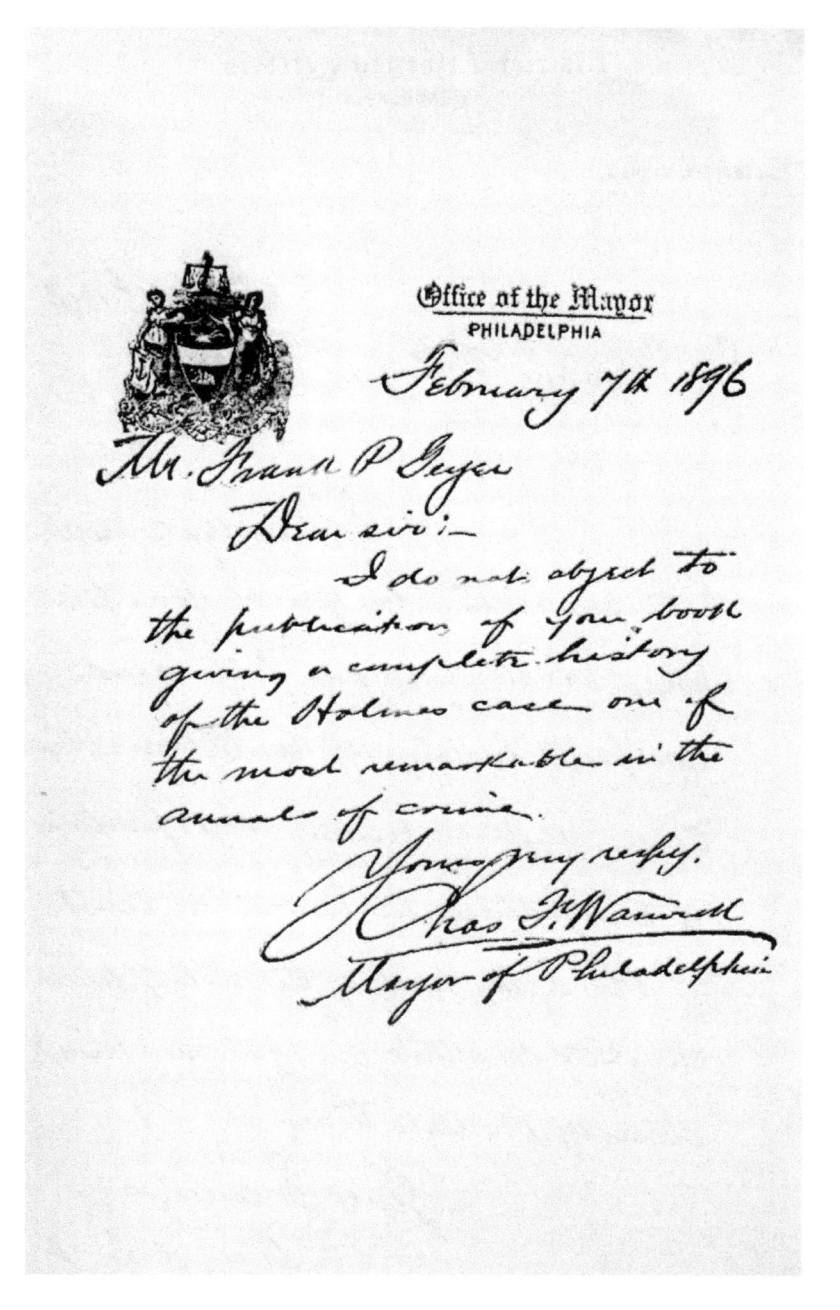

Endorsement for Frank P. Geyer's narrative from the mayor's office.

Very Truly Yours,
Frank. P. Geyer

AUTHOR'S PREFACE TO THE ORIGINAL EDITION.

It is not possible to find in the annals of criminal jurisprudence, a more deliberate and cold blooded villain than the central figure in this story, nor would the most careful research among the records of the prominent murder trials that have absorbed public attention during the past century, disclose the careful planning that made possible the apprehension of Holmes, the prosecution to an almost miraculous ending of the search for the missing children, or the equal of the forensic skill and cunning that wove the close web in which this man of many names and many murders was entangled.

That Holmes committed four murders has been proven beyond the shadow of a doubt, and that his timely arrest prevented three more murders is equally sure. If the Chicago "Castle" could give up its guilty secrets, there is more than a strong suspicion that the list of Holmes crimes would be materially lengthened. We do know that fraud, deliberately planned and coolly executed, the blackest treachery toward his associates, a long term of brutal cruelty toward the helpless woman and her children who were in his clutches, and the marvelous duplicity and falsehood practiced upon the three women who each believed herself to be his lawful wife, are to be added to the list.

A remarkable thing about a murderer who has achieved the notoriety of Holmes, is the fact that no flowers nor gifts were sent to him by morbid sympathizers. The story of the search for the missing children reads like a romance, and its almost miraculous conclusion is another proof that detective acumen and tireless patience will find the unguarded spot which always exists in the armor of the most wily criminal. The reader will echo the remarks of the learned judge, who, in charging the jury that convicted Holmes, said: "Truth is Stranger than Fiction, and if Mrs. Pitezel's Story is true— (and it was proven to be true)— it is the Most Wonderful Exhibition of the Power of Mind Over Mind I Have Ever Seen, and Stranger than any Novel I Have Ever Read."

It is fitting that this true story that outrivals fiction should be published. The tone of the narrative is wholesome. Even youth may profit by it.

CONTENTS

CHAPTER I. PAGE Who was Perry? 14

CHAPTER II. Insurance Money Claimed 18

CHAPTER III The Insurance Company, Suspicious 28

CHAPTER IV. The Clang of the Cell Door 34

CHAPTER V. The Wages of Sin 58

CHAPTER VI. In the Toils 78

CHAPTER V. "A Slippery and Subtle Knave" 84

CHAPTER VI. The Pitezel Children 89

CHAPTER IX. On the Trail 99

CHAPTER X. The Untiring Pursuit 104

CHAPTER XI. An Expert in Crime 114

CHAPTER X. The Search Rewarded 121

CHAPTER XI Forging the Links 133

CHAPTER XIV. How to Find the Boy 142

CHAPTER XV. The Detective Puzzled 147

CHAPTER XVI. The Beginning of the End 154

CHAPTER XV. "When He Came" 158

CHAPTER XVI. The Chain Complete 164

CHAPTER XIX. Justice Cried "Amen" 167

CHAPTER XX. Looking Backward 173

CHAPTER XXI. A Triple Alliance 177

CHAPTER XX. A Friend in Need 182

CHAPTER XXI. The Excluded Testimony 185

* CHAPTER XIV Chronology 190

APPENDIX I. Speech of Hon. George S. Graham 221

APPENDIX II. Motion for New Trial 270

APPENDIX III. The Decision of the Supreme Court 291

* APPENDIX IV. Holmes dies denying his guilt.... 303

* 2017 APPENDIX: H.H. Holmes rises from the grave, 2017 ... 325

* New or updated articles including information not in the original or any other reissued edition of Geyer's *The Holmes-Pitezel Case*

"Foul Deeds will rise, though all the earth o'erwhelm them, to men's eyes."

" Let guilty men remember, their black deeds. Do lean on crutches made of slender reeds."

FRANK P. GEYER

THE HOLMES-PITEZEL CASE.

CHAPTER I.

WHO WAS PERRY?

Meeting of Eugene Smith and B. F. Perry — Smith sees Holmes — Perry disappears — Discovery of a Corpse — Condition of the Corpse — Coroner's Inquest — Identification as Perry.

In the latter part of August, 1894, Eugene Smith, a house carpenter, was passing along Callowhill Street, between Thirteenth and Broad Streets, in the city of Philadelphia, when his attention was attracted by a somewhat conspicuous sign in the bulk window of the house numbered 1316. The house was one of a row of red brick, two and a half stories high, and immediately opposite the old abandoned station of the Philadelphia & Reading Railroad. The sign was made out of a sheet of muslin stretched across the window, and on it was printed in black and red letters, "B. F. Perry, Patents Bought and Sold."

Smith was an inventor and had recently patented an ingenious device for a saw sett which he was very desirous of turning into money. So stopping a moment, he decided to seek the advice and assistance of Perry, who was in the business of buying and selling patents.

When Smith walked into the store, he was greeted by a tall, raw-boned man, with a somewhat sharp countenance, who announced himself as the proprietor Perry, and who readily listened to Smith's explanation of the merits of his new saw sett. Perry requested Smith to furnish him with a model of his invention, which the latter promised to do.

The next day Smith called again, taking with him the model, the merits of which he explained more fully and in greater detail. In the course of the conversation, Smith informed Perry that he was a carpenter by trade and was anxious to secure work, whereupon Perry employed him to construct a rough counter required for business purposes, in the first floor storeroom of the house. It was while working at this counter, that Smith saw a man enter, give a sign to Perry, and pass up the stairway in the rear of the front room, into the upper or second story of the house.

Perry followed this man upstairs and shortly returned to the first floor and resumed his conversation with Smith. Smith never saw this man at the house but once, but he afterwards identified him as H. H. Holmes.

In the afternoon of Monday, September 3d, Smith called at No. 1316 to see Perry again, and to ascertain if any progress had been made in the sale of the patent. As he stepped into the store, he discovered it was vacant, and observed also that there was no one in the rear room of the first floor. Thinking that Perry was in the upper floor, or was temporarily absent upon an errand in the immediate neighborhood, Smith took a seat, and had an opportunity of observing the contents of the store. On a nail were hanging a hat and a pair of cuffs, and on the counter were several bottles and a few other articles of inconsiderable value, which appeared to make up the stock in trade of the patent dealer. After waiting a short time. Smith halloed at the top of his voice, but received no answer. He then went out and asked a neighbor if she had seen Perry about. She told him that very often Mr. Perry went around the corner to a saloon and would probably return shortly. Smith remained half an hour, and then as Perry did not return, he departed, closing the door after him. Smith was annoyed at his failure to see Perry, and also because the place had been left open and apparently unprotected, and he made it a point to return early the next morning, Tuesday the 4th inst.

No. 1316 Callowhill St., Philadelphia, Pa.

Rear of No. 1316 Callowhill St., Philadelphia, Pa.

He found the door shut, but not locked, just as he had left it. The chair in which he had si.t the day before, was in the same place he had left it, and apparently had not been moved. The hat and cuffs still hung upon the nail. He hallooed; "Perry" several times, but received no answer. He then walked up the stairs leading to the second floor, and looking towards the front room, observed a cot, but it was unoccupied. He then turned to the left and looking into the back room, his gaze met a sight that chilled his blood. Lying prostrate on the floor, with his feet towards the window, and his head to the door, was a man, dead, — the face disfigured beyond recognition by decomposition and burning, and surrounded apparently by evidences of an explosion. The sun was shining brightly through the window, and directly on the upper part of the body, and it needed no second glance from Smith to convince him of his duty to summon the police.

Leaving the house without delay, he hurried to the nearest station house and returned with two officers, who on their way, stopped for Dr. Scott, the nearest physician.

The upper part of the body was found to be much decomposed. The left arm was extended along and close to the left side, the right arm across the breast, — altogether a very peaceful posture. He was rigid and straight as if lie had been ceremoniously laid out in death. The left side of the shirt and the left breast had been burned, and the mustache on one side and the forelock of hair was singed. The body under the arm was not burned at all. From the mouth had flowed a considerable quantity of fluid, slightly tinged with blood, which stained the floor for a foot or two alongside the body.

By reason of decomposition and the burns, it seemed impossible to identify the body to a certainty, as that of Perry, although the clothing was the same which Smith had seen Perry wear. The color of the hair and the length of the body, and the general appearance was the same as Perry. At the side of the body lay the fragments of a large broken bottle, a pipe filled with tobacco and a burnt match. The tobacco in the pipe been but slightly charred. The outside window shutters were bowed, the window was up, and the fireboard at the chimney near which the body lay was open at an angle of about eight inches.

The body was at once removed to the city morgue, which is in the immediate rear of No. 1316 Callowhill Street., and on the same day the coroner's physician made an autopsy.

The brain was normal, the body well nourished, the lungs were congested, the heart empty and normal and free from clots, indicating that death had been very rapid with him. The stomach exhibited alcoholic irritation and emitted a strong odor of chloroform. Whatever caused death, caused paralysis of the involuntary muscles, as the bladder had emptied and regurgitation took place from the mouth, where the body lay.

The burns on the body as described, were also noted by the coroner's physician. An inquest by the coroner quickly followed and a verdict of death from congestion of the lungs, caused by the inhalation of flame, or of chloroform or other poisonous drug was rendered; although the coroner's physician testified that he believed death was due to chloroform poisoning. The police and the few neighbors of the vicinity discussed the case in a desultory sort of a way for some days. The coroner's jury had found the body to be that of B. F. Perry, and the question of the identification of the body as Perry appeared to be established.

But who was Perry? From whence had he come? Was he murdered or had he committed suicide? Or was he killed by the explosion of an inflammable substance in the bottle which was found broken at his side? He appeared to have just lighted his pipe. Was this the act which ignited the flame that destroyed his life? If so, how came his body to recline in sucli a peaceful attitude? But the lungs were found to be congested, and the stomach when opened, gave forth a distinct odor of chloroform. Could lie, in committing suicide, have caused the explosion when dying? If he had inhaled chloroform, how came this drug in the stomach? These and a thousand other questions were propounded, only to be unanswered. It was a mystery, and the solution did not appear to be in sight.

CHAPTER II

INSURANCE MONEY CLAIMED

Letters from Jeptha D. Howe — Cashier Cass Calls on Mrs. Holmes — Holmes Writes to Cass — Holmes Calls on President Fouse — Howe Presents Letter of Attorney from Mrs. Pitezel — Perry and Pitezel the Same — President Fouse Talks with — Holmes Meets Howe — Marks of Identification—The Body Disinterred— Howe Paid $9,715.85 Insurance Money — Affidavits of Alice Pitezel and H. H. Holmes — Smith Fails to Recognize Holmes.

In all great cities, unclaimed bodies are held at the morgue for a certain length of time, to await identification and a claimant. Perry's body lay in the Philadelphia Morgue for eleven days, and was then buried in the Potters Field.

Before the burial, however, two letters were received in Philadelphia, one by the coroner, and the other by the officers of the Fidelity Mutual Life Association. These letters came from Jeptha D. Howe, a young attorney of St. Louis, Missouri. He stated that he. represented Mrs. Carrie A. Pitezel, the wife of Benjamin F. Pitezel. That Pitezel was insured in the Fidelity Company for Ten Thousand Dollars and that his wife was the beneficiary named in the policy. That the man who was found dead at No. 1316 Callowhill Street, and who was known as B. F. Perry, was Benjamin F. Pitezel, and that he (Howe) would shortly visit Philadelphia with a member of the Pitezel family for the purpose of identifying the body, and claiming the insurance money.

The books of the company showed that a policy had been issued on the life of Benjamin F. Pitezel on November 9th, 1893, and that the insurance had been effected through the branch office of the company in Chicago, Illinois.

A communication was at once forwarded by the company to its manager in Chicago, instructing him to learn all that was possible concerning Pitezel, and particularly to ascertain the names of persons who had known Pitezel in Chicago. The situation as presented to the officers of the company at this time, aroused their suspicions, and they proceeded with caution.

The company then received word from Mr. Cass, the cashier of the

Chicago office, that the only man who knew Pitezel well, was H. H. Holmes, who lived at Wilmette, Illinois. Mr. Cass was instructed to go to Wilmette and interview Holmes. He found that Holmes was away, but he saw Mrs. Holmes, who offered to communicate with her husband. She said her husband was moving about all the time anil was not at home, but that she would communicate anything to him the agent had to say. She would not tell the agent where her husband was, although she admitted she heard from him every day or so. Mr. Cass gave the woman a clipping from a Chicago paper, which stated that Perry had been found in Chicago and she promised to send it to her husband.

On September 18th, the Chicago manager of the company received a letter from Holmes, dated Columbus, Ohio, September 17th, and the next day a second letter, dated Cincinnati, September 19th.

These two letters here given in full, exhibit the enormous capacity of Mr. Holmes for duplicity and deceit. In view of the subsequent developments of the case, they portray his many resources for meeting an occasion, and a sagacity, which would have served him well, had he chosen to earn an honest living.

Columbus, Ohio,
Sept. 17, 1894.

E. H. Cass, Esq.,

R. 46,-115 Dearborn, Chicago,

Dear Sir: —

I am in receipt of a letter from my wife, stating that you called on her in regard to Mr. Pitezel. She also enclosed me clipping from paper, which I presume you gave her. The address given in same is wrong. It should be Madison St. or Avenue on the south side of the city, and if I remember correctly, it is No. 6343, as stated in the clipping. At all events it is very near the 63rd Street entrance to the World's Fair grounds, in some hotel that was formerly used as a flat building and on E. side of Street.

Following the question asked, I would say, that I do not know who did his dental work, though I do not think he took very good care of his teeth and may have had none done.

I remember that seven or eight years ago when working for me, he had to give up work for some time on account of neuralgia in his teeth. Mr. Fay should be able to identify him readily, as he knew him quite well, as I remember Chat when Mr. Fay and I occupied an office on Dearborn Street, Mr. Pitezel was there almost daily, he having a patent coal bin on exhibition there. In a general why I should describe him a man nearly six feet high, (at least five feet ten inches) always thin in flesh and weighing from one hundred and forty-five to one hundred and fifty-five lbs., having very black and somewhat coarse hair, very thick, with no tendency towards baldness; his mustache was a much lighter color and I think of a red tinge, though 1 have seen him have it colored black at times, which gave him quite a different appearance. I remember also that he had some trouble with his knees, causing them to become enlarged directly below or in front of same, as a result of floor laying when he was in the contracting business, but whether this was a temporary or permanent affair, I am unable to state. He also had some sort of a warty growth on the back or side of his neck, which prevented him from wearing a collar when working. Aside from these points, I can think of nothing to distinguish him from other men, unless it be that his forehead was lower than the average and crown of head higher, causing one to notice same. I do remember, however, that he had, or at least had late in 1893 a boy about twelve years of age who looked so much like him, that if compared with body supposed to be his father would show the identity I should think, and if he is still unburied, there are plenty of people there who have known him intimately, among them being a Mr. Heywood, near 69th and Peoria or Paulina Streets, who is, I think, a relative; also a Mr. William Coyler or Collier living on West side, who was with him a great deal. If the identity is not cleared up by the time you receive this letter and you wish me to, I will go to Chicago any time after Wednesday next, provided you will pay my transportation theie and return. I should want same extended several days, however, so that I could stay a short time while there. I feel sure that Mr. Fay and myself could pick him out among a hundred. I would be willing to go without pay in ordinary times, but can hardly afford to do so now.

Mr. Pitezel is owing me One hundred and eighty Dollars, and if he is in reality dead, I should be glad to have that amount retained from the sum payable on his policy and apply same on my own, as I very much need it. I sent you a check from Indian Territory early in the spring to partially cover my insurance and incidentally directed it to Montreal, instead of Fidelity and it was returned to me at a time when I needed money very much to complete a trade, and used it then hoping to replace it soon.

My affairs are not in a good condition and I need insurance more than at any time. I have done a good deal for his family within the past eight years and I think if need be, I could get an order from his wife, authorizing you to retain the amount due me.

If you see fit to wire me, please do so by Western Union and I will act in accordance with your suggestions.

Yours Respectfully,

H. H. Holmes.

Holmes, of course, knew when he wrote this letter, that Pitezel's body was not in Chicago awaiting identification. He knew that it was in Philadelphia, and yet how cleverly he uses the his statement in the Chicago paper, to his advantage, and as a cover for himself! But he was anxious to be on the ground when the final act in the scheme of fraud, intrigue and deception, should be performed, and so two days later, he addresses Mr. Cass again as follows:

Grand Hotel,
Cincinnati,

Sept. 19, 1894.

E. H. Cass, Esq.,

115 Dearborn St., Chicago.

Dear Sir: —

Since writing to you yesterday, I have seen from a file of Philadelphia papers, that the supposed body of Pitezel is in the hands of the coroner there instead of in Chicago, as per clipping you sent me. I shall be in Baltimore in a day or two, and I will take an afternoon train to Philadelphia and call on your office there, and if they wish me to do so, I will go with some representative of theirs to the coroner's, and I think I can tell if the man there is Pitezel; — from what I read here, I cannot see anything to lead me to think that the person killed was other than a man by the name of Perry.

Yours Respectfully,
H. H. Holmes.

Will you kindly ask Mr. Fay to write me at Columbus, Ohio, if he will, I shall return there about Saturday.

To these letters, a polite response was sent to Holmes from Mr. Cass, stating in substance that the officers of the company were grateful to him for the information which he had so kindly furnished, and that after Mr. Holmes had finished his business in Baltimore, he would oblige them still further by coming to Philadelphia, examining the body and giving the company his views as to its identity. He was also assured that his expenses to and from Baltimore would be defrayed.

After reading this story of crime to the end, the reader is requested to turn back to these two letters and re-read them. One may then ask, if this great criminal has not proved himself to be as expert and as audacious in deceit and fabrication, as he has been bold and heartless in murder, — verily an artist in roguery

On September 20th, Holmes culled at the office of the company in Philadelphia, No. 914 Walnut Street. He saw Mr. Fouse, president of the company, and told him the correspondence he had had with the Chicago manager, of which, of course, Mr. Fouse had knowledge.

Holmes asked Mr. Fouse about the circumstances of the death, which were related to him very briefly. Holmes said it was a peculiar case and asked Mr. Fouse the cause of death, and the verdict of the coroner's jury was communicated to him. He was then asked to give a description of Pitezel which he did.

Mr. Fouse told Holmes that Mrs. Pitezel's attorney, Jeptha D. Howe, had telegraphed him that he was coming to Philadelphia with a member of the family, and the body which had been interred in the Potter's Field, would no doubt, be taken up. Mr. Fouse said he did not know precisely the time Howe would arrive and that Holmes had better leave his address, so in case the body was taken up, he could secure his (Holmes') opinion of its identity. Holmes replied that he had business in Nicetown, (a suburb of Philadelphia) and if he went away the next day he would leave word with the company, where he could be found. He also promised, if possible, to call at the office the next morning. The next day, September 21st, Jeptha D. Howe called at the office of the company and presented to President Fouse a letter from R. J. Linden, Superintendent of Police of Philadelphia, introducing him. This letter was accepted as a sufficient voucher for Mr. Howe. It had been obtained from the superintendent on the strength of a letter presented to him by Howe, and from a friend of the superintendent's in St. Louis. The letter was given to Howe to identify him, and for no other purpose. Howe produced a letter of attorney from Mrs. Pitezel, and also quite a number of letters which Mrs. Pitezel had received from her husband, while lie was living as B. F. Perry at No. 1316 Callowhill Street. He said that Pitezel had assumed the name of Perry, because he had some financial transactions in Tennessee, which for the time embarrassed him and made it advisable for him to change his name and his location. Howe did not go into this matter very minutely. Mr. Fouse told Howe that the company had become quite convinced that Perry and Pitezel were one and the same, but they were not convinced that the dead man found was Pitezel the man whom they had insured, Howe expressed astonishment at this, whereupon Mr. Fouse asked him to give a description of Pitezel, which he did. This description tallied in all respects with the description furnished.

This conversation took place in the forenoon of September 21st, and Howe informed the president that Pitezel's daughter, Alice, had come with him from St. Louis; that Mrs. Pitezel was ill from nervous prostration and was unable to make such a long journey. He was asked to bring Alice to the office after dinner. Mr. Fouse talked with Alice when Howe brought her in the afternoon. She was a girl fourteen or fifteen years of age, very reticent, embarrassed and stupid. She corroborated the descriptions given of Pitezel by Howe and Holmes. Mr. Fouse then informed Howe of the visit of a Mr. Holmes, a gentleman who claimed to be an old friend of Pitezel's, and who had been his employer in years past. He asked Howe if he knew Holmes. Howe replied he did not. At this juncture, word was received by Mr. Fouse that Holmes had returned and was in the building. Mr. Fouse so informed Howe and asked him whether he would like to meet Holmes. He said he would. Holmes was then conducted into the room, and Mr. Fouse introduced Howe to Holmes. They both accepted the introduction and met apparently as strangers. They both shook hands. Holmes, however, at once recognized Alice, and told her he supposed she recognized him, and she said she did. She had been carefully instructed in the part she was to play in the performance, and she did it well. Holmes had evidently told her that her papa was really dead, and the company would never l»ay the insurance money if they discovered that Holmes and her papa had been so intimate. Mr. Fouse then took up the statements that had been made by the three persons, Holmes, Howe, and Alice Pitezel, and then said, as they intended to disinter the body, marks of identification had better be prepared to which they all could subscribe. Before assenting to this, Howe straightened himself up and said: (referring to Holmes) Who is this man? Why is he here? What is his purpose? Mr. Fouse at once proceeded to fully and frankly explain to Howe how Holmes had come there, and referred to the letters the company had received from the Chicago manager. Howe said that this was satisfactory.

The marks of identification, — a wart on the neck, a cut on the leg, and a bruised nail of the thumb, together with certain peculiarities of the teeth were then agreed upon, and an engagement was made for all parties to report at the coroner's office the following day, Saturday, September 22d, and with the coroner's physician proceed to the Potters Field, disinter the body and look for the marks of identification. The next day the party, consisting of the deputy coroner, his physician. Inspector Perry, Howe, Holmes, Alice Pitezel, Eugene Smith, and President Fouse, all went to the Potters Field. When the party arrived, they discovered that the body had been disinterred by order of the coroner, and was in the dead house. The sight was terrifying, as the corpse was greatly decomposed.

The coroner's physician put on his rubber gloves, tore away the garments at places where the marks were supposed to be, but he was unable to find them. At this moment. Holmes pulled off his coat, rolled up his sleeves, took a surgeon's knife from his pocket, put on the rubber gloves, turned the body over, cut away the garments, washed off the skin at the back of the neck, and pointed out the wart, which he removed. He also showed the cut on the leg and the bruised nail of the thumb, which he also re moved and handing them to the coroner's physician, he requested that he preserve them in alcohol. Alice Pitezel was not permitted to witness this scene, but after Holmes had finished his self-imposed task, and after all portions of the body had been covered up, save the mouth, she was led sobbing to the table, and after looking at the teeth, said they appeared to be like her papa's.

The party then left the field and Howe asked Mr. Fouse for his opinion, and if he was satisfied. Mr. Fouse said he would hold the matter under consideration. On the following Monday, September 24th, the ofcers of the company held a conference and concluded that the identification was satisfactory and complete and so informed Howe. Howe then represented Mrs. Pitezel as being very poor and sick and greatly in need of money; that her husband had left her nothing, and he wanted to know how soon the claim could be paid. After some little consideration, the officers of the company decided to pay the claim at once, provided the expenses to which this company had been put in the effort to identify the body were deducted. To this Howe reluctantly assented, and thereupon a check to his order as attorney in fact for Mrs. Pitezel for $9715.85 was drawn and delivered to him, and the policy of insurance was surrendered. The company also paid Holmes ten dollars to defray his expenses incurred in coming from Baltimore. The company within the next two weeks received letters from Mrs. Pitezel, Alice Pitezel, Holmes and Howe, expressing their appreciation of the prompt manner in which the claim had been settled.

ALICE PITEZEL

On Sunday, September 23d, 1894, in response to the urgent request of Holmes, who said he desired to leave the city as soon as possible, the coroner permitted him and Alice Pitezel to subscribe to affidavits, in which they certify to the indentity of the body as that of B. F. Pitezel. The folioing are copies of these statements.

Benjamin F. Pitezel,

1316 Callowhill Street.

E. Alice Pitezel. I live at No. 6343 Michigan Avenue, St. Louis, Mo. I am in my 15th year. Benjamin F. Pitezel was my father. He was 37 years old this year. My mother is living. There are five children. My father came East July 20th. He first went from St. Louis to New York, and left there August 11th. We learned of his death through the papers. I came on with Mr. Howe to see the body on Saturday, September 22d. I saw a body at the city burying ground, and fully recognized the body as that of my father by his teeth. I am fully satisfied that it is he.

Signed,

E. Alice Pitezel. Witnesses,

Jeptha D. Howe.

F. Perry. Sept. 23d, 1894.

H. H. Holmes,

701 63rd Street, Chicago, Ill.

I knew Benjamin F. Pitezel 8 years in Chicago. Had business with him much of that time. More recently he had desk room in our office. I received a letter from E. H. Cass, agent of the Fidelity Co. about Benjamin F. Pitezel, sending a clipping. I came to Philadelphia and saw the body on Saturday, September 22d, at the city burial ground. I recollect the mole on the back of the neck, and low growth of hair on the forehead, and general shape of the head and teeth. His daughter had described a scar on the right leg below the knee, front. I found this on the body as described by Alice. I have no doubt whatsoever but what it is the body of Benjamin F. Pitezel, who was buried as B. F. Perry. I last saw him in November, 1893, in Chicago. I heard he used an assumed name recently. I never knew him to use any other name but his own. I found him an honest, honorable man in all dealings. Signed,

Harry H. Holmes,

Witnesses,

F. Perry. Jeptha D. Howe.

Eugene Smith was present at this disinterment and examination in Potters Field. He had seen Holmes once at No. 1316 Callowhill Street, but failed to recognize him at the exhumation of the body. Had he done so, the scheme of fraud and murder would have been disclosed then and there, and the lives of the three children saved. He says now that he had a suspicion that the man he saw at the Potters Field was the man whom he had seen at No. 1316 Callowhill Street, and that he was more than once on the point of speaking of it to Mr. Fouse, but feared making a mistake and so remained silent.

In this instance at least, silence was not the "eloquence of discretion."

CHAPTER III

THE INSURANCE COMPANY SUSPICIOUS

Inspector Gary not Satisfied — Gary Visits Major Harrigan at St. Louis. — Letter from a Train Robber — Gary Visits Hedgepeth — Search for Holmes — Pinkerton Aid Secured — Holmes Arrested in Boston — Holmes True Name Herman Webster Mudgett— Mrs. Pitezel Decoyed to Boston and Arrested — Holmes' Several Wives — Holmes Regrets His Confidence in Hedgepeth.

The Fidelity Mutual Life Association, has a detective department of its own. It is under the direction of Inspector W. E. Gary, a very shrewd, painstaking and capable officers who has had a long experience in investigations relating to life insurance risks.

Mr. Gary not only questioned the proof of the identity of the body as that of Pitezel, but he was dissatisfied with the conclusion then reached, that the man found, dead, had died as the result of an accident, as the appearances of the body with the broken bottle and pipe and the dead match at its side, seemed to prove.

The officers of the company, however, had paid the claim, and the matter was soon forgotten in the multiplicity of duties incident to the business of a great insurance company.

Early in October, about two weeks after Jeptha D. Howe departed with the check for $9,715.85, business of importance, having no relation whatever to the Pitezel case, called Inspector Gary to St. Louis, Missouri.

On October 9th, while sitting in the branch office of the company in St. Louis, a messenger called with a letter from Major Lawrence Harrigan, Chief of the St. Louis Police, stating that he, (Harrigan) had received a communication from a prisoner in the city prison, about an insurance case which the Fidelity Mutual Life Association had investigated, and suggesting that some officer of the company should at once call upon him.

This message caused Inspector Gary to visit the chief's office without delay, and there Major Harrigan handed him a letter he had received from Marion C. Hedgepeth, a prisoner who was awaiting sentence for train robbing. This letter which is here given in full will be more fully understood when the reader is informed, that Mudgett (or Holmes) was known in St. Louis, Missouri, as H. M. Howard, and that in July of 1894 he had been incarcerated in the city prison under that name on a charge of swindling in connection with the purchase and sale of a drug store.

St. Louis, Mo., Tuesday, October 9th, 1894. Major Lawrence Harrigan, Chief of Police.

Dear Sir: —

When H. M. Howard was in here some two months ago, he came to me and told me he would like to talk to me, as he had read a great deal of me, etc.; also after we got well acquainted, he told me he had a scheme by which he could make $10,000, and he needed some lawyer who could be trusted, and said if I could, he would see that I got $500 for it. I then told him that J. D. Howe could be trusted, and he then went on and told me that B. F. Pitezel's life was insured for $10,000, and that Pitezel and him were going to work the insurance company for the $10,000, and just how they were going to do it; even going into minute details; that he was an expert at it, as he had worked it before, and that being a druggist, he could easily deceive the insurance company by having Pitezel fix himself up according to his directions and appear that he was mortally wounded by an explosion, and then put a corpse in place of Pitezel's body, etc., and then have it identified as that of Pitezel. I did not take much stock in what he told me, until after he went out on bond, which was in a few days, when J. D. Howe came to me and told me that that man Howard, that I had recommended him to, had come and told him that I had recommended Howe to him and had laid the whole plot open to him, and Howe told me that he never heard of a finer or smoother piece of work, and that it was sure to work, and that Howard was one of the smoothest and slickest men that he ever heard tell of, etc., and Howe told me that he would see that I got $500 if it worked, and that Howard was going on East to attend to it at once. (At this time I did not know what insurance company was to be worked, and am not sure yet as to which one it is, but Howe told me that it was the Fidelity Mutual of Philadelphia, whose office is, according to the city directory, at No. 520 Olive Street.) Howe came down and told me every two or three days, that everything was working smoothly and when notice appeared in the Globe Democrat and Chronicle of the death of B. F. Pitezel, Howe came down at once and told me that it was a matter of a few days until we would have the money, and that the only thing that might keep the company from paying it at once, was the fact that Howard and Pitezel were so hard up for money, that they could not pay the dues on the policy until a day or two before it was due, and then had to send it by telegram, and that the company might claim that they did not get the money until after the lapse of the policy; but they did not, and so Howe and a little girl (I think Pitezel's daughter) went back to Philadelphia and succeeded in identifying and having the body recognized as that of B. F. Pitezel. Howard told me that Pitezel's wife was privy to the whole thing. Howe tells me now that Howard would not let Mrs. Pitezel go back to identify the supposed body of her husband, and that he feels almost positive and certain that Howard deceived Pitezel and that Pitezel in following out Holmes's instructions, was killed and that it was really the body of Pitezel.

The policy was made out to the wife and when the money was put in the bank, then Howard stepped out and left the wife to settle with Howe for his services. She was willing to pay him $1,000, but he wants $2,500 and so $2,500 of the money is held until they get over squabbling about it. Howard is now on his way to Germany, and Pitezel's wife is here in the city yet, and where Pitezel is or whether that is Pitezel's body I can't tell, but I don't believe it is Pitezel's body, but believe that he is alive and well and probably in Germany, where Howard is now on his way. It is hardly worthwhile to say that I never got the 8500 that Howard held out to me for me to introduce him to Mr. Howe. Please excuse this poor writing as I have written this in a hurry and have to write on a book placed on my knee. This and a lot more I am willing to swear to. I wish you would see the Fidelity Mutual Life Insurance Company and see if they are the ones who have been made the victim of this swindle, and if so, tell them that I want to see them. I never asked what company it was until to-day, and it was after we had some words about the matter, and so Howe may not have told the proper company, but you can find out what company it is by asking or telephoning to the different companies. When I asked Mrs. Pitezel's address he waited a long time and finally said it was No. 6342 S. Michigan Ave. Please send an agent of the company to see me if you please.

Yours Resp., etc.,
Marion C. Hedgepeth.

It was in compliance with this request that Inspector Gary, accompanied by a stenographer, visited Hedgepeth in the city prison and obtained from him a sworn statement, which was in effect a reiteration of the declarations made in the letter, except that in addition to all that had been disclosed by Howe after his return from Philadelphia, he told Hedgepeth that he verily believed that the body was really Pitezel's, and that Holmes had either murdered him, or Pitezel had been killed in the explosion when setting up the job of substitution.

With a copy of this letter and the statement Inspector Gary returned at once to Philadelphia and promptly reported the new revelation to the officers of the company. These gentlemen considered the story to be a fake, — a tale manufactured by a wily criminal for selfish purposes, and they refused to believe it or attach any importance to it whatever. Not so, however, with Inspector Gary. He believed the statement to be true. He pointed out matters referred to in Hedgepeth's letter, which could not have been known to Hedgepeth, and must have been communicated by either Howe or Howard, and precisely as he had related them. Hedgepeth states that the premium on the policy was sent by a telegram from New York, as indeed it was, and on the very day it was due, August 9th. How could he have known that fact? It was known only to the officers of the company and the conspirators. Gary finally persuaded the officers of the company to permit him to make a search for Holmes, and as the work progressed, proofs that the company had been made the victim of a swindle, multiplied. The aid of the Pinkerton Detective force was secured. Holmes was first searched for in Kingston, Canada, and then in Detroit, but without result. He was finally traced to Burlington, Vermont, thence to Tilton and Gilmanton, N. H. At the last named place it was found that Holmes or Howard, two of his aliases, was really Herman Webster Mudgett; that his father's home was in Gilmanton, and that he was visiting his old home while under the surveillance of detectives. He was kept under a close shadow and followed to Boston, where on November 17, 1894, he was arrested and taken to the police station.

Strange to say, his arrest was effected not on the charge of swindling the insurance company, but on a telegram from Fort Worth, Texas, charging him with horse stealing, — another of his criminal operations. At the time of the arrest, Mr. Perry, one of the officers of the company, (who had seen Mudgett at the company's office in Philadelphia, and in the Potters Field at the exhumation of the body) went to Boston. Upon seeing Mr. Perry at the city police station, Mudgett or Holmes, as we shall call him, threw up his hands and said he guessed he was wanted in Philadelphia by the Fidelity, and not in Fort Worth for the horse business. In fact he expressed a decided disinclination to revisit Fort Worth, Texas, as he knew that horse thieves and swindlers are liable to receive much more peremptory attention from the populace in that section than in the north.

Holmes had rented a house in Burlington, Vermont, for Mrs. Pitezel, who had with her, her baby and eldest daughter, Dessie, about sixteen years of age. She was brought to Boston by a decoy letter, devised by the Pinkertons and written by Holmes, and was arrested and placed in the city police station. When arrested. Holmes was found in the company of Miss Georgiana Yoke, whom he had married under the name of Henry Mansfield Howard. This lady soon proved herself to be an estimable and an honest woman. She had been cruelly and heartlessly deceived, and soon learned that she was one of several victims, for he had not only a lawful wife living near his old home in New Hampshire, but he had married at least one other woman, who honestly believed herself to be his wife.

His confidence in Hedgepeth can only be explained by his evident admiration for a man who had achieved great notoriety as a train robber. It was a weakness, which Holmes has many regretted. He has just as much deplored the other mistake he made, in omitting to pay Hedgepeth his promised reward and share of the money, for it is quite evident that while Hedgepeth told the truth in his letter to the chief of police and in his statement to Inspector Gary, his expose was in revenge for the chagrin he suffered, when he realized he was forgotten at the time of the distribution of the proceeds of the robbery.

BENJAMIN F. PITEZEL

CHAPTER IV

THE CLANG OF THE CELL DOOR

Holmes' First Confession — Admits Conspiracy to Defraud — Substitution of a Corpse — A Plausible Statement — Details of the Conspiracy.

The echo of the clang of the cell door through the corridor of the police station in Boston, had scarcely died away, before Holmes inaugurated a system of fabrications, the chief object of which was to deceive and mislead the police authorities and the officers of the company he had robbed. He admitted that a fraud had been perpetrated, and that he was one of a band of conspirators, who had successfully imposed upon a life insurance company, and had secured upwards of ten thousand dollars, by the substitution of a corpse, for the supposed dead body of the insured. He said the cadaver had been obtained from a medical friend of his in New York, whose name he refused to disclose. Holmes is greatly given to lying with a sort of florid ornamentation, and all of his stories are decorated with flamboyant draperies, intended by him to strengthen the plausibility of his statements . In talking, he has the appearance of candor, becomes pathetic at times when pathos will serve him best, uttering his words with a quaver in his voice, often accompanied by a moistened eye, then turning quickly with a determined and forceful method of speech, as if indignation or resolution had sprung out of tender memories that had touched his heart.

Here is his first confession, made November 19th, 1894, to O. M. Hanscom, Deputy Superintendent of Police, Massachusetts, and John Cornish, Superintendent of the Pinkerton Detective Agency of Boston, Massachusetts.

Boston, Mass.,

November 19, 1894.

Q. (By Mr. Hanscom.) What is Pitezel's name?

A. B. F., I think Benjamin Fuller.

Q. When did you last see Pitezel?

A. I cannot give the day. I will leave a blank and fill it in.

Q. State it in your own way.

A. Well, I saw him last in Detroit and it was Benjamin F. Pitezel. In the neighborhood of three weeks ago, but I can give the exact date by consulting my wife.

Q. Do you know where he was stopping in Detroit?

A. No, I don't know. He had been there several days before waiting for me to come there.

Q. When was the last time before that that you saw him?

A. Well I had not seen him but once since this Philadelphia occurrence and that was in Cincinnati, probably two weeks before that.

Q. You went from New York with the trunk and body?

A. Yes, sir.

Q. And turned the check over to him?

A. That was on Sunday.

Q. You know what date?

A. No, it was the Sunday nearest the first of September.

Q. After turning over to him the check for the trunk when did you see him next?

A. About ten days or two weeks, I should say, in Cincinnati.

Q. Then you gave him your instructions as ti> how to proceed with the body?

A. He had those before.

Q. Those had been given to him some time before?

A. Yes, sir.

Q. So that you did not see him after turning over to him the checks until you next met him in Cincinnati?

A. No, sir. I think there must have been two weeks. It must have been more, because it was three weeks before I went on to Philadelphia. It must have been at least ten days or two weeks after the payment of the money.

Q. You had no occasion to meet him in Philadelphia during the interim between giving him the check and the finding of the body?

A. He went right away, or was to go to New York.

Q. As soon as he prepared the body his instructions were to go to New York?

A. Yes, sir, and I went that night really within three hours after the body had landed in Philadelphia.

Q. You next saw him in Cincinnati?

A. Yes, sir.

Q. Some two weeks?

A. Well, it must have been nearer five weeks, about ten clays or so after the payment of the money. I have no means of knowing just how many clays between.

Q. How did he get possession of the three children?

A. Well, one he got in Cincinnati and the other in Detroit. The boy he took there.

Q. Did you see the child with him in Cincinnati.

A. Yes, sir.

Q. By whom was it turned over to him?

A. The three children,— or rather to be more explicit, after we came to Philadelphia to identify the body, the little child Alice, who was there with Mr. Perry about the identification, went as far as Indianapolis with me and I left her there and "went further on to St. Louis where the mother was, and as soon as the money was paid over to the attorney and given to this .woman, why a portion of it I took and the other two children and went to Cincinnati calling for this one in Indianapolis.

Q. By "this woman "you mean his wife?

A. Yes, sir. Now, when I landed in Cincinnati I had three children; two I took at St. Louis, boy and girl, and one from Philadelphia that I had just stepped off the train at Indianapolis and took from there where she had been at the Stebbins Hotel.

Q. In whose charge at the Stebbins Hotel was this child?

A. She was hardly with any one, she was fourteen or fifteen years old.

Q. Was she stopping under her own name?

A. No, under the name of Canning.

Q. You took three children and went to Cincinnati?

A. Yes, sir.

Q. Where you met the father?

A. The father, and then it was arranged, — the mother wanted to see him if she could without the children knowing he was alive.

Q. Was the mother with you?

A. No, not then, but she was to follow. I was to go to Cincinnati and get a house and have them go there and stay for the winter, all the whole family, and it was arranged that he should see her fur a few days and then he was going South where he used to be in the lumber business, but he had been drinking and before I knew it he went in where the children were stopping and saw those three, and the mother had threatened in case that they knew that he was alive she would not go any further in it, because she thought it would all come out. He is a man that drinks some. So we compromised there by his taking enough to go there and keep these three children away from the mother, so he took one of them and I took the other two to Chicago, because I had business there, thinking that it would not call anyone's attention so quick if he travelled with the boy alone as if there were three. Then I took them to Detroit and he was already there and took the other two, dressed the smallest girl as a boy, but this girl Alice is dressed, I suppose now, as a girl and there are two boys and one girl.

Q. The two boys, would that mean the eldest and the next to the eldest?

A. No, there is only one boy really.

Q. Which other one was dressed as a boy?

A. The youngest girl.

Q. How old is she?

A. Not over 11 years old.

Q. Did you get a suit of clothes in Detroit?

A. He got them.

Q. How long did you remain with him in Detroit?

A. Oh, I think 1 got in there Saturday and he went away Monday, I think. Anyway, we had intended to get the children there and let the mother know that they were there, but still he wanted to see her very bad.

Q. He did not succeed in seeing his wife in Detroit?

A. No.

Q. She did not join him there?

A. No.

Q. Did you see him leave Detroit?

A. No, I did not. I kept away wholly from him; that is, he met me. I can't think of the street, it is a street they have been repairing. We went out on the street cars.

Q. It is not really clear to my mind now why the family should be broken up, why the three children should go one way and she with the two children the other way.

A. The first intention was to have them all go to Cincinnati and stay there for the winter, get a furnished house and have her stay there until any noise might blow over, and he was going into the South on lumber business and I about my general business. When I got down there I met him. I had the three children and he had been waiting there some days and 1 stayed there with him that night, and the next day instead of doing as he agreed, he had been drinking a little and he went and saw the children which he agreed not to do under any circumstances.

Q. That, of course, gave it away that he was alive?

A. Of course, we could not get them away in a moment.

Q. Your theory was that it was necessary for the three children to accompany him for the safety of the scheme?

A. Well, if the mother knew that they knew then she would immediately throw it over as she said, and I think she will tell you so herself.

Q. At the same time I suppose there was some fear that they might in some way, betray the fact that he was still alive?

A. Well, they could not all be together and go to school; you could not depend upon 10 or 11 year old children to keep the fact: keep them from speaking among themselves or before strangers, neither could you get them to go under another name and carry it out at that age.

Q. Do you know what his next point was?

A. He was going to New York and then if he could get through on the boats, if they had not already been taken off he was going that way, and if they had he was going to go down by land as far as Key West I think, some very southern point. He knows the South, which I don't. I have been on the Eastern coast more. He had some lumber business there. And I think the safest way is to go to the railroad brokers to see if he went by boat, because he always buys these scalpers tickets when he can.

Q. About what date then do you place him in New York; according to your reckoning, what dates should he have been there?

A. I am thoroughly honest in saying that I cannot say what day, but if you will leave it I can get it. It was about a month ago.

Q. Under what name was he travelling at that time?

A. Well, T. H., or anyway it was made out of the name he used in the South, only he turned it round about. He was there under the name of Benton T. Lyman, and I think it was L. T. or L. B. Benton. Benton was the name which was agreed upon quite a while before.

Q. That is the name under which he corresponded with you?

A. I was going to address him through either Chicago or New York Personals.

Q. Had you any cipher code that he understood?

A. Yes sir, but that was only fur his writing to me, because of his going from place to place, to places where the mails did not go; very often I hardly thought it was safe. After I got his letter, anything of importance I was to put in either the Chicago Tribune, or the New York Herald in the way of a personal letter. We have done that a few times in years past.

Q. Was it agreed what the " ad" should be?

A. No, it would be in shape so that he would understand all well, or if anything new that came up should cause him to move again, it would be taken through them.

Q. Then you believe that he and the children are all alive and well?

A. Yes, sir.

Q. You have every reason to believe that?

A. Yes, sir.

Q. Would there be anything about his effects that would in any way serve to give notice if anything had occurred to him?

A. No, I am sure of that because I was in a little difficulty in St. Louis last summer, and so we talked over at that time all the names and everything. I had a good many papers on me at that time. He had allowed his beard to grow and he has new teeth. He had them all extracted. He said he was going to have them the first thing when he got to New York. He has not nearly as many as the body and that can be easily established. In fact, it is easily proven also, that I left Philadelphia also on Sunday night before the time when lie was last seen by the coroner's witnesses, — outsiders saw him after I left Philadelphia. My wife and I went through on a Pullman.

Q. If you were obliged to establish the fact, can you show any meetings with him after leaving him in Philadelphia at the time you gave him the check for the trunk?

A. Yes, sir, I think I can. While they were made as secret as they could be, we sat for a good hour in the hotel. I took the children to a certain hotel in Cincinnati and kept them upstairs, and I sat down for a good length of time in their writing room, and I was writing and they knew me well by sight there, and I think I can establish that fact.

Q. Was he there?

A. Yes, sir.

Q. You sat there with him?

A. Yes, sir. No, it was at the other hotel.

Q. What hotel?

A. Well, I would have to see a Cincinnati directory. I could pick them out.

Q. Now at any other point? How about Detroit?

A. He slipped in there where the girls stayed and I happened to be in there at the time once. We kept as far apart as we could there and I took him out of Detroit, that is, from the centre part out where the children met him, in a big trunk.

Q. The same as you had shipped his body before.

A. Yes, sir. We had a scare there. I got some word from Chicago, but it pertained to this Fort Worth matter, that officers had been there, looking for us, and I knew if they obtained a clue, they could easily trace me to Detroit, so I came out from his place there and took him outside the city almost, and took the children out in a buggy to where he was. The children were apparently with me. They knew me as their uncle.

Q. You were known to the children as their uncle?

A. They knew different, but in the house where they stayed, I was known as such.

Q. That was in Detroit?

A. Yes, sir. By getting a plan of Detroit, I could tell where it was, the streets where the girls stayed, if it became necessary to substantiate my statements, and I go there, they would know me also as being there.

Q. (By Mr. Cornish.) Where did you take the trunks from?

A. I took it more than two miles and let him out.

Q. In a house or in the woods?

A. Way outside of the city. I went to a stable and got a horse and wagon there.

Q. (By Mr. Hanscom.) Did you drive the wagon?

A. Yes.

Q. It must have been an express?

A. No, it was a buggy with sort of heavy back. I tried to get an express wagon and they had not anything except a very large one, so the trunk went on behind by tying it on. I don't think he went more than a mile in that way, a mile or two.

Q. (By Mr. Cornish.) Who helped you to put the trunk in the buggy?

A. I put in the trunk.

Q. Did you put it in alone?

A. I put it in alone.

Q. Did you take it nut alone?

A. No, all I had to do was to put the lid back when he got out.

Q. Was that on the roadway?

A. Yes, sir. Well, it was outside of the city, about two miles from the centre of the town. The occasion of it was that I thought that officers were then watching him, but not me.

Q. Did you see him after that?

A. Yes, just long enough to drive out with the children in the buggy.

Q. The children did not go with you on this first trip?

A. Oh no, I took him in a light buggy, and he waited there for the children.

Q. That same day did you drive out with the children?

A. Yes, sir.

Q. (By Mr. Hanscom.) What was the object of going out there that way?

A. I had got word from Chicago that officers from Fort Worth were there. I thought then it was on this matter, and said they had got track of both of us. He was at Fort Worth with me.

Q. Then the last time you met was when you took the children out there to see him. The last time that you actually saw him?

A. Yes. It was somewhere about 4 o'clock in the afternoon of the day that I carried him out in the trunk. He had gone across from there, from a certain place where I left him, over to another place of meeting.

Q. Did you go across the bridge?

A. No, I did not go over with him. I did not go for a couple of days. I had to wait to get them. I carried the children out to him. He was to send in a boy for the satchel. I did not take it away because I feared the officers were watching and we were only going out to ride.

Q. From that point he started?

A. Yes, sir.

Q. Towards Canada?

A. No, I don't think so. It was spoken of that he would go to Detroit after Toronto, and wait there until I could get the wife and the other two children, and he hated to go away without seeing them.

Q. Have you heard from him since?

A. No, sir.

Q. All you know about New York and about his taking a steamer for any point in the South or for South America is what had been previously agreed upon?

A. Yes, sir.

Q. And you have not heard yet?

A. No, sir, it is hardly time.

Q. Under what name was he to address you?

A. Well, I can't tell you that, any more than he asked me particularly what name, and I said it was safe enough to address me as Howard at Room 30, No. 69 Dearborn St., Chicago.

Q. Under the name of Howard or Holmes?

Q. Yes, almost any strange name to them, either those two, or some name that did not belong in the office.

Q. Was this correspondence to be sent in any care?

A. In care of Mr. Frank Blackman.

Q. Who is Frank Blackman?

A. A real estate dealer, and during my absence from the city he was having charge of my money affairs there.

Q. How many weeks ago or days ago, was this final and last meeting with him in Detroit?

A. As near as I can guess it was three weeks ago.

Q. About three weeks ago that you left Detroit?

A. Possibly a little more. I can give those dates by referring to others, that is, my wife.

Q. Have you any reason to believe that there is any mail waiting for you at this Chicago, Dearborn St. office?

A. We got some this morning. It comes as fast as it is received.

HOLMES' "CASTLE" (63d St., Chicago, Ill.)

Q. Since delivering the children to him on the outskirts of Detroit, you have not seen or heard from him directly or indirectly?

A. No, sir.

Q. Has his wife been in search of him lately?

A. Oh no, because after this break that he made in regard to seeing the children, I have had to tell her while I could get her in shape to send her to him, that he was here and there and put her off.

Q. You have put her off by telling her that her husband was at different points about the country?

A. Yes, sir, I acted under him.

Q. Such is the fact?

A. Yes, sir.

Q. And she has been to Toronto in pursuit of them?

A. Yes, sir, and Ogdensburg and Burlington, Vt. I have expected every day to get word where he was, and that was my idea of getting her here, so to ship her and the children from here.

Q. I want to know whether or not you have taken her from point to point with the understanding that she was to see her husband?

A. She was to have met him at Detroit. In fact, she was to meet him in Cincinnati.

Q. She was to have met him in Cincinnati and then she went from Cincinnati to Detroit?

A. No, sir, she went to Galva, her old home, and was to wait there until I telegraphed her and got their homes in Cincinnati.

Q. Did she do it?

A. No, sir, because when he saw the children I sent word then for her to go to Chicago and from there to Detroit. It broke her plans completely up when he saw the children. He begged of me not to let her know it, because he wanted to see her and I agreed to go as far as Detroit and take a house there and see her alone, and then let the children go and tell her afterwards.

Q. But he did not see her in Detroit?

A. No. When he was sober he saw the difficulty of having the children stay with her after he had seen them on account of their talking.

Q. (By Mr. Cornish.) You said that your wife could fill out certain blanks that you have left?

A. She remembers everything for a year past.

Q. Have you remembered where you stopped in Philadelphia?

A. Yes, it is near

Q. Was it 13th Street at the house of a Mrs. Dr. Alcott?

A. That is the name, but it is on 11th Street, unless I am very much mistaken, near No. 1900 on 11th Street. Dr. Howell is the name that I went under. The doctor s name is Alcott. (Alcorn.)

Q. At the time that you went to Detroit, your wife was in Indianapolis?

A. Well, which time?

Q. The time that you were going to meet Pitezel. Your wife left Indianapolis on October 12th, and joined you somewhere near Peru?

A. I think it was near Peru, it was an adjoining place on the road.

Q. Then you arrived in Detroit, Friday, October the 12th?

A. I will not say as to the date.

Q. That is from your wife's memorandum?

A. I think you can depend upon her.

Q. Do you remember where you stopped in Detroit? Was it Park Place?

A. Well, we first went to a hotel.

Q. No. 40 Park Place?

A. I can't tell as to numbers. It was near what they call, — yes. Park Place.

Q. And you took your meals at the Cadillac?

A. Yes, mostly.

Q. Do you know when you left Detroit to go to Toronto?

A. I think we were there just a week and two days, in Detroit.

Q. You arrived in Toronto on October 18th in the evening?

A. I don't think those dates will correspond, because I think we were at this house a week.

Q. This is taken from a memorandum book in your wife's hand. "Arrived at Toronto October 18th and went to the Walker House."

A. Then you can depend upon it.

Q. On Saturday the 20th you went to Niagara and stopped at the Imperial Hotel on the Canada side?

A. Yes, sir, that is right.

Q. On Sunday the 21st you returned to Toronto and went to the Palmer House?

A. Yes, sir.

Q. October 25th you went to Prescott and stopped at the Imperial

Hotel?

A. I don't think that was the name of the house.

Q. On October 27th you crossed to Ogdensburg. New York?

A. Yes, sir.

Q. On the 31st went to Burlington, Vermont, and took up your residence at No. 19 George Street?

A. Yes, sir. In all the places, in Ogdensburg I tried to get a suitable place to leave the family. I did not want to keep them around.

Q. Did Mrs. Pitezel go to all these places with you?

A. Well, she left Toronto the day before we did and went to Ogdensburg direct.

Q. She did not touch Prescott or Niagara, that is, only through Prescott to Ogdensburg.

A. That is all.

Q. On November 5th, did you obtain any money from your wife in Burlington?

A. She was carrying a thousand dollars for me, and, without being explicit as to date, she gave it to me.

Q. What did you tell her you were going to do with it?

A. I told her I was going East to meet someone from Chicago.

Q. You stated where East?

A. Kingston, and in fact I used it to pay bills in the East that I was owing years ago for my education in Gilmanton, N. H. where my father and mother live.

Q. So that it was expended at Tilton and Gilmanton?

A. Yes, sir.

Q. On that same day on arrival in Tilton you went to the Adams Express Office?

A. States Express, I think it was.

Q. And got a box about four feet long, two and a half feet wide, and one and a half feet thick, what did that contain?

A. That was filled with blankets and things from my buildings in Chicago, new ones, blankets and spreads.

Q. To whom did you take the box?

A. Well, I gave my part of them, in fact I guess all of them went to Gilmanton to my mother and one of my brothers.

Q. During all the time that you were at Tilton, Franklin and Gilmanton, your wife thought you were with this lawyer in Kingston?

A. Yes, sir, she did not know that I had any relatives; and I will say, that she has not known that this woman or any of the family has been going from place to place. I had to send her ahead or to follow.

Q. That is, Mrs. Pitezel?

A. Yes, sir. My wife has known nothing of the insurance matter in any way, shape or form.

Q. When did Mrs. Pitezel first become acquainted with this scheme?

A. Well, it is pretty hard to tell, because I found out a week or two ago here, that her oldest daughter had known of it in the summer; that her father had told her if anything happened to him not to be worried; that he would not be dead, and whether it was the same case with Mrs. Pitezel or not, I cannot tell, but my object in leaving Philadelphia a little ahead of when it should come out in the papers, was so to get there, to sort of break it to her, tell her if she saw it in the papers it was not a fact. Now, to the best of my knowledge and belief that was when she first knew of it.

Q. Did she know from the papers, anything about the finding of the body of Perry before you saw her?

A. They found it out in the morning in the papers, that is, the family, the entire family read it and naturally supposed it to be true.

Q. (By Mr. Hanscom.) Did it seem to be genuine grief on their part?

A. Yes, sir, the doctor even was called.

Q. Then really you believe that was the first they knew?

A. Yes, this oldest daughter was taking on just as bad as any and I know

now that she knew or supposed it was not really death.

Q. The mother is rather an illiterate, plain person?

A. Yes.

Q. (By Mr. Cornish.) Then you saw her the day she read this in the paper?

A. The night.

Q. What conversation did you have with her then?

A. I told her then that she need not worry.

Q. Did you on that evening tell her that her husband was alive?

A. Yes, I am sure of that.

Q. Then if you told her that her husband was alive, there must have been some conversation that you had with her in regard to the job that was put up in Philadelphia?

A. Oh yes, I spoke to her the next day. That is why I hastened there. In fact, I told him to hold on, not to leave the house, not prepare this body until Monday some time, but the evidence seems to show that he got scared or something and did not want to stay with it overnight.

Q. Before calling on Mrs. Pitezel did you see Jeptha D. Howe?

A. I did not see him until the next morning. I remember that I got in on the six something train and went to the office to see him and he had gone, and I saw him the following morning. I had seen him previously about the arrangement.

Q. Did you tell him of your interview with Mrs. Pitezel?

A. Yes, sir.

Q. Did he then see her?

A. I think it was the next day.

Q. Were you with him at the time?

A. Yes, sir.

Q. At her house or his office?

A. At his office.

Q. Did she go alone to his office or did you take her there?

A. I think I took her the first time and introduced her. Oh, I remember she was there in the morning waiting and we were both there waiting when Mr. Howe came on the landing there.

Q. Was there anybody at the interview or conference, except yourself, Howe and Mrs. Pitezel?

A. I don't think there was, unless a young lady that sat there, a stenographer. I am almost sure a stenographer was there.

Q. Was she engaged in taking down this conversation?

A. No, I don't think so.

Q. When was the next conference, and where?

A. I think she went there the next day at Mr. Howe's office and was there before I got there; in fact, I don't think I saw her much that date only as she came out of there just for a minute or two, on the landing to talk.

Q. Did she object very strenuously to carrying out this scheme?

A. No, not then after I explained it. She said she was in it and would do her best to carry it out.

Q. What inducements did you hold out to her to carry on this scheme?

A. It was the money.

Q. Was she promised any amount of money?

A. No, it was agreed that this money should be used to protect the property in Fort Worth, that her husband and I were both interested in.

Q. At that time was there anything stated to Howe, or by Howe, as to what his fees were to be?

A. It was spoken of and he said it would be all right, he would not set a price, but really the object he had in going to take hold of the case was to get money to liberate his other client who was in jail. (Marion Hedgepeth.)

Q. How many interviews did you have altogether with Howe, when Mrs. Pitezel was present?

A. Oh, perhaps half a dozen.

Q. Running over how many days?

A. Well, perhaps ten days, because in the meantime I went away to Franklin, I know, and then there was an interview after I got back, after he got the money.

Q. In each of these interviews in which Mrs. Pitezel was present, she knew, or was led to believe that her husband was still alive?

A. Oh yes, she did. And one thing, it was agreed between Howe and myself, that Mrs. Pitezel should not know but what he thought it was a genuine death.

Q. What was that?

A. It was agreed between Howe, the attorney, and myself, that Mrs. Pitezel did not know that he was acting in an underhand way.

Q. (By Mr. Hanscom.) Has Mrs. Pitezel received any letters from her husband since she was in Detroit?

A. I think it was since then, one in a sort of cipher. I have been in the habit for years of using cipher and they fixed one up, a simple device, using figures instead of letters. Aside from this there was none.

Q. She has received one?

A. Yes, sir, she read part of it to me.

Q. Where was it from?

A. Well, it was written, I know, in Detroit. He had me keep it so if she got anxious and worried to say he was all right.

Q. He wrote a cipher letter to his wife and that was entrusted to your custody?

A. Yes, sir. I think it was given to her in Ogdensburg, at some point on my travels since. She might not recall it, it was all in figures.

Q. (By Mr. Cornish.) You stated that there was to be some arrangements made so that you could communicate through the New York Htrald or Chicago Tribune; did you have any such communication?

A. No, sir, that was after he got away. There was no occasion then. But instead of my writing him, I was to communicate with him there and my mail was to have come from Chicago, I was not to have it direct.

Q. Now, I am going to ask you a question. From whom did you get the body in New York?

A. Well, I have refused thus far to state. I told Mr. Perry I thought I would, but if Pitezel comes up in a few days I would rather not tell that, because I was concerned years ago with this doctor, in something not exactly of this nature, but so intimately that in the position he is in, it would hurt him very much. Of course, I will if it comes right down to saving myself.

Q. I think that while you are telling this thing, you should tell the whole truth right as it is. It is a matter that must come out in time and now is as good a time as any other.

A. I think you will agree with me, that I have tried since I told Inspector Watts that I would not tell anything but the truth, that I would try to make it plain, but it is more than that. He is a man now well enough to do, so that if my wife becomes penniless, if I am shut up for a term of years, I think I can call upon him for help.

Q. Then you understand that the party who furnished you the body had no guilty knowledge?

A. They did, they knew well enough while it was being talked over; they knew from our past connection well enough, from the receipts that we got from the insurance company, he knew what the body was going to be used for. The very fact that I wanted one with a wart on the neck.

Q. Was the body placed in the trunk in the house there?

A. I'd rather not answer that. I don't want to antagonize you in the least, but for the time being I'd rather wait.

Q. Where was the trunk purchased?

A. It was a trunk that we had back and forth. It had been there in his house, an old trunk purposely, so as not to draw attention to it. I cannot tell where it was purchased, years old. The trunk belonged to him.

Q. How much money did Mrs. Pitezel give you? You said that she gave you $1,800 to be given to Pitezel?

A. It came in a lump sum. I can give you a rough guess within a few hundred dollars that was paid by the insurance company and I cannot tell. (Figures it up). In the neighborhood of $7,000.

Q. That is what she gave you?

A. I can put it in this way, that Howe gave Mrs. Pitezel just about $7,000 and she gave me $5,000 something odd.

Q. That is, that Howe gave Mrs. Pitezel $7,000 about and Mrs. Pitezel gave you $5,000?

A. Yes, and before that to pay a certain bill there.

Q. What was the bill, a bill to Becker?

A. Yes, and $400 that I was owing, attorney's fees on another matter, so directly and indirectly she caused to come into my hands about $7,000.

Q. What disposition was made of that?

A. Well, to make it clear I will have to explain the business in the South to a certain extent. We took of a party by the name of Williams, a certain piece of property to build upon, agreed to pay her $10,000 for it, and last spring from time to time we paid her $2,500. This we sent to her, and the receipt was in the shape of several pieces of paper, notes, and quite a considerable amount was sent to take them up. I forget how much, less than $5,000.

Q. Do you remember one night in Indianapolis telling your wife that you had sold certain Fort Worth property for $35,000, $10,000 to be paid in cash, and the balance in bonds and mortgages?

A. Yes, sir, this very piece of property she supposed.

Q. Now then you took a roll of bills out of your pocket, was that supposed to be part of the $10,000?

A. I think she has got the two dates confounded, because I went to Detroit to consummate this sale that she was so anxious to have made.

Q. This took place in Detroit?

A. Yes, the last time.

Q. And you told her that Blackman had $5,000?

A. The question was naturally where was the $10,000. I told her that |5,000 I sent to Chicago. I don't think I said to Blackman, though she was led to think that.

Q. Part of it you entrusted to her?

A. I gave her a thousand dollars.

Q. In Cincinnati how much did you give Pitezel?

A. In Cincinnati only a very little, a couple of hundred dollars.

Q. In Detroit?

A. I think it was $1,825, or twenty odd dollars, making the two sums $2,000 with what I had given him in Cincinnati.

Q. That is the amount that Pitezel got out of the whole affair?

A. Hardly, because he profited out of what was got out of this Fort Worth. That was all in cash.

Q. How much had Mrs. Pitezel?

A. Oh, very little, a few hundred dollars. His orders were to give it to her from time to time.

Q. How much was allowed to Jeptha D. Howe?

A. He took $2,500.

Q. Do you remember how many times you saw Pitezel in Philadelphia after or before you had taken the house on Callowhill Street?

A. Once or twice I guess before and perhaps three times, very few times publicly. I would try to meet him perhaps on the street cars or corners, I kept away purposely from his place of business.

Q. How many times did you visit the house on Callowhill Street?

A. I think three times.

Q. You went with him to buy the furniture?

A. I think I was with him when he bought the first of the furniture, but he went one way and I another, to hunt up furniture houses, and I think it was at one of those places that we had found what we bought.

Q. Who paid for it?

A. He paid for it.

Q. Do you remember the name?

A. No, I can go to it readily. It seems as though it was on 13th Street.

Q. Do you remember the man from whom you purchased it?

A. I could tell him by sight.

Q. Did you have an invoice of what you bought?

A. No, he paid. I don't think there was any bill. It was sent down the next day, and then he told me he went back again and bought some other things.

Q. Were you with him in any other store in Philadelphia, outside of this furniture store?

A. It don't seem to me as though I was.

Q. Prior to that?

A. Yes, prior, I think we went into one or two places together to see about furniture.

Q. Prior to his securing the house on Callowhill Street, where did he room?

A. It seems to me it was on Arch Street. It was near 11th. I know I had to come down from where I was rooming and go a little ways on Arch, where it said "boarding house," on Arch or Vine Street.

Q. Did you visit him in his room there?

A. Yes, I think once or twice.

Q. Had you any correspondence or made any arrangement with this party in New York in regard to securing this body?

A. I saw him personally when I was in New York just before going to Philadelphia, and then after that I went up once, I guess the Thursday before I got it on Sunday.

Q. What was the occasion of your going to New York from Philadelphia?

A. Why we found afterwards we were right in front of the morgue, but we did not know it then, and I know this man there and I had no other place to go for it.

Q. Then your purpose for visiting New York was simply to see this man in regard to getting the body?

A. Yes, I don't think there was any other business transacted there, though he sent from there some of his insurance premiums, but that was before we had gone to Philadelphia, that was paying the six months' premium or the balance, I don't know how much.

Q. That was telegraphed to Chicago?

A. Yes.

Q. Did you furnish the money?

A. Yes, in a sense, on account of his drinking some, I generally carried the money.

Q. It was sent by him?

A. I cannot tell that particular money, whether is was through him or me, but between us we furnished the money.

Q. It was telegraphed?

A. Yes, I had nothing to do with the sending of it. He went on himself to see about it.

Q. Where did you meet this party in New York about the body?

A. It was at the house — I would rather leave that out.

Q. I tell you again, that unless Pitezel is produced alive we must consider Pitezel dead.

A. I understand it and that is why I say that, which I can prove in Philadelphia to the contrary. I don't care how soon Pitezel is brought to the front now. I have almost got to do it to protect myself. It is not that I wish to go back on him by any means.

Q. (By Mr. Hanscom.) You expect in any event that there will be imprisonment go with it?

A. I certainly do. I told my wife, I begged her to go away and drop it because I expected a term at the penitentiary.

Q. Of course, it is desirable for you not to be held for the greater offence?

A. I certainly don't want to be held for murder. While I am bad enough on smaller things, I am not guilty of that and I certainly can prove in Philadelphia by records, etc., they would remember because I was sick at the time, fees to porters, etc., prove that I was out of Philadelphia; that he was seen alive after that, if I am allowed a chance to do it.

Q. (By Mr. Cornish.) I understand you to say, that you had previously had connections with his doctor in New York?

A. Yes, that is the greatest reason why at this time

Q. Of a criminal nature?

A. Well, I cannot be expected to answer that, I don't think. It was not an insurance arrangement hardly, but any way, we both profited by it.

This statement it will be observed, leaves obscure the whereabouts of the three children. He places them in South America with their father, and describes one of the girls as being dressed as a boy. The main purpose of the interview was to ascertain, whether Pitezel was alive or dead, and if alive, how the substitution of a dead body, obtained in New York, had been effected. The fate of the children was overlooked for the time. That they had been murdered was not dreamed of; in fact, the case was too fresh, and opportunity had not yet arrived for either the police or the detectives of the company to verify or disprove the statements of the prisoner. The authorities were yet groping in the dark.

CHAPTER V

THE WAGES OF SIN

Mrs. Pitezel Questioned by the Police— Her Pitiable Condition — Complicity in the Plot — Tries to Shield Her Husband — Prepared for His Disappearance — Believed Him Alive— Gives Holmes $7,000— Had Parted with Three Children — Other Details of the Examination — The Prisoners Taken to Philadelphia — Holmes Tries to Bribe Detective Crawford — Committed for Trial — Howe Brought from St. Louis — H. H. Holmes, Benjamin F. Pitezel, Carrie A. Pitezel and Jeptha D. Howe Formally Indicted by the Grand Jury.

Poor Mrs. Pitezel! What a wretched plight she was in! Her husband had disappeared; Alice, Nellie and Howard were in unknown hands, her other two children, Dessie, her eldest daughter, and her year old infant, were without a protector, and she was in prison, under suspicion of having been a party to a conspiracy to cheat and defraud an insurance company.

After Messrs. Hanscom & Cornish had obtained the statement from Holmes, given in full in the previous chapter, they turned their attention to Mrs. Pitezel. She occupied a cell in the same police station in which Holmes was detained, and her grief and surprise over her arrest and incarceration were so great, that the hearts of the officers were moved to pity.

It is to be regretted, that in this interview, Mrs. Pitezel was not as truthful and as frank as she subsequently became with the authorities in Philadelphia. She was evidently inspired by a desire to shield her husband, whom she then believed to be alive, notwithstanding her statement to the contrary. Her denial of her complicity in the scheme to cheat and defraud the insurance company by the substitution of a body, was untrue.

She had been informed of the scheme from its inception, both by Holmes and her husband, and although at first she earnestly and sincerely advised against it and pleaded with her husband not to join Holmes in such a nefarious piece of business, she ultimately acquiesced in it, and was quite prepared for the disappearance of her husband for a time, in accordance with an understanding between them. When Howe paid to her, her share of the money, about 17200, she believed the plot had been successfully carried out; that her husband was alive, and would ultimately disclose his whereabouts to her and would, when prudent, return to his home.

This much may be said for her. She was leading a miserable existence in poverty, with a large family of five children. She was in ill health, and tied by marriage to a crook, a man whose instincts were low and criminal, — much given to drinking alcoholic stimulants excessively, and who had been for years a close associate and companion of Holmes'. Her participation in the crime, however, was without excuse, and she was properly apprehended and charged with conspiracy. It was her plain duty to have prevented the consummation of the scheme at all hazard, — even if a bold stand for truth and honor had caused a separation from her husband.

Her punishment, however, has been severe, much more dreadful than any that could have been inflicted by the law, and while some may condemn her, many will not hesitate to pity one, who now carries with her such a weight of woe.

Upon being questioned by the officers, she answered as follows:

Q. (By Mr. Hanscom.) Where is your home?

A. My home is in Galva, Ill.

Q. Now this matter about the death of your husband and the identification of the body, the collection of the insurance, etc., when was the matter first brought to your attention?

A. Why, I saw it in the paper first.

Q. You saw that a death had occurred?

A. Yes.

Q. The death of whom?

A. B. F. Perry.

Q. And did you understand at the time that your husband was living in Philadelphia under the name of Perry?

A. Yes, sir.

Q. Did you know what street and number he had located on?

A. No. 1316, I think, Callowhill Street.

Q. Before the time that you got this news from the press or in some other way, had you known anything about this scheme?

A No, they did not tell me anything about it.

Q. Nothing had been said to you about it?

A. No, they did not tell me anything about it.

Q. Have you one of your daughters here with

A. Yes, sir.

Q. Is she the eldest daughter?

A. Yes.

Q. Is she the one that went to identify her father?

A. No, she is not the one.

Q. After seeing the death in the paper, who was the first to speak to you about it?

A. Mr. Becker was the first one that I spoke to. He saw the account in the paper, of course, and he was our groceryman and I talked to him about it.

Q. Where were you living then?

A. In St. Louis.

Q. What street and number?

A. It is Carondelet; it is a part of St. Louis.

Q. How long had you been living there?

A. Oh, we moved there in May; about the first of May. Well, maybe it was the middle of May.

Q. Did Mr. Holmes come to your house soon after the announcement of the death to see you?

A. I think it was a week after.

Q. Now what did he say to you about it? He then told you the scheme, did he, that your husband was not dead?

A. Why, I told him that I saw something in the paper in regard to my husband and I wanted to know if that was my husband and if it was true, and he said, "You need not worry about it, there is no use in worrying about that," and he would not say much more about it. He went and talked with the children and only stayed a little while that evening and went away.

Q. Up to that time had you mourned your husband as dead?

A. Yes, sir.

Q. Did you believe he was dead?

A. Yes, I believed he was dead.

Q. Had you taken any steps in the matter?

A. I spoke to Mr. Becker and he went down to the police, and then there had been one or two reporters out.

Q. But a week had elapsed?

A. I think it was about a week, I won't be positive about that.

Q. Had you sent any word to Philadelphia?

A. No, I had not.

Q. Had you written?

A. No, I did not try it, I did not know what to do.

Q. What did Mr. Becker tell you to do?

A. He thought I had better employ an attorney and have it attended to.

Q. Did you employ an attorney?

A. I did not just then, not right that day.

Q. Did you make any arrangements to recover the body?

A. No, I did not.

Q. Had you received a telegram or any word from Holmes before he called upon you?

A. No, I did not.

Q. Had it been talked over with you that such an occurrence might take place, that is, that your husband might absent himself and let the report go out that he was dead? Had such a report ever reached you?

A. No, not up to this time.

Q. Never had been talked over with you?

A. No.

Q. Had you no intimation, not the slightest sign that it had been talked over?

A. Not before that, I had no knowledge of what was to be done.

Q. Had you any money by you at the time this occurred?

A. No, I did not have but little.

Q. How much did you have?

A. Five or six dollars, I think.

Q. He had not sent you much money?

A. No.

Q. Well, on this first visit that Holmes, or Howard, whoever he is, made to you, did he tell you before lie went out that your husband was living, that you need not worry about it?

A. Well, he spoke to that effect, I don't know as those were the exact words.

Q. Did he ease your mind regarding the death of your husband before he went away, telling you that your husband was not dead?

A. Yes.

Q. Did he go into the story that your husband was insured?

A. No, he did not go into the story then.

Q. Did you know that your husband had an insurance on his life?

A. I knew he had an insurance on his life, but I did not know whether it was all paid or not. It was not paid up, and I did not know even when I heard of the death, whether it was all paid up.

Q. Did you know the amount of the insurance?

A. I did at the time he insured.

Q. How much?

A. $10,000.

Q. Who collected that money?

A. Mr. Howe.

Q. As your attorney?

A. Yes.

Q. Did he turn that money over to you?

A. Well, most of it was turned over to me.

Q. What did you do with it?

A. Well, Mr. Howard had some of it.

Q. How much did Mr. Howard have of the $10,000?

A. I don't know exactly that.

Q. You understood they paid the full amount, $10,000?

A. Yes,

Q. After Mr. Howe had made the payments then you turned over a large portion of that money? This is not an effort to entrap you. We simply want to get at the facts.

A. Well, I understand you, and am trying to give you the facts as well as I can.

Q. How much of that $10,000 did you turn over to Howard, (Holmes)?

A. I don't know as I can tell you the exact amount.

Q. Can you remember?

A. No, I can't.

Q. Was it $7,000?

A. It must have been pretty well on to that.

Q. He states it was about $7,000.

A. Well, that is correct, I think.

Q. Did you turn over that money to any other person than him?

A. No, no person only what the attorney and the expenses were, that was all.

Q. How much did that amount to, the attorneys and the expenses? Can you remember that?

A. No, I can't. They made out a memorandum of it, Mr. Howe did. He just made it out, and I don't know, they got into a kind of fussing about it, and, by the way, they did not give me the statement of it.

Q. You did not get that?

A. No, I have no statement of it at all.

Q. After having paid the expense and $7,000 more or less that you gave Howard, what portion of the $10,000 had you left?

A. Well, I guess about $500.

Q. You had really about $500 out of the whole business?

A. Yes.

Q. Do you know how much of it your husband had?

A. No, that is something I can't answer, for I don't know.

Q. When did you last see your husband?

A. I saw him last the 9th day of July, and I have not seen him since.

Q. The 9th day?

A. It was either the 8th or 9th of July that he left home in the evening, and I went down to the Union Depot and that was the last.

Q. In St. Louis?

A. Yes.

Q. Did he correspond with you after that?

A. Up to the time that I saw it in the paper he did, but I have never heard from him since, only just what Mr. Howard says, that is all.

Q. Now, what has Mr. Howard said to you about the whereabouts of your husband since that time?

A. Well, the only place that I know of where he has been, is Montreal and Toronto.

Q. How do you know that he was in Montreal?

A. I don't know for a certainty, I could not swear only as I have heard it.

Q. From whom?

A. From Mr. Howard.

Q. That he was in Toronto and Montreal?

A. Yes. 7

Q. Has he told you that you would meet him at any other place?

A. He said I might see him at Detroit, or Toronto, or Burlington, but I have never seen him.

Q. Then you had hopes when you went to Burlington, that you might meet him?

A. Yes.

Q. And failing to find him in Burlington, where did you expect then to see him?

A. Well, I don't know. I gave up all hopes of seeing him.

Q. He has kept you moving, hasn't he?

A. Yes.

Q. I wish to ask you one question direct. Do you believe now that your husband is alive?

A. Well, there must be something in it. I am sure I could not swear to it for I don't know for a fact that he is alive. All I know is, what you have been telling me, and what he has been telling me, and that is all I know.

Q. But he has kept you moving from point to point; I would like to have you tell it in your own way.

A. Well, I have been moving from one point to another. I have been just heartbroken, that is all there is about it.

Q. Yes, I know, we are sorry for you. Can you tell me the points in the order of them, how you have been moving about since you left home?

A. I went to my parents, from there to Chicago, from Chicago to Detroit, and from there to Toronto, from there to Ogdensburg, from there to Burlington.

Q. And that is where you were yesterday?

A. Yes, Burlington.

Q. Have you had confidence in Howard all the way through, that he would finally take you to your husband?

A. Why, I thought so.

Q. Has your confidence ever been shaken?

A. Well, sometimes I thought maybe he was fooling me or something.

Q. By the way, did you have a cipher, anything in the shape of a cipher, by which your husband could communicate with you privately, any system of communication, numbers, characters?

A. Oh no, we do not write that way.

Q. You never wrote that way?

A. No.

Q. Did you ever expect to get any such letter from your husband, written in any mysterious way, ciphers of any kind?

A. No.

Q. Did Holmes ever read to you at any time since the money was collected, say at the time you were in Detroit, did he ever read anything to you, purporting to be a letter from your husband written in cipher, did you receive something of that kind?

A. Well, I think he did have something of that kind that was written in that way, and said it was from him. That is all I know.

Q. Was it in any envelope?

A. No, I guess not.

Q. Did you see the paper that he had?

A. Why, it was just a small piece of paper.

Q. He read something to you from that paper?

A. Yes.

Q. Did you have the paper in your hand?

A. No.

Q. What did it say?

A. Why, just said that he was well and all right and I need not be worrying all the time.

Q. You went to Detroit, expecting to meet your husband there?

A. Yes.

Q. When he read that letter to you, do you remember where you were then?

A. In Toronto, I think.

Q. You went to Detroit and from Detroit to Toronto?

A. Yes.

Q. In Detroit did you expect to meet your husband there?

A. I thought I would see him, he said I would.

Q. How many of the children had you with you? Just had the little girl and the babe?

A. Yes.

Q And the other three children were with whom, so far as you know?

A. They were at Covington.

Q. With whom?

A. I don't know who they were with. I asked him the name and he simply told me who they were with, said she was a widow, a nice woman.

Q. Now, how long ago was it that you parted with these three children?

A. I have not seen Alice for two months, and have not seen the others for

Q. Alice went away first?

A. Yes sir.

Q. She went to identify the body of her father?

A. Yes, sir.

Q. And you have not seen her since?

A. No.

Q. In whose keeping was she, into whose charge did you give her at the time she went on to view the body?

A. Mr. Howe took her.

Q. Who is he?

A. He is the lawyer, the attorney.

Q. That was acting for you?

A. Yes, sir.

Q. A St. Louis man?

A. Yes, sir.

Q. Do you know where his office is in St. Louis?

A. Well, it is in the Commercial Building.

Q. Into his keeping you placed the girl?

A, Yes, they wanted me to go, but I was very sick at the time.

Q. And Alice went on with him?

A. Yes. Well, he turned Alice over to Mr. Holmes then, and he brought her on to Covington.

Q. Did you see her in Covington?

A. No, sir, I was not in Covington at all.

Q. Have you some friends in Covington?

A. No, sir.

Q. You have not seen her since she went on to view the body?

A. No, sir, I have not seen her since.

Q. Into whose custody did you place the other two?

A. He took the other two, that is, Holmes, took them from St. Louis to Covington, where Alice was.

Q. You don't know whether they actually went to Covington or not?

A. No, I am just telling you.

Q. That is right. What was his reason for taking them? What reason did he give?

A. The only reason was he said he would take them there and I could go home and make my parents a visit, and not to be bothered with them, because my parents were getting along in years, and he would take the children and then I could go over there when I got through visiting.

Q. He was going to take them to meet Alice?

A. Yes, sir.

Q. And that they would all be stopping with some widow lady.

A. Yes.

Q. Did he give the name?

A. No, sir, I told you he did not.

Q. Did he say anything about that they were going to Covington to meet their father?

A. No, sir, he did not say that.

Q. Has he ever told you since then, that they were with the father?

A. No sir.

Q. Then you still believe that they are in Covington?

A. No, sir, he told me he took them to Toronto, that is all I know about it. I don't know where they are. All I know is that he said he would take them from Covington to Toronto.

Q. You understood from him that they are there?

A. At Toronto.

Q. With friends of his, or whom do you believe them to be with, your husband?

A. No, he said he would give them to some friends there. I don't know whether he has.

Q. We believe this man to be a very bad man, and we want to get at all the truth.

A. Well, that is as far as I know. I can't tell you anything more, because I don't know.

Q. You did not understand then that these children were going to join their father?

A. No, sir.

Q. Has he ever told you about dressing one of the girls in boy's clothing?

A. No, sir.

Q. He never told you about those things?

A. Well, I have one boy.

Q. There is a boy and two girls?

A. Whoever told you that?

Q. We have been talking with him. We are not doing anything to undertake to make you feel bad, we are trying to get at the matter and sift it. He has kept you moving about the country from point to point, and you look as though you had been through a good deal and we want to get all the light we can. We don't believe in this man very much. That is why we are asking you these questions.

A. Do you know where the children are?

Q. No, that is one of the things we want to find out. We want to find them as much for your sake, as well as for any other reason in the world. In fact, we may say that all these questions that are being asked you now regarding these children are in your behalf. Holmes is locked up in this very building, and we have been talking with him.

A. I thought maybe I would see the children here.

Q. Holmes is locked up, you knew that, didn't you?

A. I didn't know it until I came up here.

Q. He has not given you to understand that the children were with their father?

A. No.

Q. Is there anything else that you can think of that he has said about the whereabouts of the children?

A. That is the last that I know about it.

Q. You have met him a number of times at these different points?

A. Yes.

Q. He has kept you moving on?

A. Yes.

Q. (By Mr. Cornish.) Have you heard from Alice since she has been away?

A. I have not heard from her from Covington since I was home.

Q. Have you received a letter from her from Covington?

A. Yes, sir.

Q. Had she written it herself?

A. Yes, sir, she and Nellie had written it themselves.

Q. Did you keep the letter?

A. No, I did not keep the letter.

Q. Do you remember what they said?

A. Well, they said they were well and the woman was real good to them, said she was an awful kind lady, that they would like to see mama, and wanted to know how the baby was, if it could talk yet and how grandma and grandpa were and they hoped they would see mama soon. I think that is about the extent of it.

Q. That was sent where, to Galva?

A. Yes.

Q. Did you receive any letters from them from any other point except Covington?

A. No, I think not.

Q. Did you get any from them from Toronto?

A. No, sir.

Q. The only correspondence you had from them was in Covington?

A. Yes, sir.

Q. And that was during the time you were in Galva?

A. Yes, sir.

Q. Did you ever write to your children?

A. Why, certainly.

Q. How often?

A. Well, I wrote them several letters while I was home in Galva.

Q. (By Mr. Hanscom.) But you only heard from them once?

A. Well, I think I got two letters.

Q. (By Mr. Cornish.) How did you direct your letters?

A. Directed them to Alice Pitezel, Covington, Ky.

Q. Did you mail it yourself?

A. My father mailed it.

Q. Have you written to them since at Covington or Toronto?

A. Why, yes, I have sent them several letters.

Q. Who did you send them by, mail them yourself?

A. No, I did not mail them myself.

Q. Who mailed them?

A. Holmes mailed them, I suppose. I had given them to him to mail.

Q. Did you write to your father and mother at Galva?

A. Yes, sir.

Q. Did you mail any of them?

A. I mailed one from Chicago.

Q. Have you written to them since? When you were in Toronto and Detroit and those other places?

A. Yes, sir.

Q. Did you mail those?

A. No, sir.

Q. Who did?

A. I gave them to Mr. Holmes to mail.

Q. Who suggested that you should employ Jeptha D. Howe as counsel?

A. Mr. Howard. (Holmes).

Q. The first time that he called upon you in St. Louis did he suggest that you employ Mr. Howe?

A. No, not that night.

Q. The next day?

A. I don't remember that I saw him the next day, I think it was two days after that.

Q. Then he suggested that you should employ Mr. Howe?

A. Yes, I think it was a couple of days, I can't give it exactly.

Q. You went by the name of Adams in Detroit, Toronto and Ogdenshurg?

A. Yes, sir.

Q. And by the name of Cook in Burlington

A. Yes, that is right.

Q. Did Mr. Holmes tell you to use those names?

A. Yes, sir.

Q. Where were you stopping in Burlington?

A. Winooski Avenue, No. 26, I think.

Q. How many times did you see Holmes in Burlington?

A. Well, that is kind of a hard question to answer, I don't remember, four or five times.

Q. Did he call at the house?

A. Yes sir, but he never stayed any length of time.

Q. Did he give you any money there?

A. No, sir.

NO. 26 WINOOSKI AVENUE, BURLINGTON, WHERE HOLMES
INTENDED TO KILL PITEZEL'S FAMILY

Q. Did you receive a package from him last Saturday by express?

A. Yes, sir.

Q. What did that contain?

A. It contained two tickets, railroad tickets.

Q. And a letter?

A. A short letter in it.

Q. What did the letter contain?

A. Just for me to pick up my things and come to Lowell Sunday night, and then Sunday morning this Mr. Lane came and gave me another letter from him, that just stated for me to come straight on to Boston, that he would see me through.

Q. You have told all you know about this matter?

A. Yes, I have told about all I can remember, it is mixed up anyway.

Q. Did you make any attempt to find the children there in Toronto?

A. They were not there when I was there.

Q. After you had left, lie told you that they were there?

A. That was when I was in Burlington, he said they were there.

Q. That was the first that you knew of the children being in Toronto?

A. That was the first I knew that they were there, and this letter came for me to come on down here, and, of course, that ended it.

Q. How did he explain to you that the children had left Covington for Toronto? Why did he change their location?

A. Well, he said he thought it would be better to have them up there, and I could go and see them there, that they would be closer to me. I thought, of course, I should go there to see them.

Q. Where were you, when he told that they were in Toronto?

A. I was in Burlington. It is just lately.

Q. He did not tell you where they were in Toronto?

A. No, sir.

Q. Whether they were in school or at a private house?

A. No, sir, I could not find them if it was a case of life and death.

Q. When your husband went away from St. Louis, did he tell you that he was going to Philadelphia or Chicago?

A. He went to Chicago. He told me that he was going there to dispose of some lumber. He did not say he was going to Philadelphia when he went away.

Q. And then you heard from him in Chicago that he was going to Philadelphia?

A. Yes, sir.

Q. That was under the name of Pitezel?

A. Yes, sir.

Q. Did he tell you in that letter from Chicago, that he was going by the name of Perry? A. No, sir.

Q. In the letter after that?

A. Yes, sir.

On Monday, November 19, 1894, Thomas Crawford, one of the detectives of the Bureau of Police of Philadelphia arrived in Boston, with warrants for the arrest of Holmes and Mrs. Pitezel, both of whom, however, consented to go to Philadelphia without the formality of a requisition from the Governor of Pennsylvania. The party consisted of Detective Crawford, Inspector Perry of the Insurance company, H. H. Holmes, Miss Yoke, whom he had married under the name of Howard, Mrs. Pitezel and her infant and Dessie Pitezel. On the journey, Holmes reiterated his statement that Pitezel was alive, and in South America, and that the children were with him. That he had given Pitezel $1,600 and had sewed $400 in Alice's dress or chemise. He said he left Alice in Indianapolis, (after taking her to Philadelphia) and then got the other two children and brought them to her. He then took them all to Detroit, where they met Pitezel, and then the latter and the three children sailed for South America. He said he and Pitezel were to keep track of each other through the personal column of the New York Herald.

He said to Dessie Pitezel: "Don't worry Dessie, you and your father will meet before long, and you will see your sisters and your brother." He told her she might expect to see her father in Philadelphia. He reiterated to Crawford his story of the manner in which the corpse had been obtained in New York, and laughed at the bungling manner in which Pitezel had left the body; that he had particularly instructed Pitezel how to place the body, to put the chloroform in its mouth and to press the sides, so as to work it down the throat; that Pitezel had left the body with its hand across the breast, looking as if it had died a peaceful death, whereas the man was supposed to have died a horrible death. He said he instructed Pitezel how to fix the bottle and the pipe, so as to have it appear as if in lighting the pipe the benzine had exploded and killed the man. On the train Holmes asked Crawford, if he believed in hypnotism. Crawford said "No." He said he could hypnotize people very easily, and wanted to try his powers on Crawford, but the invitation was declined. The sort of hypnotism Holmes was most proficient in was best exhibited when he offered to give Crawford $500 dollars for a purpose not stated, but quite well understood. That bait was also declined.

On Tuesday, November 20th, 1894, the party arrived at the Central Station, City Hall, Philadelphia. Holmes and Mrs. Pitezel were given a hearing and were at once committed to prison to await trial. Dessie

Pitezel and the baby, were placed in the kind care of Benjamin Crew, Esq., Secretary of the Society to Protect Children from Cruelty. Within the next few days, Jeptha D. Howe was brought on from St. Louis, on the charge of conspiracy and was held in $2,500 bail to answer at court. In due time the case reached the office of George S. Graham, Esq., District Attorney. In this office an indictment was prepared, charging H. H. Holmes, Benjamin F. Pitezel, Carrie A. Pitezel, and Jeptha D. Howe with having fraudulently and wilfully conspired to cheat and defraud the Fidelity Mutual Life Association, out of the sum of $10,000 dollars, by means of the substitution of a body for that of Benjamin F. Pitezel. This indictment was formally presented to the Grand Jury and a true bill was found, and the matter rested in that shape until Holmes created another sensation by making a second so-called confession.

CHAPTER VI

IN THE TOILS

The Insurance Company Not Idle — Efforts to Locate Pitezel— Holmes in His Cell — The Arch-Scoundrel Changes His Base — Sends for the Superintendent of Police — Admits Lying — Pitezel Dead and the Children in London — Holmes' Second Confession in Detail — Efforts to Verify or Disprove It — The Children Still Missing — Groping in the Dark — Thomas W. Barlow, Esq., Retained for the Insurance Company — A new Indictment — The Trial — Holmes Happy — Sentence Deferred.

Between the arrest of these parties and their indictment, the officers of the Insurance Company were not idle. Mrs. Pitezel soon learned the wisdom of sincerity and truthfulness, and became communicative, and day by day the history of the crime was laid bare. Every effort was made to locate Pitezel and to find the children, and no expense was spared in running out all sorts of clues. While this was going on, Holmes was occupying his solitary cell in the county prison. He had been for years a very busy man and never before had such an opportunity for reflection and self-examination. As time passed, the probability that Pitezel was not only not alive, but had been murdered at No. 1316 Callowhill Street, pressed itself upon the officers of the Company, and the District Attorney as well, and this impression soon found its way to Holmes in his prison cell. He now discovered that a change of base was necessary. He remembered a conversation that had taken place between him and Inspector Perry, after his arrival in Philadelphia. In this interview, Mr. Perry a-ked him this question: Who helped you to double up the body in New York City and put it in a trunk? Holmes said: "I did it alone. It is a trick I learned at Ann Arbor, Michigan, while studying medicine there."

Mr. Perry knew that when the body which had been found at No. 1316 Callowhill Street, was removed to the morgue, it was straight and rigid and two men had carried it, one at the head and the other at the feet, — so another question was asked Holmes: "Can you tell me where I can find a medical man or a medical authority, which will instruct me how to re-stiffen a body after rigor mortis has once been broken? "To this inquiry. Holmes made no answer.

On December 27th, 1894, Holmes sent for R. J. Linden, Esq.,

Superintendent of Police of the Department of Public Safety of Philadelphia. He told the superintendent that he was very sorry he had been so untruthful in his former statements, when he had declared that Pitezel was alive, and was in South America, and that the children were with him. He said he was now prepared to tell the truth, the whole truth and nothing but the truth; that Pitezel was not alive, but dead, and that it was really Pitezel's body which had been identified in the Potters Field; that the children were not with their father, but with Miss Williams, who had taken them to London, where they could easily be found. He then dictated to a stenographer, the following statement, which is called by the police. Confession No. 2.

Statement.

I contemplated defrauding the insurance company in August or September, 1893, in connection with Benjamin F. Pitezel. No one else was in the plot until July, 1894. Mrs. Pitezel was then informed of it by Pitezel. About August 1st, on my release from jail in St. Louis, I outlined the conspiracy to Howe and showed him how L intended raising money to liberate Hedgepeth from jail, I having told Hedgepeth of it while in jail and agreed to raise $300 to help him out. Howe at that time had no idea of joining in the conspiracy. I went from St. Louis to Chicago to raise some money there, and went to New York where I got $600 from Minnie Williams. I then arranged with Pitezel that he should provide a retreat to stop at after the conspiracy was consummated and also to get his teeth altered. Leaving him in New York, I came to Philadelphia to look for a house. I took part of No. 1905 North Hill Street. Three days later Pitezel came and took the house No. 1316 Callowhill Street, which he furnished partially with chemicals and bottles to represent a patent dealer. I visited this house I think four times besides the day on which he died. I visited the house about the last of August and stayed five or six hours. At that time Pitezel was despondent. I found he had been drinking and took him to task for it. He remarked that he guessed he had better drink enough to kill him and have done with it. He borrowed $15 from me and I left about 4 o'clock. To the best of my knowledge I next saw him on the following Saturday, September 1st, at the Mercantile Library, and quite late that evening he came to my house on North 11th Street and said he had received a telegram that his baby was sick and he had to go home. I said we had better arrange how his business should be run and he told me he could get a party to come to the place. I raised no objection to his going. When we got the arrangements all made he said: "You will have to let me have some money to go with."

I asked him where the $150 were that he told me he had a few days ago. He said: "Well I haven't got it." I could not give him any at that time. This was about 9 o'clock in the evening. I promised to go down in the morning, but before leaving we arranged that I should go in his place and take care of the sick baby and start the body there. The next morning, Sunday, about 10:30, 1 went to his house. I had been provided with a key to go in with. I found no one there either on the first or the second floor, where his sleeping apartment was. He had a cot there which I do not think he ever made up. I went over to the Mercantile Library and stayed there about an hour, and then went up on Broad Street where I had a private mail box, but did not get any mail, bought a morning paper and went back to the Callowhill Street house. I found no one there and knew that no one had been there while I was away. I went upstairs and laid down on the cot and read the paper. It was probably about 12 o'clock when I got back. After reading the paper for about a half hour, I went to his desk to write some letters, and found there a scrap of paper with a figure cipher on it that we used, and it said: "Get letter out bottle in cupboard."

I kept that piece of paper until in Toronto, where I used it in sending a cipher to Mrs. Pitezel and tried to imitate his figures. I got the letter and it told me that he was going to get out of it, and that I should find him upstairs, if he could manage to kill himself. I went upstairs and looked in the clothes press on the second floor, which was the only place I had not been on that floor. Not finding him there I ran up to the third story, opened the door, and saw him lying on the floor apparently dead. I felt his pulse and laid my hand on his and found it was cold. His eyes were partially closed. I then had to leave the room on account of the fumes of chloroform being so strong. I went and opened the window in the other room and came back and started to go in again, but had to give it up, and went to the second floor again. As soon as I could, I did go in again and found that he was lying on his back with his left hand folded over his abdomen and his right hand lying at his side. I did not keep the letter which was in the bottle, but destroyed it with other papers the next day on the train going from Philadelphia to St. Louis. I removed the furniture from the third story room and took it to the second story leaving the body until the last. Then I brought the body down into the second story, and arranged it in the way it was found. This was about 3 o'clock. I had arranged with Pitezel, that when he should place the substitute body, a bottle should be broken which it was supposed that he had in his hand when the explosion occurred, and that the fragments should be scattered around the room. I held the bottle up and broke it with a blow of the hammer upon the side. That bottle contained benzine, chloroform and ammonia, which was to be used for burning the floor to indicate that an explosion had occurred. I took some of this fluid and put it upon his right hand and side, and on the right side of his face and set fire to it. I then arranged the articles that he had taken from his pocket putting them back again, and hung his vest in the second story bedroom, and the coat in the first story where he had been in the habit of keeping it. I gathered together the rubber tube, towel, and a bottle of chloroform and left the house as soon as I could, about a quarter of four. I then went to Broad Street station and found that the train for the west would leave in thirty minutes, and another at 10:25 P. M. I went immediately to No. 1905 North 11th Street and packed my things, and started for St. Louis that night. I found a letter to Mrs. Pitezel in his clothing, which I took with me and put with the other papers in my inside vest pocket. I think I threw away the key to the house, which I had and put back the regular key where lie usually kept it, and instead of locking the door, I left it open a few inches. I got to my house about 5 o'clock. My wife was not well, and I went to work and straightened things and got the packing done before it was dark. When I found the body, the pockets of the pants were turned out, and his knife and the key of the house were lying on a chair. Up to this time, Howe was in the conspiracy. The following Wednesday night I got to St. Louis, and on that day I had seen in a St. Louis paper, a report that the body had been found. I went immediately to Howe's office, having made up my mind, that as he knew of it, I had better let him settle up the insurance. He was not there. I went to Mrs. Pitezel's and found that they had also seen the report. The children were greatly worried, but Mrs. Pitezel was not, as she believed that the scheme had been carried out. We talked the matter over a couple of hours, and I came back that night and saw Howe and explained what had been done, not telling him that it was Pitezel, but leaving him to believe that the plan of placing a substitute had been carried out, and retained him on behalf of Mrs. Pitezel to procure the money from the Company, He suggested that she have some of her neighbors write first, inasmuch as it would not look well for her to immediately run off and get a lawyer; this was done. At the time of the discovery of the body, a towel was over his face. The tube was fastened to the bottle by a cork with a quill; then he had tied around a string to keep the chloroform from running too fast. I think the rubber tube was four or five feet long. I took the tube with me. His wife asked me what that was for. I think I took the cork and quill out of the house also.

(In answer to questions): It did not occur to me when I found that Pitezel was drinking, to give him a little chloroform. I had nothing to do with his taking the chloroform.

This statement Holmes reiterated to the officers of the company and efforts to verify or disprove it were renewed with vigor. January, February, March and April of 1895, came and went, and yet the most earnest work failed to discover the children, or obtain any clue of them, after they had disappeared from Toronto on October 25th, 1894, to which place they had been traced. Furthermore if it was Pitezel's body that was found in the Callowhill Street house, there was no substitution, and an indictment charging the conspirators with having substituted a body, would not meet the case.

At this juncture, the officers of the Company, under the advice of District Attorney Graham, retained Thomas W. Barlow, Esq., a member of the Philadelphia bar. The District Attorney had associated Mr. Barlow with him in many cases in previous years, and they were in thorough accord. A brief of all the facts of the case was carefully prepared and eventually a new indictment was found, charging H. H. Holmes, Marion C. Hedgepeth, and Jeptha D. Howe, with having conspired to cheat the Insurance Company, by alleging that one B. F. Pitezel, who had been insured in said company had died as the result of an accident. This indictment was ingeniously constructed to meet the facts of the case, within the grasp of the Commonwealth. If a body had been substituted and Pitezel was alive, it was good; if the body found was really Pitezel's and he was dead and had committed suicide, it was equally good, as a clause in the policy made it null and void, in case of self destruction. It was then determined to hold any further investigation of the case in abeyance, until a trial should be had under this new bill, the prisoner convicted, and remanded to prison to await sentence.

On June 3d, 1895, the prisoner was called for trial on the new bill. He was defended by able counsel, who presented a bold front on behalf of their client on the first day of the trial. On the second day they weakened and advised their client to plead guilty. This he did with alacrity, as he thought the end of his troubles was in sight. He was informed by his counsel, that the maximum term of imprisonment in Pennsylvania for conspiracy, was two years, and if he pleaded guilty he might possibly get less. The prisoner hastened to take advantage of such a comfortable means of retreat. He really looked happy when the Judge said he would not sentence him then, but would consider his case at a later day.

In the Court Room closely observing the prisoner, was Detective Frank P. Geyer, of the Bureau of Police of Philadelphia. Mr. Geyer had been requested to be present by the District Attorney and Mr. Barlow. A few days later, Mr. Barlow was made Special Assistant District Attorney, and the great work of uncovering one of the greatest criminals of modern times immediately commenced.

CHAPTER V

"A SLIPPERY AND SUBTLE KNAVE"

Holmes' Interview with the District Attorney — The Humanity of Justice — Holmes Urged to Produce the Pitezel Children — His Apparent Candor — Disposition of the Children — Four Hundred Dollars Pinned in Alice's Dress — Nellie Disguised as a Boy — The Loudon Address — Holmes and Miss Williams Agree upon a Cipher — The New York Sunday Herald — Correspondence with Scotland Yard.

Holmes was removed from the court room to an apartment in the City Hall, designated as the cell room, where prisoners are detained after trial, or while waiting their conveyance to the county prison. As Holmes sat cheerfully chatting with one of his counsel, a message reached them from the District Attorney, requesting a conference at once, touching the whereabouts of the children. This meeting took place in Mr. Graham's office. In the middle of the office was a long table. Holmes and his counsel sat on one side of this table, and Mr. Graham and Mr. Barlow on the other. The District Attorney opened the conference by informing Holmes, that the officers of the Commonwealth were very anxious to find the Pitezel children and restore them to their mother; that he had decided to abandon the case against Mrs. Pitezel, as she had suffered quite enough for any part she had reluctantly taken in the perpetration of the fraud on the Insurance Company, and that he intended to set her at liberty without delay; that the uncertainty of the fate of Alice, Nellie, and Howard, coupled with the death of her husband, (of which she and all parties were now quite convinced), had almost dethroned her reason, and that every instinct of humanity dictated a pressing necessity for haste in any effort which could be made to bring her children to her, and that the immediate recovery of the children would remove a growing suspicion that they had been foully dealt with.

"It is strongly suspected, Holmes," said District Attorney Graham, "that you have not only murdered Pitezel, but that you have killed the children. The best way to remove this suspicion, is to produce the children at once. Now where are they? Where can I find them? Tell me and I will use every means in my power to secure their early recovery. It is due to Mrs. Pitezel and to yourself, that the children should be found. You were arrested in November last and you said the children were with their father in South America. It is now May, and we have heard nothing of them. We know your November statement to be untrue, because I am quite convinced that their father died on the second day of September last, at No. 1316 Callowhill Street. You subsequently said that Pitezel was dead and that you gave the children to Miss Williams in Detroit, and you have furthermore given several variations from this last statement. I am almost persuaded that your word cannot be depended upon, yet I am not averse to giving you an opportunity to assist me in clearing up the mystery which surrounds their disappearance and their present abode, and I now ask you to answer frankly and truthfully. Where are the children?"

While Mr. Graham was talking. Holmes listened quietly and attentively, and made no response until he was sure that the District Attorney had paused for a reply. He then said with every appearance of candor, that he was very glad of the opportunity thus afforded him to assist in the restoration of the children to their mother.

"The last time I saw Howard," he said, "was in Detroit, Michigan. There I gave him to Miss Williams, who took him to Buffalo, New York, from which point she proceeded to Niagara Falls, After the departure of Howard, in Miss Williams' care, I took Alice and Nellie to Toronto, Canada, where they remained for several days. At Toronto I purchased railroad tickets for them for Niagara Falls, put them on the train, and rode out of Toronto with them a few miles, so that they would be assured that they were on the right train. Before their departure, I prepared a telegram which they should send me from the Falls, if they failed to meet Miss Williams and Howard, and I also carefully pinned in the dress of Alice, four hundred dollars in large bills, so Miss Williams would be in funds to defray their expenses.

"They joined Miss Williams and Howard at Niagara Falls, from which point they went to New York City. At the latter place. Miss Williams dressed Nellie as a boy, and took a steamer for Liverpool, whence they went to London. If you search among the steamship offices in New York, you must search for a woman and a girl and two boys, and not a woman and two girls and a boy. This was all done to throw the detectives off the track, who were after me for the insurance fraud. Miss Williams opened a massage establishment at No. 80 Veder or Vadar Street,

London. I have no doubt the children are with her now, and very likely at that place."

Holmes said further that he and Miss Williams had agreed upon a cipher, which they were to use in communicating with each other in the personal column of the New York Herald, and that if an advertisement were prepared in accordance with this cipher, very doubtless she would be heard from in a very short time, and the children recovered.

He further denied with great emphasis, that he had killed Pitezel, or had harmed the children and became almost tearful when he exclaimed to the District Attorney, "Why should I kill innocent children?"

The conversation then became general, during which time Holmes exhibited no embarrassment whatever until he was asked by Mr. Barlow: "Please give me the "name of one respectable person to whom I can go, either in Detroit, Buffalo, Toronto, Niagara Falls, or New York, who will say that they saw Miss Williams and the three children together." This question staggered him for a moment, but he quickly recovered himself and said in an injured tone, that the question implied a disbelief in his statement. He was promptly told that it certainly did, and furthermore, that the speaker believed his entire story to be a lie from beginning to end. This drew a vehement protest from Holmes and he declared his readiness to furnish the cipher, with which an advertisement in the Herald should be made up, and by means of which the children would be recovered.

He was told to prepare the cipher and he said he would send it to the District Attorney from the prison.

A day or two later, this letter was received by District Attorney Graham, from Holmes:

May 29, '95.

District Attorney Graham.

Dear Sir: —

The adv. should appear in the New York Sunday Herald and if some comment upon the case can also be put in body of paper stating absence of children and that adv. concerning appears in this paper, etc., it would be an advantage. Any word you may see fit to use in adv. will do and if a long one, only one sentence need be in cipher as she will know by this

Fac-Simile of Holmes' Letter to District Attorney Graham.

that it must come from me as no one else, unless I told them, could have same. Perhaps the first sentence should be — Important to hear before 10th. Cable. Also write to Mr. Massie. AplbcRun — nb — CBRc — etc.

The New York Herald is (or was a year ago) to be found at only a few places regularly in London.

Very Respectfully,

H. H. Holmes.

REPUBLICAN republican
ABCDEFGHIJ klmnopqrst uvwxyz.

CbepBc Thus Holmes

The suggestions contained in this letter were strictly complied with. The Philadelphia correspondent of the New York Herald, was taken into the confidence of the District Attorney's office, and an article was prepared, commenting upon the case and published in the same edition, Sunday, June 2d, 1895, in which the following advertisement in the personal column appeared:

"MINNIE WILLIAMS, ADELE COVELLE. GEKALDINE WANDA.-AplbeuRun nb CBKc EBLbvB lOtli PREeB ABnucu PCAeUcBu RubuPB. Also write pk PRaaAB cbepBa. Address, GEORGE S. GRAHAM, City Hall, Philadelphia, Penn., U. S. A."

This cipher would have conveyed to Miss Williams, the following message: IMPORTANT TO HEAR BEFORE 10th CABLE RETURN CHILDREN AT ONCE. ALSO AplbcnRun nb CBRc EBLbiB 10th PREeB ABiuicu PCAeUcBu Ru buPB. Also WRITE MR. MASSIE. HOLMES. write pk PRaaAB. CbepBa. Address, etc.

It was determined to open a correspondence with the Scotland Yard offices in London, and ask their aid in searching for the children. It was soon discovered, however, that there was no Veder or Vadar Street in London and a request for the assistance of the police authorities in that city was abandoned for the present.

CHAPTER VI

THE PITEZEL CHILDREN

Holmes' Story not Credited — Nettie and Minnie Williams — Holmes Declares Minnie Murdered Her Sister — The Search for the Children Decided upon. The Route Proposed — Holmes' Cunning — Important Clues— Release of Mrs. Pitezel — Mrs. Pitezel's Statement — Nitro-Glycerine — Holmes' Letter to Mrs. Pitezel — Detective Geyer.

No one in the District Attorney's office believed a word of the story that Holmes had told about the children, and it was determined to make a patient and persistent search among the cities in the West for information or clues which would lead to their recovery if alive, or the discovery of their bodies if dead. It was a gigantic task and almost a hopeless one, but neither its great size nor the strong improbability of success, was permitted to interfere with the plans which were then perfected.

Rumors of the remarkable disappearance of two sisters, Nettie and Minnie Williams, had become current. They had been last seen in the company and under the protection of Holmes, and a piece of real estate in Fort Worth, Texas, of which they were owners, was found to have been conveyed to Benton T. Lyman, (which was an alias of Benjamin F. Pitezel) and into the possession and control of Holmes. Holmes had admitted his intimacy with these women and told a startling story of the Holmes type, describing his return one night to the home of the Williams sisters, of his discovery that Minnie in a moment of rage had killed Nettie and how he had shielded the former, by taking Nettie's body out on the lake at Chicago and quietly sinking it. This story, as untruthful and as improbable as any he ever told, had left an impression upon the minds of the officers of the Insurance Company and of leading police officials. They reasoned, and with some force, that while they were quite ready to believe that Holmes had killed the little Pitezel children, they did not think it possible that such an astute and wily criminal, had left a trace behind him, and that most probably the bodies of the children had been sunk in some lake or river, just as Nettie Williams had been. They further reminded the District Attorney and his Assistant, that the children had disappeared in October, 1894, and it was then June, 1895, and it was hardly to be expected that after such a lapse of time a clue which would lead to the discovery of their bodies or the means adopted in disposing of them, could be discovered.

The proposition therefore, to go over the route taken by Holmes, in company with the children, starting from Cincinnati, thence to Indianapolis, Chicago, Detroit, Toronto, and Burlington (Vermont) savored very much of a wild goose chase, and would be moreover a waste of time and money. After Holmes had been arrested in Boston, the detectives of the insurance company had traced the children to Cincinnati and thence to the cities above named, until Detroit was reached, when Howard disappeared. The two girls with Holmes, were then traced to Toronto, when they disappeared, and so it looked very much as if the story Holmes had told of having given Howard to Miss Williams in Detroit, and then sent the girls to her from Toronto, was true.

Holmes however did not tell this story until after he knew that the insurance detectives had discovered the houses he had rented in Detroit and Burlington and so he adjusted himself to the situation from time to time as it arose.

The newspapers were regularly served to Holmes in the county prison and he employed his time in keeping pace with the news as it came to him.

A few important clues had, moreover, been overlooked. When he was arrested, a tin box containing title and other papers and private memoranda, were found. Among the papers Avere ten or twelve letters from Alice and Nellie, written to their mother and grandparents from Cincinnati, Indianapolis, and Detroit, and which they had evidently given to Holmes to mail. A number of letters written by Mrs. Pitezel in Detroit and Toronto, were also found in the box. She said she had given them to Holmes to mail and was surprised when informed that they had been found in his box. These letters constituted a very important clue and they will be given in their proper place in this narrative. The other clue was a small bunch of keys, found by Miss Yoke (Mrs. Howard) in her trunk and surrendered by her to the officers.

District Attorney Graham and his Assistant, Mr. Barlow, were not affected by any pessimistic view of the situation. They did not believe that a man could kill three children and escape discovery. They believed that the children were alive or in hiding, or if they had been murdered all previous efforts to find them had been unskillfully made, and they resolved to undertake a careful and patient search for the blunder which a criminal always makes between the inception and the consummation of his crime.

About this time the District Attorney, as already stated, determined upon the release of Mrs. Pitezel. She had given a full, frank and truthful statement of all she knew of the case. She stated she had given Holmes about $6,700 of the $7,200 she had received from Howe, and Holmes had given her a note drawn to the order of B. B. Samuels for $16,000. Here is an exact copy of this note.

THE WORTHLESS PROMISSORY NOTE. (*Given by Holmes to Mrs. Pitezel.*)

There was no endorsement on the back of this note.

That after she had given Howard and Nellie to Holmes, to take to Cincinnati, to join Alice, she had gone to the home of her parents in Galva, Illinois. That in response to a letter from Holmes, she went on October 13th, 1894, to Deivoxt, where he said she would meet her husband.

That upon her arrival in Detroit, Holmes met her and said, that Ben had found it impossible to remain in Detroit, and had gone to Toronto. That on October 18th she went to Toronto, where Holmes told her, that Ben got frightened because of his belief that the detectives were after him, and had gone to Montreal. He showed her a note written in cipher, which he said Pitezel had sent to her. That under the advice and direction of Holmes, she journeyed with her children wearied and worn out with travel and anxiety, to Prescott, thence to Ogdensburg, and finally to Burlington, Vermont, where Holmes rented a house for her, — he giving her name as Mrs. Cook, and his own as Judson, and alleging that she was his sister; that while in Burlington, Holmes, brought a package of nitro-glycerine to the house and placed it in the cellar. That he wrote her a note requesting her to carry the package to one of the upper floors, which she did not do. That while in the Burlington house. Holmes came there and went into the cellar, and after a while she followed him and found him removing some boards on the cellar floor. She says he exhibited much confusion when he found her observing him, and shortly after left the house.

On June 19, 1894, Mrs. Pitezel entered her own recognizance to appear when wanted, and was at once set at liberty. On the day of her discharge, she received the following remarkable letter from Holmes:

Philadelphia, June 17th, '95.

Mrs. Carrie A. Pitezel.

Dear Madam: —

I have been exceedingly anxious during the last mouths to communicate with you, but have been completely headed off in every direction. I learn that you will shortly be set at liberty, and I shall take this letter to City Hall with me and then give it to my attorneys to be sent to you, as the prison regulations do not prohibit my doing so. I have been repeatedly called cruel and heartless during the past six montlis, and by those who were at the very time doing more than I, that was both cruel and heartless towards you. Within ten days after you came here arrangements were made with my attorney to furnish bail for you and a house to live in. We were refused permission to see you, although you remember coming here from Boston, it was promised I should see you. Later I offered to make arrangements with your lawyer for the same. Mr. Barlow of the District Attorney's office, told me I could do nothing and that I need not worry myself about you as you are being cared for. Within three days after you came here you had been made to believe so much from others that you forgot that for years I had done all I could do for you and yours and that it was hardly likely that all at ouce I should turn and do all I could against you.

Facts you should know are as follows: Ben lived West, and while drunk at Ft. Worth, Texas married a disreputable woman by the name of Mrs. Martin. (Write E. Otto, also Boarding House bet. Houston and Throckmorton Sts., on 1st St., where they lived as Mr. and Mrs. Lyman.) When he became sober and found what he had done, he threatened to kill himself and her, and I had him watched by one of the other men until he went home. When we straightened up the bank account, he had fooled away or been robbed by her of over $850 of the money we needed there so much. Later he wanted to carry out the insurance work down in Mississippi, where he was acquainted, and I went there with him, and when I found out what kind of a place it was, would not go any further with it there and told him so, and he said if I did not, he would kill himself and get money for you, etc. To get him out of the notion. I told him I would go to Mobile and if I could get what was wanted would do so, if nut, I would go to St. Louis and write for him to come. I did not go to Mobile. Was never there in my life. When I reached St. Louis I wrote him, and in the letter he left me after he died, he said he tried to kill himself with laudanum there, and later I found out this was so. (Henry Rogers, Prop, of Hotel at Perkinsville, Ala.) Where lie was very sick. He also wrote you he was sick there, I think you told me. Here in Phila. we were not ready. He got word baby was sick and he had to own to me he had drank up the $35.00 I gave him extra in N. Y., and then I told him I would settle up everything, as if we carried it out, he might get to drinking and tell of it. He begged me not to do it, and at last I concluded to try again, but thought it best to have him think for a week or two that I was not going on with it, so lie would sober up and be himself. I blame myself for this and always shall, for the next day when I went to his store I found him as I have described, and Perry or the detectives have got the cipher slip he left me, or at all events, it was in the tin box they took. He asked me to get you a house in Cincinnati, on ac. of good schools, etc., and I did so, but did not dare take you there after Howe and McD. threatened my arrest, and so made arrangements with Miss W. to live with you. She took Howard with her from Detroit because he would quarrel with the girls if no grown person was with them, and he wanted his father's watch and Alice wanted to keep it, and so I took it, telling them I wanted to show it to you and Dessa, and bought all three of them each a cheap watch. When I found the conditions in Toronto were not as Miss W. thought they were, and I was getting word from Chicago every day that I was being followed, I thought best to go out of the country altogether, and the Ins. Co. know the children A. and E. were at their hotel at 1 o'clock the afternoon you left Toronto, and between then and when I saw you at 4 o'clock at the store where I was buying some things for them, I had been to my wife's hotel twice and was with you again at 6:30, and had meantime started the children to Miss W. and eaten my supper. From that time until my arrest in Boston, if I could now be allowed to sit down with you and my wife, I could show where every half hour was spent. In Boston I recvd. letter from Miss W. that they would leave there in a few days, and if the detectives would now go, as I beg of them, they could trace out the N. Y. end of the matter and stop all the unnecessary delay and expense. This would spoil their theories and would not be a sufficiently bloodthirsty ending of the case to satisfy them it seems. As soon as they got a house and were settled, they were to send word and you were to then go to them, and this was why I wished you to take a furnished hduse so you could get rested and not be at hotels. I made arrangements for Miss W, to tell you all, when you Avere settled. If you had known they were following you, you would have been worried, and I think you will remember I tried to do all I could to keep you from it, and we had to get rid of the old trunks and get the things into bundles, so there would be no checking. There is a bundle of yours now at the Burlington Depot marked with the name you Avent by there, which I have forgotten. I was as careful of the children as if they were my own, and you know me well enough to judge me better than strangers here can do. Ben would not have done anything against me, or I against him, any quicker than brothers. We never quarrelled. Again, he was worth too much to me for me to have killed him, if I had no other reason not to. As to the children, I never will believe, until you tell me so yourself, that you think they are dead or that I did anything to put them out of the way. Knowing me as you do, can you imagine me killing little and innocent children, especially without any motive? Why, if I was preparing to put them out of life was I (within an hour before I must have done it if ever) buying them things to wear and make them comfortable, even underwear for them to take to Miss W. for Howard, (which I can prove I bought in Toronto,) if as they would have you believe, Pat had taken him and killed him weeks before. Don't you know that if I had offered Pat a million dollars, he would not have done a thing like this. I made a mistake in having it known that Miss W. killed her sister, as it tends to make her more careful about her movements, but I could hardly do otherwise, when I was accused of killing them both. Now after they get done trying to make the case worse than it is, you will find that they will trace the children to N. Y. and to the steamer there. Next to you, I have snffered most about them, and a few days ago gave the District Attorney all facts I could, and if nothing comes of it soon, I hardly expect anything new to occur until I can be taken to Ft. Worth and arrange the property so Mr.

Massie, her old guardian, can take lier part of the money to her in London. By advertising, if she knows there is money for her, and it comes through Mr. Massie safely, she will find some way, (probably through her Boston friend,) to get it. As long as there is nothing to gain, she will hardly come out openly and lay herself liable to arrest. I dislike fearfully to go to Ft. Worth to serve a term, as the prisons there are terrible. I had rather be here five years than there one, and in going, there is no better way to have you know I am still willing to do all 1 can for you and yours. I blame the Company here for keeping you shut up six months in this den, for worrying you about your children not being alive and for their trying to separate my wife from me, for these things do not concern them, but I have never blamed them for otherwise making me all the trouble they can. I would do the same with another if the tables were turned. As matters now stand, I have got here, in Illinois and in Texas, between fifteen and twenty years of imprisonment awaiting me. If the children can be found, I want to finish here and in Illinois first, hoping by that time the Texas matters may blow over or that I may die; but if they are not found before my sentence expires liere, if any arrangement can be made so papers can be filed in Texas to bring me back here or to Illinois, after I have served this first small charge in Texas, so I do not have to stay and serve the others there until after my northern term is served, I will go and do all I can to both get the property straightened there, so you can leave a small income and arrange for recovery of the children. Ben's death was genuine and you were entitled to the money, and if it had not been for H. and McD., you would to-day have been in Cincinnati with all the children.

About the money — Ben asked me to use most of it to pay debts and arrange so some steady income should come to you from the South. The note you got in St. Louis was made by him in the spring and some money was due on it. We were owing Miss W. about $5,000. T gave $1,000 to her in Detroit (also $400 to Alice in Toronto) and you have no reason to think I was not intending to take care of you then, more than in years before, and now if I can get to Ft. Worth without running risk of staying there more than one year, I will soon straighten so as to get you money while I am there in jail. Mr. Shoemaker went there two weeks last winter and started matters, but until I can go there and be taken into court, nothing more can be clone I fear. There are some letters at the City Hall that I promised Alice I would save for her, as I did not dare let her carry them with her, and if after they get through with them, you can get them, I wish you would do so, also Ben's watch. Howard has the other things. I don't know what you will do meantime, if you gain your liberty here, but rest assured I will do all I can at the earliest possible moment. So far as the children's bodily health is concerned, I feel sure I can say to you they are as well to-day as though with you, also that they will not be turned adrift among strangers, for two reasons. First, Miss W., although quick tempered, is too soft hearted to do so; second, if among others where their letters could not be looked over and detained, they would write to their grandparents, (not to you, as I instructed Miss W. from Boston in answer to her letter to me. if she heard of my or our arrest, to have children think we were lost crossing to London.) They have no doubt written letters which Miss W., for her own safety, has withheld.

If there are any questions you wish to ask me, make a list of them and send to one of my attorneys. I have refrained from asking you any, lest you would think that the object of my letter. I have no desire to do anything to cause your lawyer or the prosecution any unnecessary work or annoyance, and if you write me, shall isimply answer questions asked. Shall not advise or question you, nor would 1 have done so if allowed to have seen you during past months, though it would liave saved them much unnecessary delay and expense to have had us eliminate some of the features of the case by comparing memories. I, at least, hope your suffering here is nearly ended.

Yours Truly

H. H. Holmes.

The foregoing narrative substantially presents the case, known to, and considered by the District Attorney's office at the time arrangements were perfected, which permitted of the release of Mr. Geyer from his routine duties in the Police Department. He had been for twenty years an esteemed and trusted member of the Philadelphia Detective Bureau. He had had a vast experience in detective work, and more particularly in murder cases and justly enjoyed the friendship and confidence of the District Attorney, and his assistant, as much because of his high personal character, as his skill and dexterity in his profession. Funds to defray the expenses of the search were readily furnished by the officers of the Insurance Company, notwithstanding their belief that little more could be accomplished than threshing over old straw. On the evening of June 26th, 1895, full of hope and courage Detective Geyer started on his journey. But we will let him tell his own story.

DETECTIVE GEYER'S NARRATIVE.

CHAPTER IX

ON THE TRAIL

Defective Geyer Undertakes the Search — Arrival at Cincinnati — Searching Hotel Registers — Holmes Located at two Hotels under Two Aliases — Hotel Clerk Recognizes Photographs of Holmes and the Children — Holmes Rents a House under Another Alias — Holmes gives Away a Stove —Geyer Starts for Indianapolis.

About the time of the trial and conviction of Holmes, I was sent for by Mr. Barlow, to call upon him at the District Attorney's office. On my arrival there, I was informed that Mr. Graham had decided to send me West to make a search for the missing Pitezel children. Arrangements were then made with the snperintendent of police to detail me for the task, and preparations were completed for the start. Several conferences were held with the officers of the insurance company, and the District Attorney and his assistant, and I soon became familiar with every point of the case. Eight months having elapsed since the children had been heard from, it did not look like a very encouraging task to undertake, and it was the general belief of all interested, that the children would never be found. The District Attorney believed, however, that another final effort to find the children should be made, for the sake of the stricken mother, if for nothing else. I was not placed under any restrictions, but was told to go and exercise my own judgment in the matter, and to follow wherever the clues led me. I was well piovided with money, and with a Godspeed and well wishes from all Avho weie interested, I started on my journey.

I left Philadelphia on Wednesday evening, June 26th, 1895, for Cincinnati, Ohio, arriving there on the 27th at 7.30 PM, registered at the Palace Hotel, and after partaking of some lunch, I proceeded to police headquarters, where I met my old friend, Detective John Schnooks. I explained to him the nature of my visit to Cincinnati, and he requested me to call in the morning and have a conference with Superintendent Philip Dietsch. An hour or two was spent with Schnooks rehearsing some of our old stories, after which I returned to the hotel for a good night's rest. Bright and early the next morning, I arose and after eating a hearty breakfast, I started for the city hall, where I met Superintendent Dietsch. One half hour or more was spent with him going over the case and givhig him my reasons for believing that Holmes had had the children in Cincinnati, Ohio. Reaching his hand under his desk, his finger was placed on a touch button that summoned a messenger from the detective department, who was instructed to send Detective Schnooks into the office. A moment or two later Schnooks made his appearance, and the superintendent instructed him to render me all the assistance in his power, in the effort to locate the children. Bidding the superintendent good day, Schnooks and I left the office and commenced the greatest search I have ever had in my twenty years' experience in the detective business. When I left Philadelphia, I was provided with photographs of Holmes, Pitezel, Alice, Nellie, and Howard Pitezel, Mrs. Pitezel, Bessie and the baby, also of Mrs. Pitezel's trunk, (the one Holmes borrowed from her in Detroit, Michigan, saying that he wanted it for the purpose of getting Ben out of the town, as the detectives were onto him), a photograph of a missing trunk which belonged to the children; also of a trunk belonging to Mrs. Howard. As I knew that Holmes had left St. Louis on September 28th with the two children, Nellie and Howard, I suggested to Schnooks, that we first search the hotels around the depots to see if a man registered there on that day, who had three children with him, a boy and two girls. We called at a number of hotels, but met with no success. We finally struck a cheap hotel at No. 164½ Central Avenue, known as the Atlantic House, and upon examining the register, we discovered that on Friday, September 28th, 1894, there appeared the name of Alex. E. Cook and three chihlren. The photographs of Holmes and the three children were shown to the clerk, who could not say positively that they were the photographs of the people who had stopped there, but thought they resembled them very much. Recalling to my mind that Holmes had Mrs.

Pitezel living in Burlington under the name of Mrs. A. E. Cook, I felt convinced that I was on the right track. The clerk informed us that these parties only remained overnight, leaving the following morning. Thanking the clerk for his kind attention, we left the hotel and continued our search among such hotels as we had not visited, and when we arrived at the Hotel Bristol, corner of 6th and Vine Streets, we discovered that on Saturday, September 29th, 1894, there appeared on the register the name of A. E. Cook and three children, Cleveland. They were assigned to room No. 103, a room which contained two beds. Mr. W. L. Bain, a clerk at the liotel, recognized the photographs of Holmes and the children, as the party who registered there under that name. The register showed that they left the Bristol on Sunday, September 30th.

Knowing that Holmes was in the habit of renting houses in most every city he visited, I determined to give up the search among the hotels and make some inquiry among the real estate agents and ascertain whether he had rented a house in Cincinnati. After visiting quite a number of them, we called at the office of J. C. Thomas, No. 15 East 3d Street. His clerk informed us that Mr. Thomas had gone to his home in Cnmminsville, a suburban town about five miles from Cincinnati. A photograph of Holmes was shown the clerk, who had a distinct recollection of having seen the original in the office with a small boy. The photograph of Howard was then produced and he identified it as the boy who was with Holmes. The clerk was unable to give us any further information in regard to the renting of the houses, as the books were locked up, and Mr. Thomas had the keys. We then determined to go to Cumminsville and find Mr. Thomas, so off we started, and when we reached Cumminsville, we were unable to locate our man, — nobody appeared to know him, and in consulting the directory his name did not appear in it, (probably he had not lived there long enough.) We returned to Cincinnati someWhat disappointed, and as it was after business hours, we were compelled to give up the search.

The next morning we were at the real estate office of Mr. Thomas again, and as soon as he arrived, we lost no time in consulting him. We showed him the pictures of Holmes and Howard Pitezel, which he immediately recognized as that of a man who had a small boy with him, and who rented a house from him at No. 305 Poplar Street, on Friday, September 28th, 1894, paying $15 in advance for it and giving the name of A. C. Hayes. Mr. Thomas informed us that his tenant had only remained in the house about two days, when he left for parts unknown, but suggested that we call on Miss Hill, who lived at No. 303 Poplar Street, (next door), as he thought she would be able to give us some information concerning him. We immediately left for No. 303 Poplar Street, where we met Miss Hill, whom we found to be very willing to tell us all she knew about the strange tenant. She said there was really very little to tell. The first she noticed of him was on Saturday morning, September 29th, when a furniture wagon was driven in front of No. 305 Poplar Street and a man and small boy alighted. The man took a key out of his pocket, and after opening the door of No. 305, a large, iron cylinder stove, such as is used in barrooms or a large hall, was taken out of the wagon and carried into the house. As there was no other furniture taken in, it aroused her curiosity and she spoke of it to several of her neighbors. She was doubtless observed by Holmes doing this, for on the next morning, September 30th, (Sunday) he rang her bell, and told her he was not going to occupy the liouse and that she could have the stove.

Having located Holmes and the children at two hotels in Cincinnati, and discovered the two false names he assumed. Cook and Hayes, I felt justified in believing that I had taken firm hold of the end of the string which was to lead me ultimately to the consummation of my difficult mission. I was not able to appreciate the intense significance of the renting of the Poplar Street house and the delivery of a stove of such immense size there, but I felt sure I was on the right track and so started for Indianapolis, from which point several of the children's letters found in Holmes' tin box had been dated.

THE POPLAR STREET HOUSE, CINCINNATI, OHIO.
(*Where Holmes intended to murder the children.*)

FRANK P. GEYER

CHAPTER X

THE UNTIRING PURSUIT

The Search in Indianapolis — Holmes Took Alice Pitezel to Cincinnati — The Three Canning Children Identified as the Pitezel Children — Mrs. Holmes Registered as Mrs. Georgia Howard — Represents Her Husband as Wealthy — Holmes as an Uncle — Holmes' Schemes to Get Rid of Howard — The Children Homesick — Chicago — The Search for a Trunk — Geyer Calls on Phimmer — Plnmmer Admits Knowing Holmes, bnt Denies Ever Seeing the Children— A German Chambermaid Recognizes Photographs of the Children — How the Children Passed Their Time— The Picture of the Trunk Identified— Holmes as Harry Gordon — Mrs. Gordon — Interview with a Janitor — The Williams Girls Again — Search for a Bricklayer.

Saturday evening, June 29th, at 7:30 o'clock, I arrived at Indianapolis, Indiana, registering at the Spencer House. After partaking of a lunch, I started out in search of police headquarters, which I found to be located on Alabama Street, south of Washington Street. Entering the building, I met Captain Splann, who is in charge of the detective corps. Introducing myself, I told him what my business was in Indianapolis and he requested me to see Superintendent Powell. About this time a report came in that a man had been shot and killed in the Jiorthern part of the city, and that the murderer had escaped. The captain was compelled to start for the scene of the murder, and invited me to accompany him, which I did. On our arrival at the house, we learned that the man was not dead, but was suffering from the result of a pistol shot wound in the neck. The usual preliminaries were gone through with, and after obtaining an accurate description of the would-be murderer, we left the house in search of Superintendent Powell and while looking for him, I met several of the city detectives. Captain Splann gave them a description of the man who was wanted, and requested them to make search for him at once. Shortly after we met the superintendent, who advised me to call at police headquarters the next morning, telling me that he would detail a good man to aid me, and that he would render me all the assistance in his power.

Sunday morning, bright and early, I called at police headquarters, where I met Superintendent Powell, who introduced me to Detective David Richards and informed me that he had assigned him to assist me in my investigation in Indianapolis. Richards and I retired to a private room and after explaining the case to him we left headquarters to continue the search for the missing children.

I suggested to Richards that we first make inquiry among the hotels near the Union Depot and on going to the Stubbins House and examining the register, we found that on September 24th, 1894, was an entry in the name of Etta Pitsel, St. Louis, Mo., and that the hotel records showed she left on the morning of September 28th. Further inquiry elicited the fact that the girl was brought there by a man known to Mr. Robert Sweeney, the clerk, as Mr. Howard, and that on Friday morning, September 28th, he had received a telegram from Mr. Howard, dated St. Louis, requesting him to have Etta Pitsel at the Union Depot to meet St. Louis train for Cincinnati, Ohio. This was the day Holmes left St. Louis with Nellie and Howard Pitezel, telling their mother that he was going to take them to Indianapolis, where they would be taken care of by kind old lady. Mr. Sweeney fully identified the picture of Alice Pitezel, as the girl who stopped at the Stubbins House; also that of Holmes, as the man whom he knew as Howard and to whom he had given Alice Pitezel on the St. Louis train for Cincinnati, Ohio.

Feeling confident that Holmes had returned to Indianapolis, I continued to search among the hotels. The register of a number of hotels was examined in the neighborhood of the depot, but we failed to get any further information regarding the children. We then went to the place known as the Circle, where there are several hotels. We called upon the proprietor of the Hotel English, and asked permission to examine his register of September, 1894. Turning to September 30th, we discovered on the register the three Canning children, Galva, Illinois, room No 79.

Mr. Duncan, the clerk was shown the pictures of the children who were registered there under the name of Canning, and positively identified, them. He also identified the picture of Holmes, as that of the man who had brought them there and who took them away on the next morning, Monday October 1st. Knowing that the children's grandparents' name was Canning and that they lived at Galva, Illinois, I was convinced that I was on the right track, and with renewed energy, I determined to find out where they were taken to on Monday morning, October 1st. Every hotel and lodging house in Indian apolis was searched, but no record could be found of where the children had stopped. Finally it dawned upon Richards that in September, 1894, there had been on Meridian Street within fifty feet of the Circle, a small hotel known as the Circle House. This hotel had been closed for a long time, but we determined to find the proprietor, a Mr. Herman Ackelow. Inquiry around the Circle as to where we could find him, brought forth the information that he had moved to West Indianapolis, but that we could find his clerk, a Mr. Reisner, near the Union depot. Off we started at once to find the clerk and located him in a hotel south of the depot, and ascertained from him that the register and all the records belonging to the Circle House, were in charge of an attorney named Everett. We then made arrangements with Mr. Reisner to meet us at the lawyer's office the following morning, Monday, July 1st, 1895. According to promise, Richards and I were at lawyer Everett's office at 9 AM on Monday, where we met clerk Reisner. The register was produced, and turning over to October 1st, found a similar entry to that in the Hotel English, three Canning children, Galva, Illinois, room No. 24. Mr. Reisner in looking over the cash account, informed us that they had left there October 6th. It was easily observed that the books of the Circle House were kept without much system, consequently we had to rely on dates given us by Reisuer as being accurate.

In making my search among the hotels, I discovered that Holmes had his wife registered at the Circle Park Hotel under the name of Mrs. Georgia Howard. The entry was made September 18th, and she remained there until September 24th. This was the time when Holmes, with Howe and

Alice Pitezel was in Philadelphia for the purpose of identifying Pitezel's body. While at the Circle Park Hotel, Mrs. Howard became very intimate with the proprietress, a Mrs. Rodius. She informed her that her husband was a very wealthy man, and that he owned real estate and cattle ranches in Texas; also had considerable real estate in Berlin, Germany, where they intended to go as soon as her husband could gel his business affairs into shape to leave.

The Circle Park Hotel is also situated in the place known as the Circle and is within one hundred feet of the Circle House, where Holmes had the children. September 30th, Mrs. Howard's name re appears on the Circle Park Hotel register and she remains there until October 4th, showing that she was almost within speaking distance of the Pitezel children, yet she was in absolute ignorance of it.

I suggested that we go to West Indianapolis and have an interview with Mr. Herman Ackelow, the former proprietor of the Circle House, to see if he could throw any light upon the whereabouts of the children. When we reached West Indianapolis, we found that Mr. Ackelow was running a beer saloon. It did not require a great deal of ceremony to introduce ourselves, after which I spoke to him about the children. He had a distinct recollection of them and recognized the photograph of Holmes as the man who brought them and took them away from his hotel. Holmes represented to Mr. Ackelow, that he was their uncle, — their mother, who was a widow, Avas his sister, and that she would be with them in a few days. Holmes said that Howard was a very bad boy and that he was trying to place him in some institution, or bind him out to some farmer, as he wanted to get rid of the responsibility of looking after him.

Mr. Ackelow also informed me, that on numerous occasions he had sent his oldest boy up to the children's room to call them for their meals. His son would return to him and tell him that he found the children crying, — evidently heartbroken and homesick to see their mother, or hear from her.

From the fact that Holmes had told Mr. Ackelow that he wanted to get rid of Howard, I came to the conclusion at once that he had murdered him, but where, up to this time, I was unable to determine.

In an interview I had with Mrs. Pitezel in the Moyamensing Prison, Philadelphia, she told me that the trunk the children had with them when they left her at St. Louis, Mo., was missing. I then interviewed Holmes, as to what he had done with it, and he informed me that he had left it in a hotel on West Madison Street, about fifty feet from the corner of Ashland Avenue, Chicago, Illinois.

Information had also been sent me by the Fidelity Company, that their general manager in Detroit, Michigan had positive information that Holmes and the boy were seen in Detroit, Michigan, where Holmes had rented a house.

While I felt somewhat reluctant to leave Indianapolis, as something seemed to tell me that Howard never left there alive, I decided I would abandon the search there for the time being, and go to Chicago, Illinois and see if I could verify the trunk story. At 11:40 AM, July 1st, 1894, I left Indianapolis, Indiana, for Chicago, Ill., arriving there at 5:30 PM, and registered at the Imperial Hotel. After supper I went to Police Headquarters, and after going through the usual preliminaries of introducing myself, I informed the captain in charge of Detective Headquarters, why I was in Chicago. He listened with much interest to my story and requested me to call early in the AM, when he would introduce me to Inspector Fitzpatrick.

Tuesday morning, July 2d, I called at Police Headquarters, and learned that the Inspector had been detained on some business and would not be at the office for some time. I was then introduced to Detective Sergeant John C. McGinn, and was informed that he was assigned to assist me in my investigation in Chicago.

The story of the finding of the body at No. 1316 Callowhill Street, and the mysterious disappearance of the children was all told to McGinn. We then left Police Headquarters, and I suggested that we call on Wharton Plummer in room No. 1218 Chamber of Commerce Building. Plummer was Holmes' attorney and had represented him in some of his business ventures. Holmes had informed me prior to leaving Philadelphia, that Plummer had taken dinner with him at the hotel where the children were stopping on West Madison Street, and that he (Plummer) had seen the girls. Entering the office, I handed my card to Mr. Plummer, who requested us to be seated. I then opened up a conversation with him regarding Holmes and the missing children. He admitted having seen Holmes in Chicago about the time referred to and said that he met him on the North side, and thought it was on Division Street, and that they went into a restaurant and had some lunch. He positively denied having been at the hotel where Holmes stopped, and declared most emphatically that he had never seen the children.

Having learned in Indianapolis, that the chambermaid, Caroline Klausmann, who had charge of the room in the Circle House, which the children occupied, had moved to Chicago, I determined to locate her if possible. We learned that she was stopping at No. 223 West Clark Street and upon making inquiry at the above number, we ascertained that she was employed at the Swiss Hotel, on Wells Street between Ohio and Indiana Avenues. We then proceeded to the Swiss Hotel where we met Miss Klausmann, whom I found to be a middle aged German woman, unable to speak English. As I was familiar with the German language, I explained when I came to see her and showed her the photographs of the children. She recognized them at once, and with tears in her eyes described to me how they would employ their time while she was at the hotel in Indianapolis. She said that the children were always drawing pictures of houses, or engaged in writing, and that she frequently went into their room and found them crying. Observing that they were alone at the hotel, she naturally believed they were orphan children, and when she found them crying, she thought they were crying over the loss of their father and mother. She said it grieved her very much to think she was unable to speak English, so that she might have sympathized with them. She identified the picture of the missing trunk, as the one the children had with them at the Circle House. After leaving Miss Klausmann, we concluded we would go to the West side and endeavor to locate the hotel where Holmes claimed to have left the missing trunk.

We went to West Madison Street and Ashland Avenue, but were unable to locate any hotel as described by Holmes. However, we made a search of the register of every hotel within a mile of where Holmes had said the children had stopped, but were unable to locate them. We returned to the City Hall, and after a half hour consultation, we agreed to return to Ashland Avenue and West Madison Street and make another search for the hotel. We did not find a hotel, but succeeded in finding a lodging house, about fifty feet from the corner of Ashland Avenue on West Madison Street, just as described by Holmes. This house had been occupied at that time by a Miss Jennie Irons, whom we found about five blocks further west on West Madison Street. The photographs of Holmes and the children were then shown to Miss Irons, but she failed to identify the children, but thought she had seen the man. Subsequent developments have proved that Holmes, under the name of Harry Gordon, occupied apartments with Miss Irons in 1893, having with him a woman who was known as Mrs. Gordon, and has been since identified as Miss Emily Cigrand, a woman who mysteriously disappeared from No. 701 Sixty-Third Street, Chicago, the house that has since become famous as "The Castle."

As Holmes had lived with Miss Irons, he had no difficulty in describing the place to me. However, neither the children, nor the trunk had been there.

As there was nothing to be learned from Miss Irons, I concluded that my next move would be to visit Pat Quinlan, Holmes' janitor at the block, Sixty-third and Wallace Streets, opposite Englewood Station. So getting on a cable car, we started for Quinlan's home, and on our arrival there we discovered there was only one entrance to the upstairs of the big building. Going up a dark winding stairway, we reached the second story, and knocking at the door, we Avere requested to come in. Quinlan is a man about five feet, eight or nine inches, slim build, light curly hair, sandy mustache, and looks to be about thirty-eight years old. I presented my card to him and he requested me to be seated, after which I began my conversation about Holmes and the missing Pitezel children, trying to impress Quinlan all the while, that I believed he knew all about them. Quinlan told me the last time he saw Holmes, was in the fall of 1894, on the North side in Chicago. He was with another man, whom Quinlan says he did not know. Quinlan spoke to Holmes and said: "Hello, where did you come from?" Holmes answered and said: "I have just come from home." Quinlan thought he meant Wilmette. I questioned Quinlan closely in regard to the Pitezel children. He admitted that he knew them very well, but positively denied knowing anything whatever of their whereabouts, and that if he did know he would be only too willing to render all the assistance he could to locate them. He expressed his belief, that if the body found at No. 1316 Callowhill Street was that of Pitezel, that Holmes had murdered him, and subseqnently murdered the children, and if such were the case. Holmes should be hung for it, and that he, (Quinlan) would only be too willing to spring the trap. Quinlan said from what he had read of Holmes since the case has gained publicity, he sincerely believed that Holmes set fire to the block and intended to destroy him and his family.

During my last interview with Holmes in Moyamensing Prison, he told me he had given the children to a man named Edward Hatch, who was formerly a bricklayer and had done odd chores around the block in Chicago. He said that Quinlan and Dr. Robinson were well acquainted with him, so while at Quinlan's, I thought I would take advantage of the opportunity, and question Pat as to what he knew about Hatch. He informed me that he knew a bricklayer by that name, who had done some work for Holmes, and that he was a hardworking, industrious man. I then told him about what Holmes had said about giving Hatch the children. Quinlan denounced Holmes as a dirty, lying scoundrel and said that Hatch would not be guilty of doing anything that was wrong. I also interviewed Quinlan in regard to the Williams girls, who were formerly at the Castle. He said he knew Minnie and had met her at the block. No.

701 West Sixty-third Street, and that Holmes introduced her to him and his wife, as his cousin, and also introduced her to Mrs. Holmes as his cousin. He said positively, that he never saw Nettie Williams after this case was made public.

I next interviewed Dr. Robinson, the proprietor of the drug store on the first floor in the Castle. He had no recollection of knowing a man named Hatch, but said he had seen both Minnie and Nettie Williams together at the block in June, 1804, and saw Minnie there alone about one month later. The Doctor's opinion of Holmes was not a very good one.

The story Holmes gave me about Hatch and the children, was his very latest, and was told immediately after he learned that I was about to make a new search for the children. He had always stuck to his romance about giving them to Minnie Williams, but he was evidently anticipating the possibility of just what followed, so he rigged up the Hatch tale and arranged it to suit possible future developments.

The next move we made was to try and locate Hatch. We found by consulting a directory, that a man by the name of Edward Hatch, a bricklayer by trade, lived at No. 6248 Sangamon Street. This is about six blocks from the Castle, so we concluded to go there at once and see if we could find him. On our arrival at the house, we found that it was occupied by a colored family and that Hatch had moved out about ten months before. Inquiry was made in the neighborhood, but no one appeared to know where he had gone. We then visited a Mr. Glenister, who resides on Union Street above Twenty-eighth Street, who is the Secretary of the Bricklayers' Union and tried to ascertain from him if there was such a person connected with their Union as Hatch. Mr. Glenister searclied the records for us, but was unable to find the name. We then went to a number of buildings in course of erection and made inquiry among the brickhayers, but no one appeared to know a man by that name, who followed the trade of a bricklayer.

I then decided to leave the search for Hatch in the hands of Detective McGinn, and to go to Detroit.

NELLIE PITEZEL.

CHAPTER XI

AN EXPERT IN CRIME

Detroit — Holmes Rents a House — Howard with Him — Alice and Nellie at the New Western Hotel — Holmes as G. Howell — Search in Holmes' House — Alice and Nellie Again Identified — Picture of the Trunk Again Recognized — Mrs. Pitezel at Geis' Hotel — Under Great Mental Strain — Mrs. Pitezel and Her Children but a Few Blocks Apart — Holmes' Skillful Plotting.

On Wednesday morning, July 4th, I left Chicago for Detroit, Michigan, arriving there at 6 PM and registered at the Hotel Normandie. I went at once to police headquarters, where I met Detective Thomas Meyler, an old personal friend of mine, to whom I explained the nature of my visit. I was then introduced to the captain in charge and repeated my story of the missing children. He requested me to call in the morning and see Superintendent Starkweather.

Early on the morning of the 5th, I was at police headquarters, where I met the superintendent who assigned Detective Tuttle to assist me in my search in Detroit. The same old story was told to him and off we started.

The first place at which we called was at the office of the Fidelity Mutual Life Insurance Company, where we met Mr. Frank R Alderman, the general manager for Michigan. After obtaining from him the name of the real estate agent who rented a house to Holmes, we left the office and went to No. 60 Monroe Street, where we met a Mr. Bonninghausen, the agent referred to. Handing him my card, I requested a private interview which he granted, and after propounding several questions to him, I learned that on or about the 13th of October, 1894, a gentleman called at his office, representing that he wanted to rent a house for a widowed sister who had three children. He said he desired a house that was on the outskirts of the city, if it were possible to get one.

This just suited the agent, as he had a house at No. 241 E. Forest

Avenue in which he had a personal interest, and which had been without a tenant for a long time. The agent identified the photograph of Holmes, as that of the man who inquired for the house and said that Holmes took the number and was informed that he would find the keys at Mr. McAllister's drug store on Forest Avenue, which is just a few doors below No. 241. About two hours later Holmes returned to Mr. Bonninghausen's office and informed him that the house was just what he wanted. He paid five dollars in advance, and said that when his sister arrived, which would be in tliree or four days, he would return and pay six months' rent in advance, as he did not intend living with her, and wanted to see that she was properly provided for. Mr. Bonninghausen said he was under the impression that Holmes had a small boy with him when he rented the house, describing him as a boy about nine or ten years old. A Mr. Moore, who was in the office at the time Holmes rented the house, and who by the way is the present occupant, corroborated Mr. Bonninghausen as to Holmes having the boy Howard with him while in Detroit.

Leaving the real estate office, I was somewhat impressed with the belief that my theory, that Howard had never left Indianapolis alive, was wrong. However, I decided to make a search among the hotels, and see if I could locate the children, suggesting to Tuttle that we first visit those near the depot. The first few we visited failed to give us any further information, but when Ave examined the register of the New Western Hotel. P. W. Cutter, proprietor, we discovered the name of Etta and Nellie Canning, St. Louis, Mo., room No. 5, made October 12th, and evidently about midnight. The photographs were shown Mr. Cotter, who positively identified the girls as having stopped there, and that of Holmes as the man who had brought them there, registered their names, and who called the next day and took them away. Mr. Cotter was quite positive that there were but two children and that they had no trunk with them. The register of the Circle House in Indianapolis, showed that the children had left that hotel on the 6th of October, and they appeared to have arrived in Detroit, Michigan, October 12th. this was a matter for serious consideration, as it made an interval of six days to be accounted for between Indianapolis and Detroit.

Having satisfied myself that the two girls had been in Detroit, I determined to try and locate Holmes, and ascertain if the boy had stopped with him, so we continued our search among the hotels, and on the register of the Normandie, I found an entry October 12th, 1894, "G. Howell and wife, Adrian." Having become thoroughly familiar with Holmes' handwriting and knowing that the name "G. Howell "was one of his many aliases, I felt convinced that it was his registry. The photographs of Holmes and his wife were shown the Clerk, who was not positive as to Holmes, but was sure that the woman had stopped at the hotel about that time. The record of the hotel proved that Holmes and his wife left there October 13th after supper.

After leaving the Normandie, I decided to visit the house No. 241 East Forest Avenue. On arriving there we were met by Mrs. Moore, who very kindly admitted us to the house and gave us the privilege of examining the cellar. I found that it was divided into three parts. The front which extended across the entire width of the house, had a cemented floor and contained a wood and coal bin, and a large portable heater about four feet in diameter. The part in the rear to the west side of the house, was used as a wash room, having a large stationary washtub in it and a board floor. The part to the east side was used for storage purposes, and it also had a cement floor and cellar steps leading to kitchen on first floor. A careful examination of both the cement and board floor, proved that they had not been tampered with.

There was a dijor opening out of the wash room to a stairway, which leads to the back yard, and is covered with a cellar door. The stairway was encased by a brick wall, which served as a foundation for a rear porch. This foundation is about three feet six inches above the cellar floor and it was discovered after Holmes left the house, that a hole had been dug back of the wall facing the cellar steps, about four feet long, three feet wide, and three feet six inches deep.

Mr. Boninghausen and Mr. Moore having informed me that they had seen a boy with Holmes when he rented the house, Detective Tuttle and I searched every spot of ground adjacent to the premises to see if the earth had been disturbed, but we could find no evidence of it. We then made an examination of the cellar heater and discovered the door to be thirteen inches wide and eight inches high, and the cylinder about four feet in diameter, but there was no evidence, nor had there been, that the furnace had been used for any improper or unusual purpose, so Mr. Moore said. I called on Dr. McAllister who had possession of the keys. I showed him the picture of Holmes, and he identified it at once as that of a man to whom he had delivered the keys. We then returned to Police Headquarters, and after a short consultation, we decided to keep up the hunt for Alice and Nellie, and also to locate Holmes and his wife. I had a memorandum of the address given by Aliee in her letter written in Detroit, October 14th, 1894, at No. 91 Congress Street. This house was kept by Mrs. Lucinda Burns. She distinctly remembered having accommodated two little girls, who came there on October 13th and left October 19th. She said a gentleman had called on her on the morning of the 13th of October, rented the room and paid one week's rent in advance, after which lie left and returned again in less than an hour, bringing the little girls with him. He introduced them to Mrs. Burns as Miss Annie and Miss Amy.

Mrs. Burns said the children were never out of their room and occupied their entire time reading and drawing. They had no trunk with them, but each carried a small satchel. They were very quiet and reserved, and at no time did they reveal their identity.

When shown the pictures of Holmes, and Nellie and Alice Pitezel, she identified the girls at once as the children who had stopped with her, and Holmes as the man who had rented the room for them.

Not having been able to trace Holmes to any other hotel, we concluded to try the boarding houses, so away we journeyed, and the reader can imagine the task in going to many, many houses, ringing the bells, showing the pictures and telling the story to every person who came to the doors. We finally located a house at No. 54 Park Place kept by a Mrs. May Ralston, who when shown the pictures of Holmes and his wife, identified them as a couple who had come there in October, 1891, paid the rent for a room for one week, but only remained four or five days. While at Ralston's they were known as Mr. and Mrs. Holmes, and he represented that they were members of the theatrical profession. The pictures of the trunks were shown Mrs. Ralston and she picked out the picture of Mrs. Howard's canvas covered trunk as the one the couple had in use at her house.

The disappearance of the children's trunk was the source of much annoyance to me, and I determined, if possible to locate it. Several days were spent among expressmen, freight depots, omnibus companies, express offices, hackmen, and liverymen, but we could get no clue to it.

Mrs. Pitezel having informed me that she had stopped at Geis's Hotel while in Detroit, I determined to go there and interview the proprietor and others connected with the hotel, from whom I might obtain information which would be of service to me in the effort to locate the children. I found in looking over the register, that the only party who had stayed there, and who would answer the description of Mrs. Pitezel, Dessie and the baby, had registered on October 14th, 1894, in the name of Mrs. C. A. Adams, and daughter, Chicago, room No. 33. Miss Minnie Mulholland, the housekeeper, identified the picture of Mrs. Pitezel, Dessie and the baby as the parties who had registered there in October under the name of Adams, and had occupied No. 33, having with them two trunks, one a large top flat trunk, and the other very small. Miss Mulholland identified the picture of the flat top trunk I showed her, as one similar to that which Mrs. Pitezel had with her while at the hotel.

Miss Mulholland in describing Mrs. Pitezel, alias Adams, says she looked like a woman who was bowed down with trouble. She was never out of her room, and was apparently suffering great mental anxiety. She occupied a back room, but as Miss Mulholland had a room facing the street, she consented to allow her the use of it during the day. When Mrs. Pitezel said she was going to leave, Miss Mulholland told her she would send for the omnibus company to move her trunk for her. Mrs. Pitezel objected to this, and said that she would look after that herself, and went out and employed an ordinary car man. This was evidently done so that the detectives could not trace her baggage through the express office. In doing this, she was acting under instructions from Holmes, who never transferred his baggage by express, but always secured a man on the street to do it.

Geis's Hotel is not more than three or four blocks from Mrs. Burns' house at No. 91 Congress Street.

The children, Alice and Nellie had arrived at the last named place on October 13th, and Mrs. Pitezel and Dessie and the baby had registered at Geis's on the 14th, so it become perfectly evident that the mother, Alice and Nellie were in Detroit at the same time, and but a few blocks apart, the former supposing her children to be in Indianapolis, and the latter led to believe by Holmes that their mother was in Galva, Illinois. At this very time the children wrote a letter from No. 91 Congress Street to their grandparents at Galva, in which they sent a message to their mother. In both places I learned that the travellers on this sad journey kept close within their rooms.

What falsehoods, what fabrications were made up hy this accomplished liar, to induce or force the little girls to keep in doors may never he told, unless he for once speaks the truth. To Mrs Pitezel, of course, he held up the terrible possibility of Ben being traced by tile detectives through her movements, hence the necessity for seclusion.

I found that Mrs. Pitezel and the two children who were travelling with her, Dessie and the baby, had left Geis's Hotel on October 18th, and Alice and Nellie from No. 91 Congress Street on October 19th, and that Holmes and his wife from No. 54 Park Place on October 18th.

It must have taken very careful management to have moved these three separate parties from Detroit to Toronto, without either of the three discovering either of the others, but this great expert in crime did it, and did it successfully. His wife (or Mrs. Howard, who supposed she was his wife) was in total ignorance of the whole scheme. She was not only unaware of the proximity of Alice and Nellie, and of Mrs. Pitezel and her other two children, but she did not know them and had never seen them, and supposed that her husband (Holmes) was travelling from city to city selling leases upon an alleged patent copier, or collecting moneys from corporations and merchants using such copiers. This was his story to her, and it is the only bright spot in this entire story. It might be said to the credit of Holmes, that although he had deceived and betrayed this woman into marrying him, when he had a lawful wife (and still another woman who called herself his wife) living, he never permitted Miss Yoke to discover that he was a swindler or worse. He evidently desired to hold her respect for him until the very last.

I concluded my search in Detroit on Sunday, July 7th, and in the evening of that day, took the train for Toronto, at which place I arrived the next morning at half past nine o'clock.

CHAPTER X

THE SEARCH REWARDED

Arrival at Toronto — The Telltale Register — G. Howell and Wife Again — The Children in Toronto — H. Howell and Wife — Geyer Plans a Campaign — Meets the Newspaper Men — The Aid of the Press Invoked — A Disheartening Search — The House in a Field — The Pile of Loose Dirt — Sales of Half-tickets — Geyer Visits Prescott and Niagara Falls— Back in Toronto— Holmes Traced to No. 16 St. Vincent Street — Spades are Trumps — The Search in the Cellar — Finding the Bodies of Alice and Nellie Pitezel — Disposition of the Remains — The St. Vincent House Besieged by Reporters and Sketch Artists.

I WAS not a stranger in Toronto. My business had previously called me to that city on several occasions, and so when I arrived at the station, I directed the cabman to take me to the Rossin House, where I had stopped before. After breakfast and a short rest from my long and tiresome ride, I gathered up my bundle of papers and photographs and proceeded to the police headquarters.

On entering the detective department, I met another old friend, Alf Cuddy and after shaking hands with all the boys, whom I had met before, I was taken into the office of the ever kind, affable and courteous inspector, Mr. Stark, to whom I told the oft repeated story. He listened to me very attentively, and then took me into the room of Chief Constable Grassett, whom I had not had the pleasure of meeting before. To him I presented my letter of introduction from the superintendent of police of Philadelphia, and recounted to him the object of my errand. The chief assured me that his department would do everything in their power to assist me, and sent a messenger for Inspector Stark to come into the room. He instructed the inspector to detail a man to work with me as long as he was needed. Tlianking the chief for his courtesy and attention, I returned with the inspector to the detective department, where my old friend Cuddy was assigned to help me out in Toronto. This suited me very well, as I knew Cuddy to be an energetic fellow and not afraid of work, and willing to keep on until every clue had been run out, and the investigation either a success or a failure. Into a private room we went, and I narrated the entire story to Cuddy, so that lie would know what lie was doing.

HOWARD PITEZEL.

Proceeding as I did before, I thought it wise to examine the registers in the hotels around the Grand Trunk Depot, and we first wended our way to the Walker House and asked permission to see the register of 1894. We were informed that it had been packed away in the storeroom, but if it was important they would send a bell boy to get it. We told the clerk we would consider it a great favor if he would do so, and in a few minutes we had the register in our possession. Turning over the leaves until we came to October 18th, we found that "G. Howell and wife, Columbus," had registered for supper that day and left after dinner on the 20th, occupying room No. 14.

Our next visit was to the Union House. There the same request was made and complied with, and on the 18th of October we found the name of "Mrs. C. A. Adams and daughter, Columbus." Having located Holmes and Mrs. Pitezel, the next thing to do was to locate the girls, so we continued our search among the hotels, until we reached the Albion, and upon examining the register there found the names of "Alice and Nellie Canning, Detroit." This registry was made October 19th and had evidently been written by one of the girls.

The photographs of the girls were then shown to Mr. Herbert Jones, the chief clerk of the hotel, who positively identified them as the pictures of the children who were brought to the hotel by their porter, George Dennis, on Friday evening, October 19th. Mr. Jones also informed us that on the morning following their arrival, a gentleman called to see them and was there on almost every succeeding day during their stay at the hotel, with the exception of Sunday. The picture of Holmes was shown Mr. Jones. He recognized it as the man who called at the hotel for the children in the mornings of the days they stopped at the hotel. He said this man took the children away with him for the day, but they usually returned alone in the evening for supper. On the morning of the 25th of October, this same man called as usual at the hotel, paid the children's board bill, took them away with him, and that is the last time they were seen by him or any one in the hotel.

Holmes having left the Walker House on the afternoon of October 20th, and knowing that he was in Toronto as late as the 25th, I determined to discover whether he had registered and remained in another hotel, — so I continued my search until we arrived at the Palmer House, and there, under date of October 21st, we found him registered under the name of "H. Howell and wife, Columbus," room No. 32.

So thoroughly convinced was I that Holmes had rented a house in Toronto, Ontario, that after hearing Mr. Jones' story, I wrote in my report to the Superintendent of Police in Philadelphia, dated at Toronto, July 9th, 1895, the following:

"It is my impression that Holmes rented a house in Toronto the same as he did in Cincinnati, Ohio, and Detroit, Michigan, and that on the 25th of October he murdered the girls and disposed of their bodies by either burying them in the cellar, or some convenient place, or burning them in the heater. I intend to go to all the real estate agents and see if they can recollect having rented a house about that time to a man who only occupied it for a few days, and who represented that he wanted it for a widowed sister."

Inspired by the belief that perseverance and energy would bring forth some good result, I determined to get a Toronto directory and prepare a list of real estate agents, and interview each and every one of them, — so on Wednesday morning, July 10th, I went to Police Headquarters, where I met Cuddy and suggested my idea to him. It was a big task, yet it had to be done, so in we started upon the directory, — Cuddy reading off the names while I copied them. It took some time to prepare the list, and when finished we started, first going to those who were in the business portion of the city. It took considerable time to impress each agent with the importance of making a careful search for us, and before we knew it, night was upon us and the real estate offices were closed. Seriously meditating as to the best method to pursue to arouse the citizens of Toronto, I then determined to meet the newspaper men, give them my views of the case and explain to them my theories, so that the matter would be brought before the public, and the story of the disappearance of the children read in every household in the city. That night I was besieged by a number of reporters who called at my room in the Rossin House. I gave them the whole story, and told them I was prepared to let them have the photographs of Holmes and the children, and would esteem it a favor if they would publish them. I also requested them to call the attention of real estate agents and private renters to the matter, so that if any person had rented a house under such circumstances as I described, I would be glad to have them communicate with me. The next morning every newspaper published in Toronto, devoted several columns to the story of the disappearance of the children, and requested all good citizens to forward any information they might have to Police Headquarters, or to me at the Rossin House.

Thursday morning, July 11th, Detective Cuddy and I continued our search among the real estate agents. We found a majority of them prepared to meet us, for they had read the morning papers and our task was thus facilitated very much. In the afternoon, we decided to visit several suburban towns, known as Mimico and North and South Parkdale, so away we went singing the same old story to each and every agent we came across. However, we kept fighting on, hoping against hope, with no word or sign of encouragement. Another day went by and there was not the slightest clue to give us a grain of comfort. On our return to Police Headquarters, we received word that a man giving the name of Holmes had rented a house on the outskirts of the city, — a house that stood in the middle of a field, and was surrounded by a board fence six feet high. This house was situated at Perth and Bloor Streets. We wanted nothing more, and away we journeyed. We found the house situated as already described, and occupied by an aged couple with a son about twenty years old. After introducing ourselves as officers, we ascertained from the old gentleman, that they had only lived there a few months, and did not know who occupied the house the previous October. We explained to them our suspicions and said that we believed that Holmes had murdered the children, and had buried them somewhere under the house. "That accounts for that pile of loose dirt under the main building," said the old man. "Get a shovel" was Cuddy's suggestion, so the old man led the way to show us how we could get under the house, while the young man went in search of a shovel. He soon returned, and taking off our coats, we crawled into a small hole and were soon underneath the floor of the main building. The floor was not more than two feet above the earth, and it did not take us long to discover what the old gentleman meant by the pile of loose dirt. As it was getting dark, we requested that some light be furnished. The boy crawled out from under the floor and in a short time we had several coal oil lamps burning and commenced digging, feeling positive that we would unearth the children. A hole was dug about four feet square, when it was decided to give it up for the night and return the next morning. Friday morning, July 12th, I called at Police Headquarters and met Cuddy, and proposed to him that we go and see the agent who rented the house Perth and Bloor, and see if he could identify the photograph of Holmes as the man who had rented the house. The agent was not a very early riser, consequently our patience was taxed in waiting for him. However, when he came and looked at the picture, he said that it was not the man. Again were we disappointed, and the balance of the day was spent at the Grand Trunk Depot, in trying to ascertain if there had been any half tickets sold on the morning of the 25th of October from Toronto to Suspension Bridge. The ticket agent treated us very courteously, and examined his records and found that on that day, there had been only one whole ticket sold for Niagara Falls, or Suspension Bridge. In answer to a question, whether a conductor would take a whole ticket for two children, he said he would, so we were unable to say positively that Holmes had not sent the girls to the Suspension Bridge to meet Minnie Williams, as he claimed to have done, — he going as far as Parkdale. We then endeavored to learn through the freight office, what amount of baggage was shipped to Prescott, Canada, on the night of the 25th of October and the morning of the 26th. We learned that two pieces had been sent there on the night of the 25th, and one piece on the morning of the 26th. This corresponded with the amount of baggage carried by Holmes and Mrs. Pitezel, and convinced me that Prescott was the place they had gone to, and in the event of not meeting with success in Toronto, I determined that Prescott would be my next stopping place. As Flolmes had left the Walker House on the afternoon of October 20th, and his whereabouts from that time until the afternoon of the 21st not being known, I was impressed with the belief that he had taken his wife to Niagara Falls; so on Saturday morning, July 13th, I concluded that I would go there and see if I could locate them, and if so, ascertain whether they had the children with them. Taking the boat to Lewistown, and from there the trolley cars, I arrived at Niagara Falls, (Canada side) about eleven AM, and began a search among the hotels, and in a short time my labor was rewarded by locating them at King's Imperial Hotel, where they arrived on the afternoon of the 20th, and left on the afternoon of the 21st. There were no children with them, and they had evidently gone there simply to view the Falls. I returned to Toronto and visited a number of the newspaper offices for the purpose of examining their files, and made a list of private renters who advertised their houses to rent, as I intended to call upon every one of them in person. I was so positive that Holmes had disposed of the children in Toronto, that I could not think of leaving, until I had made a more extended search. That evening I met Cuddy, and we discussed our plans for Monday morning.

Sunday, July 14th, was devoted to writing home and to meditating over the case, and the probable chances of success.

Monday morning, July 15th, I went to Police Headquarters and joined Cuddy, He appeared to be somewhat more cheerful than usual, and when I suggested that we would start out and search among the private renters, he informed me that they had received another report about a man who had rented a house on St. Vincent Street, whose description corresponded with that of Holmes, and he suggested that we run this clue out before doing anything else. Notwithstanding his fine spirits, he remarked that he guessed it would prove to be a wild goose chase, similar to the many that we had already enjoyed. In looking over the newspaper files, I discovered that there was a house to rent at No. 16 St. Vincent

Street and to inquire of Mrs. Frank Nudel, at No. 54 Henry Street. Detective Cuddy was personally acquainted with Mr. Frank Nudel, who is connected with the Educational Department of Toronto, and he suggested that we stop and see him before going to the St. Vincent Street house. We found Mr. Nudel, who told us that his wife was the owner of the house No. 16 St. Vincent Street and that she had rented it to a man some time last October, who only occupied it for about one week. Thanking him for this information, we started for the St. Vincent Street house, but instead of going to No. 16, we called at No. 18 to see an old Scotchman named Thomas William Ryves, who had notified one of the inspectors of police that a man answering Holmes' description, and whose picture with the Pitezel girls he had seen in the Toronto papers, had occupied the house No. 16, next to him, and had told him he had rented it for a widowed sister, who was at Hamilton, Ontario, and that he expected lier there in a few days. We found Mr. Ryves a very pleasant old man to talk to, and after propounding the usual questions to him, lie immediately recognized the photograph of Alice, but he was not positively sure of Holmes. He said he never got a good look at Nellie and could not say whether or not it was her picture. He told us that the man asked him to loan him a spade, as he wanted to arrange a place in his cellar for his sister to put potatoes in. He said that the only furniture that was brought to the house was an old bed and mattress, and a big trunk. The trunk was taken away from the house, but the bed and mattress were left there. By this time we had heard sufficient to convince us that we were on the right track, and bidding the old gentleman good day, we requested him to meet us again at his house in one hour. We lost no time in going to Mrs. Nudel's house, and ringing the bell the summons was answered by her daughter. We asked if Mrs. Nudel was at home and received an answer in the affirmative;

"Tell her," I said, "we want to see her at once, it is very important."

We were requested to take a seat in the parlor, and in a few minutes Mrs. Nudel made her appearance, and without giving her a cliance to say much, I produced the pliotograph of Holmes, and asked her if she had ever seen the original of that picture. Mother and daughter both looked at it at the same time, and answered together,

"Why, yes, that is the man who rented the St. Vincent Street house last October and only occupied it for a few days."

NO. 129 ST. VINCENT STREET, TORONTO, ONT., WHERE HOLMES MURDERED THE PITEZEL CHILDREN

Mrs. Nudel said the man represented that he wanted it for a widowed sister, who was coming on from Detroit, Michigan. This seemed too good to be true, and our anxiety to examine the house was so great, that we hurriedly thanked her and left. We at once returned to No. 18 St. Vincent Street where we met Mr. Ryves anxiously awaiting for our return. Requesting him to loan us a shovel, he went into the house and came out with the same spade he had loaned to Holmes. We rang the bell at No. 16 St. Vincent Street. The door was opened by the lady of the house, a Mrs. J. Armbrust. Mr. Ryves introduced us and told her we would like to go into the cellar. She kindly consented and ushered us back into the kitchen. Lifting a large piece of oilcloth from the floor, we discovered a small trap door, possibly two feet square in about the centre of the room. Raising this, I discovered that the celhir was not very deep but it was very dark, so I asked Mrs. Armbrnst to kindly provide us with some himps. In a short time she had them ready, and down into the cellar we went. The cellar was very small, about ten feet square, and not more than four and a half feet in depth.

A set of steps almost perpendicular led to it from the old-fashioned trap door in the middle of the kitchen floor.

Taking the spade and pushing it into the earth, so as to determine whether it had been lately dug up, we finally discovered a soft spot in the southwest corner. Forcing the spade into the earth, we found it easy digging, and after going down about one foot, a horrible stench arose. This convinced us that we were on the right spot, and our coats were thrown off, and with renewed confidence, we continued our digging. The deeper we dug, the more horrible the odor became, and when we reached the depth of three feet, we discovered what appeared to be the bone of the forearm of a human being. Throwing some dirt into the hole, in order to keep down the stench as much as possible, we left the cellar and went into the kitchen, where I had a conference with Cuddy and advised him to communicate with Inspector Stark and tell him of our discovery and have him suggest over the telephone what undertaker we should employ to remove the bodies. Cuddy acquiesced in what I said, and we started for the nearest telephone, which we found in a telegraph office on Yonge Street, a short distance from the St. Vincent Street house. Cuddy called up the inspector, told him of our discovery, and requested him to recommend an undertaker to take charge of the bodies. The inspector after congratulating us, told us to go to B. D. Humphrey, an undertaker on Yonge Street, and make any proper arrangements with him. We found Mr. Humphrey at his establishment, and requested him to assist us in the exhumation of the bodies. I suggested to him to take several pairs of rubber gloves with him, as the bodies were in such a state of putrification, it would be impossible to lift them out of the hole without them. We then returned to the St Vincent Street house, accompanied by Mr. Humphrey and into the cellar we went again. Mr. Humphrey after preparing himself for the task, jumped into the hole already made by Cuddy and myself and assisted us in the work. In a short time we unearthed the remains of the two little girls, Alice and Nellie Pitezel.

Alice was found lying on her side, with her hand to the west. Nellie was found lying on her face, with her head to the south, her plaited hair hanging neatly down her back. While we were making preparations to lift them out of the hole, a messenger was dispatched to Humphrey's undertaking establishment to send two coffins to No. 16 St. Vincent Street. In a short while the wagon arrived and the coffins were taken into the kitchen, and we proceeded to lift the remains out of the hole. As Nellie's limbs were found resting on Alice's, we first began with her. We lifted her as gently as possible, but owing to the decomposed state of the body, the weight of her plaited hair hanging down her back, pulled the scalp from off her head. A sheet had been spread in which to lay the remains, and after we succeeded in getting it out of the hole, it was placed in the sheet, taken upstairs, and deposited in the coffin.

Again we returned to the cellar, and gently lifting what remained of poor Alice, we placed her in another sheet, took her upstairs, and placed her in a coffin by the side of her sister. The bodies were immediately removed to Mr. Humphrey's establishment, after which they were sent to the nioigue. By this time Toronto was wild with excitement. The news had spread to every part of the city. The St. Vincent Street house was besieged with newspaper men, sketch artists, and others. Everybody seemed to be pleased with our success, and congratulations, mingled with expressions of horror over the discovery were heard everywhere.

I then telegraphed the first result of my search to District Attorney Graham and to superintendent of the Philadelphia police, and thus it was proved that little children cannot be murdered in this day and generation, beyond the possibility of discovery.

NO. 241 EAST FOREST AVENUE, DETROIT, MICHIGAN, WHERE HOLMES INTENDED TO MURDER HOWARD PITEZEL

CHAPTER XI

FORGING THE LINKS

St. Vincent Street — Fair Without, a Charnel House Witluu— The Little Wooden Egg— Clothing Identified— Great Excitement in Toronto — Mrs. Pitezel Summoned from Galva, Illinois — The Preliminary Inquest — Arrival of Mrs. Pitezel — A Mother's Anguish — Mrs. Pitezel Identifies the Bodies — Mrs. Pitezel's Testimony — Testimony of Mr. Ryves — The Burial — Mrs. Pitezel in Kind Hands.

The house where the children were found, is a quaint little two-story cottage of an old and simple style of architecture. It stands back a few feet from the sidewalk, — the narrow plot of lawn in front being enclosed with a wire net fence five feet high and beautified with a few blossoming flowers. A veranda tastefully decorated with a clinging clematis, adds much to the homelike appearance of the place. The front doorway opens into a hallway, which divides the house in half and continues to the kitchen. The cottage contains six medium sized rooms, below, including a kitchen and a pantry, three on either side of the hall, and there are four small rooms above. A single gable window looks from the upper story to the street. At each end of the house are three small windows, none of them much larger than the window in the front. The back yard is small, and is reached from the kitchen by a short set of steps.

Feeling somewhat fatigued over the day's work, I determined to spend the evening at the Rossin House in writing to my superintendent and others, and to map out a plan for the next day, as our work was not completed. As the bodies were badly decomposed, personal identification might be difficult and I determined if possible to find some evidence which would aid in establishing their identity, — so I concluded to learn if possible, who had occupied the house after Holmes had left it. The next day, after meeting Cuddy at police headquarters, we started off to find the tenant who succeeded Holmes in the St. Vincent Street house. We were not long in ascertaining, that after Holmes had left, the house had been occupied by a family named MacDonald, who only remained a very short time, but no one was able to tell us where they had moved to. However, hy diligent search we located them at No. 17 Russell Street. We called at their home, where we met Mrs. MacDonald and after introducing ourselves, told her the object of our visit. She said that all she had found at the house No. 16 St. Vincent Street, was an old bedstead and mattress. I then questioned her as to whether she had any children, and she informed me that she had a boy about sixteen years old who was not at home at that time. I requested her to send him to police headquarters as soon as he arrived home, and bring with him anything he had found in the St. Vincent Street house. Bright and early the next morning young MacDonald, appeared at police headquarters with a little wooden egg, which when parted in the middle, would disclose a snake, which would spring out. He said he had found this egg in a small leather caba, in one of the closets on the second floor. I had been supplied with a list of the playthings the children had with them, and one can imagine my surprise and elation when I found in this list, a description of just such an egg as the MacDonald boy found. It was one of the links which contributed to making the identification sure. Another link in this chain was supplied by Mrs. Armboust. The children were found buried in a nude condition, and the manner in which their clothing had been disposed of was one of the points of my inquiries. A part of a waist, and what appeared to be a piece of ribbon were found when the children were exhumed. When Mrs. Armbrust was cleaning the house after moving in, she noticed some rags and straw hanging from the chimney in the north front room. These she pulled down and found a part of a striped waist of a grayish color, a piece of a woolen garment of brownish red, and a part of a dress of bluish color. The straw had been lit but had not burned, as the clothing had been shoved into the chimney too tightly. A pair of girl's button boots were found in the wood box; also one odd boot and other parts of the clothing of a female. All this had been thrown away by

Mr. Armbrust, but they answered the description of the clothing worn by the Pitezel girls, given by their mother.

The missing trunk had not been forgotten during all this time, and it was frequently spoken of by Cuddy and myself. After having heard from Mr. Ryves, that a large trunk had been brought to the house, the idea suggested itself to us, that possibly Holmes might have murdered the boy in Detroit, placed him in the trunk, and shipped him to the St. Vincent Street house to dispose of the body. I determined if such were the case, not to leave Toronto until I had satisfied myself on this point, — consequently we employed several men to dig up every inch of the entire cellar and we thoroughly examined the barn and outhouses, but without result.

The finding of the bodies, as I have said before, caused great excitement in Toronto, and if the good people of that city had been furnished with an opportunity, I am sure they would have made sliort shrift of Holmes. Preparations were made for the inquest, which was to be conducted by Coroner Johnston, and in the meantime I was receiving dispatches from District Attorney Graham, of Philadelphia, regarding Mrs. Pitezel, who was at Chicago, Illinois, and whom he had instructed to go to Toronto, Canada, to meet me, and if possible identify the children.

On Tuesday morning, July 16th, Coroner Johnston summoned a number of jurors to be present at the morgue that evening at half-past seven o'clock, also requesting my attendance there at the same hour. This was to be the preliminary inquest to view the bodies.

7:30 PM we all appeared at the morgue, and Coroner Johnston opened the inquest, after which the jury was sworn. Then the superintendent of the morgue was sent for and everything being ready, the coroner directed the jury to examine the bodies. In the dead house they went, but I assure you that their stay was a very limited one, as the odor from the decomposed remains was unbearable, and Coroner Johnston adjourned the inquest until Wednesday evening, July 17th, to be held in the Police Court, City Hall. On Wednesday evening I attended the inquest and was requested to recite the story of Holmes, and the insurance swindle, and the disappearance and the finding of the children. I was kept on the witness stand about two hours and a half, and then after hearing several other witnesses, the investigation was adjourned to await the arrival of Mrs. Pitezel. Thursday morning, July 18th, I received a dispatch from her, stating that she had left Chicago and was on her way to Toronto. I watched all incoming trains during the day, and at 7:30 PM I again went to the Grand Trunk Depot, and was surprised to see so many people there. This was due, however, to the fact that Mrs. Pitezel had been interviewed by a number of newspaper men before leaving Chicago, and they had wired her time of departure for Toronto to the Toronto papers. Shortly after my arrival at the station, the Canadian Pacific train from Chicago came in, and I observed Mrs. Pitezel getting off the car. I had a difficult task to make my way through the crowd to reach her, but as quickly as possible I placed her in a carriage and took her to the Rossin House, where I had made arrangements to have her placed in a room opposite my own, and I requested that no one should disturb her. Mrs. Pitezel reached her room in an absolutely prostrated condition. The chambermaid had very kindly volunteered to render her such assistance as was possible, and after applying restoratives, she soon revived sufficiently to talk to me. Amid her tears and moans, she said,

"Oh, Mr. Geyer, is it true that you have found Alice and Nellie buried in a cellar?"

I did all I could to calm her, and told her to prepare for the worst. She told me that she would try to bear up with it and would do the best she could. I then told her as gently as possible, that I had found the children, but did not describe to her their horrible condition, nor under what circumstances they were discovered. After remaining with her a short time, I asked several of the ladies connected with the hotel to visit her room and say a comforting word to her, which they did, and it seemed to have a good effect upon her.

Friday morning, July 19th, I knocked at Mrs. Pitezel's door, and I found that she had improved. She said she had not slept very well, but felt somewhat rested. I then left her and told her I would go out and make arrangements for taking her to the morgue during the day to look at the children. I then went to Police Headquarters and met Cuddy, after which we called at Coroner Johnston's house. He informed us that he would have the bodies so arranged that we could bring the mother to look at them at four o'clock that afternoon. Cuddy and I then returned to the hotel, where every care that human forethought could suggest, had been taken to prepare Mrs. Pitezel for the awful task necessity imposed upon her. I told her that; it would be absolutely impossible for her to see anything but Alice's teeth and hair, and only the hair belonging to Nellie. This had a paralyzing effect upon her and she almost fainted. At -i PM we had a carriage at the Rossin House, and I informed her that we were ready to proceed to the morgue. In a few minutes she was ready, and after supplying ourselves with brandy and smelling salts, we started for the morgue, where we found a number of curious people on the outside awaiting our arrival. Mrs. Pitezel was seated in the waiting room, while I went into the dead house to see that everything was in readiness, before we conducted her in.

I found that Coroner Johnston, Dr. Caven and several of his assistants, had removed the putrid flesh from the skull of Alice; the teeth had been nicely cleaned and the bodies covered with canvas. The head of Alice was covered with paper, and a hole sufficiently large had been cut in it, so that Mrs. Pitezel could see the teeth. The hair of both children had been carefully washed and laid on the canvas sheet which was covering Alice. Coroner Johnston said that we could now bring Mrs. Pitezel in. I entered the waiting room and told her we were ready, and with Cuddy on one side of her, and I on the other, we entered and led her up to the slab, upon which was lying all that remained of poor Alice. In an instant she recognized the teeth and hair as that of her daughter, Alice. Then turning around to me she said, "Where is Nellie?" about this time she noticed the long black plait of hair belonging to Nellie lying in the canvas. She could stand it no longer, and the shrieks of that poor forlorn creature are still ringing in my ears. Tears were trickling down the cheeks of strong men who stood about us. The sufferings of the stricken mother were beyond description. We gently led her out of the room, and into the carriage. She returned to the Rossin House completely overcome with grief and despair, and had one fainting spell after another. The ladies in the hotel visited her in her room and spoke kindly to her, and expressed their sympathy with her in her sad bereavement and this seemed in a measure to ease her mind. At 7 PM, I received word from Coroner Johnston, that if it were possible, he would like to have Mrs. Pitezel attend the inquest that evening and give her testimony. While I did not think she was in a fit condition to leave the hotel, I communicated to her what Dr. Johnston had said, and she said she thought she would be able to go and get through with it. About 7:30 PM I called a carriage and we started for the City Hall, where I gave Mrs. Pitezel in charge of the matron and then went into the court room and informed Coroner Johnston that Mrs. Pitezel was ready to testify. He requested me to bring lier into the room, whereupon Detective Cuddy and I led her in and placed her on a seat beside the Coroner, and in a few moments, after taking the necessary oath, she began her story. For two hours and a half this poor woman was kept on the stand and prodded with all kinds of questions. So weak did she become, that at times her voice was inaudible, and several times we feared she would totally collapse. Finally the Crown's Assistant Attorney thought he had heard enough and consented to allow her to leave the stand. She was returned to the matron's room and was scarcely there, when she became hysterical, and her shrieks for Alice, Nellie and Howard, could have been heard a block away. Several doctors present at the inquest immediately prescribed for her, and after working with her about one hour, we got her in a condition to move her to a hole.. The matron at the City Hall was a professional nurse, and volunteered to accompany Mrs. Pitezel to the hotel and remain with her during the night, if I so desired it. I was only too willing to have her join us and render the poor woman all the assistance and sympathy possible. I sent for a carriage and we returned to the hotel, where Mrs. Pitezel spent a terrible night.

The story as revealed by the witnesses at the inquest was very clear, after it had been unravelled. Holmes and his wife had left Detroit on October 18th, arriving in Toronto the same day, registering at the Walker House as G. Howell and wife, Columbus. Mrs. Pitezel and Dessie and the baby, left Detroit the same day, but two hours later, registering at the Union House under the name of Mrs. C. A. Adams and daughter.

Alice and Nellie left Detroit the following day, October 19th. Holmes met them at the Grand Trunk Station and turned them over to George Dennis, a hotel porter, who took them by direction of Holmes to the Albion Hotel, where they remained until the morning of October 25th. Holmes called for the girls on the morning of the 20th and returned them to the hotel about six o'clock in the evening of the same day, and this he repeated every morning and evening except Sunday until the morning of the 25th, when he took them away finally, for they did not return. He paid for their board every morning and the last payment was made on the 25th.

On October 20th Holmes rented the house No. 16 St. Vincent Street of Mrs. Christiana Nudel, and said he wanted it for his widowed sister, who was coming from Detroit. He rented the house for six months, at ten dollars for the first month, and twelve dollars per month for the remainder of the term. He took the key and went away Mrs. Nudel heard nothing more until nearly the end of the month, when she learned that the house was empty, and that the key had been left with Mr. Ryves, the next door neighbor.

Mr. Ryves saw the little girls on the veranda of the house and once in the yard. He saw Holmes there. Holmes told him different stories. The first day he met him he said he was renting the house for a sister who was coming from Hamilton. He said she had a family of four children, and that he would board with them as he had secured a situation in Toronto. He brought a trunk with him first, and later on a mattress and bedstead Avere brought and remained on the veranda for two days. The day Ryves saw the girls in the yard, Holmes came over and borrowed a spade from him, saying that lie was going to fix a place ill the cellar to hold potatoes.

He borrowed the spade about four or five o'clock in the afternoon and returned it between eight and ten o'clock the next morning, handing it over the fence to Mr. Ryves. Mr. Ryves never saw the girls again after seeing them in the yard. The day after Holmes returned the spade, he came to the house and removed the trunk, and left the key with Mr. Ryves. The latter went into the house the next day and into the cellar to look where the potatoes were to go and he found fresh earth scattered around the bottom of the cellar and some loose boards lying on top. Mrs. Pitezel identified the little wooden egg as a trinket which Alice had, and which she used to carry in a little leather caba.

Nothing could be more surprising than the apparent ease with which Holmes murdered the two little girls in the very centre of the city of Toronto, without arousing the least suspicion of a single person there. It startles one to realize how such a hideous crime could be committed and detection avoided. Surely if the investigation and search for the children had not been made by the Philadelphia authorities, these murders would never have been discovered, and Mrs. Pitezel would have gone to her grave without knowing whether her children were alive or dead. This was the one consolation she had in the very darkest hour of her life. She knew the fate of her unfortunate daughters— the mystery of their disappearance had been solved, and the only remaining problem was the discovery of her little son, Howard. She could not believe he was dead, and clung fondly to the hope that he would ultimately be found alive.

Holmes was successful in maintaining the same conditions in Toronto, as he had in Detroit. Mrs. Pitezel was at the Union Hotel, and Alice and Nellie at the Albion, although each party was ignorant of the proximity of the other.

On the afternoon of July 19th, 1895, the remains of the little girls were buried in St. James' cemetery, the expense being borne by the authorities of Toronto. It was a sad scene. In the meantime I received orders from District Attorney Graham to return to Detroit and resume my search for the boy Howard. I left Toronto, Sunday, July 20th, (in company with

Mrs. Pitezel) and arrived in Detroit on the afternoon of the same day. Mrs. Pitezel did not stop in Detroit, but continued on to Chicago in charge of some good women, of a Christian Endeavor Society, who volunteered to see to her.

I had finished a part of my task, and the fulfillment of the other part now confronted me. Where was the boy Howard? Had he been placed in some institution, as Holmes had intimated his intention of doing, or was he hidden in some obscure place beyond reach or discovery? Was he alive or dead? I was puzzled, nonplussed, and groping in the dark. I could not turn back, — I was directed to go on, and I determined to do so, hoping that patience and persistent hard work might finally lead me to the light.

REAR OF NO. 241 EAST FOREST AVENUE, DETROIT, MICHIGAN

CHAPTER XIV

HOW TO FIND THE BOY

Geyer Again in Detroit — Where is Howard Pitezel?— Did He Leave Detroit Alive? — Reviewing the Evidence — Another Search at No. 241 E, Forest Avenue — Geyer Does Some Hard Thinking — Review of Holmes' Movements — Copy of Letter From Alice to Her Grandparents, Found in the Possession of Holmes — Its Pitiable Tale — Holmes' Fiendish Treatment of Both Mother and Children — A Friend Warns Holmes to Leave Detroit — The Murder of the Children Postponed — The Furnace Theory.

About 5 PM I went to the Detroit Police Headquarters, where I met Detective Meyler, who, after congratulating me upon my success in Toronto, informed me that the Superintendent would not be in his office until the following morning.

That Sunday evening I spent in recounting to Meyler the story of finding the girls, after which I retired for the night.

Monday morning, July 22d, I reported at Police Headquarters and met Superintendent Starkweather, who agaiu detailed Detective Tuttle to assist me in Detroit. I decided to go over with greater care, the evidence which proved Howard to have been seen in Detroit, and called with Tuttle on Mr. Frank R. Alderman, the manager of the Fidelity Mutual Life Association for Michigan. When the case was first investigated by the detectives of the insurance company, Mr. Boninghausen, the real estate agent who rented No. 2-11 E. Forest Avenue to Holmes, said that the latter was accompanied by a small boy, but when I called upon him again, in company with Mr. Alderman, he declared that he had no absolutely positive recollection of the matter, but that Mr. Moore, who subsequently rented the same house, had said that he had noticed a boy with Holmes. This knocked out one of the supports of the Detroit theory, and we then sought out Mr. Moore and found him at No. 241 E. Forest Avenue.

Mr. Moore said that he had never been positive about the presence of the boy with Holmes. Several persons with children were in Mr. Boninghausen's office at the time, and he said he tliovght one of them, a small boy, was with Holmes, but he was not sure.

At this time we made, with Mr. Moore's permission, another thorough search of the premises, No. 241 E. Forest Avenue, including the barn, outhouses and yard, and I felt fully convinced that if the boy had been murdered there, his body had been consumed in the large furnace of the house.

We then went to the Wabash railroad station to ascertain the number of half tickets, which arrived from Chicago at 11:15 PM, on October 12th, 1894. An effort was made to find the cancelled tickets of this date and train, but they had all been destroyed. I was still very much at sea about Howard, and I did some very hard thinking on the subject. Time and time again I reviewed the facts known to me. Holmes arrived in Detroit on the evening of October 12th. He sent the girls into the station and told them to remain there and wait for him. He then rejoined his wife, (who was also with him, but ignorant of the presence of the children) and took her to the hotel. He then left his wife and returned to the station and took the girls to the New Western Hotel, where they were registered as Etta and Nellie Canning. The next day, the 13th, he moved them to a boarding house kept by Mrs. Lucinda Burns, No. 91 Congress Street. At this house Alice wrote a letter to her grandparents, which she gave to Holmes to post, and which he, as usual, omitted to do. This was one of the letters found in the possession of Holmes when he was arrested.

This letter was unsigned, but it was written by Alice, because it is in her handwriting and she refers to her sister Nell. The letter enclosed two pages of note paper, on which the children had made rude drawings of houses, one of which bore the caption "Uncle Tom's Cabin." This was copied from a picture in Mrs. Stowe's book, which the girls had. Under the drawing of the cabin was written, "All these pictures was drawn at No. 91 Congress Street, Detroit, Mich."

This letter is dated October 14th, 1894, just two days subsequent to their arrival in Detroit, and on the very day their mother, (Mrs. Pitezel), their sister Dessie, and the little baby, Wharton, arrived in Detroit, where they were to meet Pitezel, so Holmes said. This little party registered at Geis's Hotel, as Mrs. C. E. Adams and daughter. Geis's Hotel is not over five blocks from No. 91 Congress Street, so when this poor child Alice, was writing to her grandparents to Galva, Illinois, complaining of the cold, sending a message to her mother, asking for heavier and more comfortable clothing, wishing for little Wharton, the baby who would help them to pass away the time, — while this wearied, lonely, homesick child was writing this letter, her mother and her sister and the much wished for Wharton, were within ten minutes' walk of her, and continued there for the next five days. More than that, — this unparalleled villain who had robbed the Insurance Company of Ten Thousand Dollars, and in turn fraudulently secured Sixty-Seven Hundred Dollars of the swag from Mrs. Pitezel, was at that very moment making arrangements to kill the girls and bury them at No. 241 East Forest Avenue. The hole which he had dug, (which he admitted he had dug to bury therein, he said, a tin box containing valuable papers, — a hole four feet long, three and a half feet deep and three feet wide) was intended as a grave for the little girls. This was the reason he did not purchase them any warmer clothing, notwithstanding it was coming winter. It was unnecessary to spend any money for clothing, when they were to die so soon.

The reason this plan was not executed in Detroit, was because of a notice he received from one of his Chicago friends, who knew of the insurance swindle and from whom he received a friendly tip, warning him that detectives were on his track. This notice came to him by telegram and caused him to move his field of operations to Toronto.

To me the significant part of this letter was the expression, "Howard is not with us now." Why did not Alice say to her grandpaients where they had separated from Howard? A simple phrase or sentence would have told the story. I believe these children, after leaving Indianapolis and reaching Detroit, the city to which Holmes had brought her mother, and sister and her little brother, were kept in a state of fear or apprehension. The evident design of Holmes was to keep the children in ignorance of the proximity of their mother and he quite likely told them that if their identity were discovered, their father, who was being hunted by detectives, would be apprehended. They gave their name as Canning, (the name of their grandparents) at his suggestion, and kept close indoors just as he advised. The proposed boat ride they speak of in their letter, and which was not taken because the weather was too cold, was deferred most likely by their supposed friend.

In one of his numerous statements made in prison to various persons, and to District Attorney Graham, Holmes said he had given Howard to Miss Williams in Detroit, who had taken him tu Buffalo. I did not believe a word of the Williams part of this statement, but still my suspicion of Mr. Holmes' character for truth and veracity did not assist me in clearing up the veil of mystery which surrounded the disappearance of the little boy.

The hole in the cellar of the Forest Avenue house, and the great size of the cellar furnace, the expression in the letter I have quoted, and the uncertainty of Mr. Moore's memory as to the presence of a boy in Boninghausen's office, became the basis of numerous theories. One idea clung to me tenaciously. I could readily imagine Howard separated from his sisters the night of the arrival of the party in Detroit: of Holmes taking him to a quiet place until he was wanted; of the renting of the Forest Avenue house and the digging of the hole; of the discovery by Holmes of the great size of the cellar furnace, which caused him to change his proposed means of disposing of the body; of the murder and incineration of the corpse by the method so readily at hand.

Nothing had ever been discovered in the furnace by the new tenant, Mr. Moore, which indicated that a body had been consumed therein, — so after the fullest consideration of all that the most persistent search could reveal, I finally concluded that the separation from Howard had taken place prior to the arrival of Alice and Nellie in Detroit, and not after, and I decided to search for him elsewhere, and wired to Philadelphia my purpose to return to Indianapolis.

LETTER FROM ALICE PITEZEL TO HER GRANDPARENTS (FOUND IN HOLMES POSSESSION WHEN ARRESTED)

CHAPTER XV

THE DETECTIVE PUZZLED

Once More in Indianapolis — Days of Fruitless Work — Everybody Willing to Aid — Scores of People Suggest CluesHas the Clever Criminal Outupitted the Detective? — Copies of the Children's Letters — Keen Analysis of their Contents — The Evidence of an Envelope — Geyer Ordered to Chicago — Chicago Police Dig up the Skeleton of a Child — The Skeleton is not Hovrard's — Geyer Goes to Philadelphia for Consultation and Rest.

I LEFT Detroit on the afternoon of July 23d, and arrived in Indianapolis the next morning, having been delayed on the route at Peru, Indiana. I again registered at the Spencer House and lost no time in going to police headquarters, where I met Superintendent of Police Powell, to whom I confided my purpose of resuming my search for the Pitezel boy in Indianapolis. Detective Richards was again detailed to assist me, and we at once mapped out a plan of operations. We procured a directory of the city and made a list of every real estate agent in Indianapolis and vicinity and commenced to interview every one of them with the hope of finding a house that had been rented early in October of 1894, to a man who wanted it for a widowed sister, and who occnpied it but a short time. Holmes had given this "widowed sister" story in Cincinnati, Detroit, and Toronto, and I believed he had told the same falsehood in Indianapolis.

Our search continued in this manner for days, yet I learned nothing which gave me the least assistance in obtaining the clue for which I was so anxiously seeking. The newspapers had published columns of the Toronto story and my return to Indianapolis was heralded abroad in conspicuous head lines. All of the papers published pictures of Holmes and Howard Pitezel, and it seemed as though every man, woman and child in Indiana was alert and watchful, and aiding me in the work of finding the missing child.

Scores of citizens called upon me at the Spencer House, making suggestions and giving me many supposed clues, all of which were faithfully run out. The number of mysterious persons who had rented houses in and about Indianapolis multiplied from day to day, and Detective Richards and I were not permitted to rest a moment. Days came and passed, but I continued to be as much in the dark as ever, and it began to look as though the bold but clever criminal, had outwitted the detectives, professional and amateur, and that the disappearance of Howard Pitezel would pass into history as an unsolved mystery.

About this time I received a communication from Assistant District Attorney Barlow, who was holding up the Philadelphia end of the line with great hopefulness and patience. He sent me an analysis of three of the children's letters written from Indianapolis, which threw more light upon the matter, and brought me more closely to the track of the destroyer of innocent children. These three letters now given, are exact copies of the originals.

Indianapolis, Ind ,

October 6, 1894.

Dear Mamma, Geandma and Grandpa: — We are all well here. It is a little warmer to-day. There is so many buggies go by that you cant hear yourself think. I first wrote you a letter with a crystal pen, but I made some mistakes and then I am in a hustle because Mr. H. has to go at 3 o'clock I don't know where. It is all glass so I hafto be careful or else it will break, it was only five cents. Mr. H. went to T. H. Indiana last night again. Their was a poor boy arrested yesterday for stealing a shirt he said he had no home the policeman said he would buy him a suit of clothes and then send him to a reform school. The patrols are lots different here than they are in St. Louis & Chicago, they couldnt get away if they wanted to. We hafto get up early if we get breakfast. We have awful good dinners pie fruit and sometimes cake at supper and this aint half.

They are all men that eat at the tables we do not eat with them we have a room to ourselves. They are dutch but they can cook awful nice. Their is more bicycles go by her in one day than goes by in a month in St. Louis. I saw two great big ostriges alive and we felt of their feathers they are awful smooth | they are black with white tails they are as big as a horse. Why have buffaloes got big rings in their noses for I want Grandma and grandpa to write to me. Is the baby well and does he like coco I want you to all write why dont you write mama. I will close for this time goodby wte

Yours truly, Nellie Pitezel

over

Alices eyes hurts so she wont write this time.

Indianapolis Ind.

Oct. 6th 1894. Dear Mamma.

We are all well except I have got a bad cold and I have read so much in Uncle Tom's book that I could not see to write yesterday when Nell and Howard did. I am wearing my new (ders) dress today because it is warmer to day. Nell Howard and I have all got a crystal pen all made of glass five cents a piece and I am writing with it now. I expect Grandma and Grandpa was awftd glad to see you. The hotel we are staying at faces right on a big wide bulvard and there is more safties and bugies passing than a little bit and how I wish I had a safty. Last Sunday we was at the Zoological Garden in Cincinnati, O. And I expect this Sunday will pass away slower than I dont know what and Howard is two dirty to be seen out on the street to-day. Why dont you write to me. I have not got a letter from you since I have been away and it will be three weeks day after tomorrow. It is raining out now quite hard. Nell is drawing now. The hotel is just a block from Washington Street and that is where all the big stores are. There is a shoe store there And there has been a man painting every day this week. They give these genuine oil painting away with every

$1.00 purchas of shoes with small extra charge for frames. You cant get the pictures with out the frames though I wish I could get one you dont know how pretty they are. We go there every day and watch him paint. He can paint a picture in 11 minutes aint that quick. Nell keeps joring the stand so I can hardly write I mad half a dozen mistakes on the other side just because she made me. This letter is for you all because I cant write to so many of you I guess I have told all the news so good bye love to all and kisses

Your loving daughter

E. Alice Pitezel.

P. O. Write soon Howard got a box of collars and took one out and lost box and all the contents.

Monday morning.
Do Mamma

Just got a letter from you saying that the babe was cross and Dessa and Grandma was sick. How is Grandpa I hope you will all feel better I thought you would not be home sick at all when you got there but it seems as though you are awful homesick Who met you at the depot did you get there Saturday or Sunday. I dont like to tell you but you ask me so I will have to. H. wont mind me at all He wanted a book and I got life of Gen. Sheridan and it is awful nice but now he dont read it at all hardly. One morning. Mr. H. told me to tell him to stay in the next morning that he wanted him and he would come and get him and take him out and I told him and he would not stay in at all he was out when he came. We have written two or three letters to you and I guess you will begin to get them now I will send this with my letter that I wrote yesterday and didnt send off Hope you will all keep well

continued I have just finished Uncle Tom's Cabin and it is a nice book. I wish I could see you all. This is another cold day. We pay $12.00 a week for our room and board and I think that is pretty cheap for the good meals we have Yesterday we had mashed potatoes, grapes, chicken glass of milk each ice cream each a big sauce disli full awful good too lemon pie cake dont you think that is pretty good. They are Germans. I guess I will have to close so good bye, love to all and kisses. Write soon keep well Yours Truly

E. Alice Pitezel.

In Mr. Barlow's view, these letters negatived the statement made by Mr. Ackelow, the proprietor of the Circle House, that the children had left that hotel on October 6th. The first letter written by Nellie, is dated October 6th. The next letter written by Alice, is also dated October 6th, but it was evidently written the day after Nellie had written her letter and should have been dated the 7th.

"Alice's eyes hurts," writes Nellie, "so she won't write this time." "I have read so much in Uncle Tom's book," writes Alice, "that I could not see to write yesterday when Nell and Howard did."

October 6th was on Saturday, the next day, was of course, Sunday, the 7th. It is quite evident, that Alice wrote on Sunday, the 7th, because she speaks of wearing her new dress; that she expects "this Sunday to pass away slower than I don't know what," that "Howard is too dirty to be seen out on the street to day, etc." If there is any doubt that this letter was written on Sunday, October 7th, it is completely dispelled by the third letter with its simple heading, "Monday morning," without any date affixed in which she speaks of having written two or three letters to her mother, and "I will send this with my letter I wrote yesterday and didn't send off," and that they had ice cream and an extra good dinner the day before. This letter was evidently written, Monday, October 8th, and the children had evidently continued at the same hotel, the Circle House, and had not left it on October 6th.

I again interviewed Mr. Ackelow the Circle House proprietor, and examined the books of the hotel with greater care and soon discovered, that the last payment of their board was made on October 10th, on which day they had left, and not on October 6th, as first stated. As I had ascertained to a certainty that the children had arrived in Detroit on the evening of October 12th, I found I was hot on the track, and with only forty-eight hours to be accounted for. Howard had disappeared in the forty eight hours, and either in Indianapolis, or between that city and Detroit. The Monday morning letter was of great significance in its relation of Howard's alleged misbehavior. "One morning Mr. H. told me to tell him to stay in the next morning, that he wanted him and would come and get him and take him out and I told him and he would not stay in at all, he "was out when he came."

This is precisely what Holmes did at the Albion Hotel in Toronto; he called for the girls and took them out on the morning of October 26th, and they never returned. Poor little Howard, if he had known the fate that was in store for him, he would have continued to stay out "when he came."

Mr. Ackelow told me that Holmes spoke of Howard as a mischievous boy and hard to control, and said he intended placing him in some institution or in some good home on a farm.

Holmes told this story so that when Howard was separated from his sisters, his disappearance would arouse neither curiosity nor suspicion. It worked well too, because neither Mr. Ackelow nor any attache of the hotel was able to say, whether Howard left before or at the same time the girls left.

Mr. Barlow further informed me, that the envelope which had enclosed a letter written by Alice to the Fidelity IMutual Life Insurance Association, thanking them for the prompt payment of the insurance policy had been mailed on October 11th, and was postmarked "Chic. Richmond & Cin. R. P. O.," — a government post route between Chicago, Indianapolis, Cincinnati and Detroit. Thus it appeared reasonably certain, that the party were on a train somewhere between these cities on October 11th.

Thursday morning, August 1st, I received a telegram from District Attorney Graham, directing me to go to Chicago and have an interview with the police authorities in the city, who were reported to have dug up the skeleton of a child at Holmes' Block, No. 701 West 63rd Street, Chicago. That evening I left Indianapolis and reached Chicago the next morning (Friday). At police headquarters, I met Chief Brandenaugh and Inspector Fitzpatrick, with whom I had a conference lasting several hours. I heard enough to convince me that they had not found the remains of Howard.

Another telegram then reached me from Mr. Graham, requesting me to return to Philadelphia for a consultation, and I immediately left on the Pennsylvania Limited, arriving home the next day at 4:17 PM

I went direct to the District Attorney's office in the City Hall, where I was warmly greeted by Mr. Barlow, who informed me that I had been summoned home for a few days rest and for consultation, and that I was to resume work in the case again as soon as the preparations for a fresh start were completed.

Mr. Barlow's confidence in our ability to find Howard never faltered. The mere fact that I had searched every real estate office in Indianapolis, and had for days run out every supposed clue presented, and had failed to find even a trace of the boy, had no effect upon him. He believed that skill and patience would yet win, and said, that when Mr. Graham and he and I met on Monday, we would consider further plans for searching in Indianapolis and vicinity, and if not successful there, then among the junction towns between Chicago, Indianapolis, Cincinnati and Detroit.

CHAPTER XVI

THE BEGINNING OF THE END

Consultation in the District Attorney's Office — Holmes Again Questioned — The Monumental Liar Repudiates His Former Statement — Introduces the Mysterious Hatch — A Fresh Start — W. E. Gary Associated with Geyer — Chicago Again — The Janitor of the "Castle" and His "Wife Interviewed — Outlying Towns Searched for Clues — Third Return to Indianapolis — Kindness of Authorities and Citizens — Nine Hundred Clues Run Out— Irvington, Ind.— The Veil About to Lift.

Monday morning, August 3d, I met the District Attorney and his assistant in their office in the city hall, and remained in consultation with them the greater part of the day. After Alice and Nellie had been found in Toronto, Holmes had been brought to the city hall in Philadelphia and vigorously examined in the hope of securing from him some admission which would assist me in finding Howard, but not a word did he say, which threw a particle of light upon the matter. His former statement in which he had given with great detail, the particulars of his meeting with

Miss Williams, and how he had given Howard into her care in Detroit, whence she had taken him to Buffalo, he repudiated, and he now introduced the mysterious Hatch. According to Holmes, Hatch was the miscreant who had probably shed the blood of innocent childhood, and not he, and he was willing, he said, to do all in his power to ascertain what this bad man Hatch had done with Howard.

This examination, which had been conducted by Mr. Barlow, was fully related to me, but we obtained not a grain of comfort from anything that this king of fabricators had said.

The officers of the insurance company now took a new grip on the case, and expressed their determination to hold on until the mystery which shrouded the disappearance of the little boy was cleared up, so the preparations for a fresh start included the assignment of Mr. W. E. Gary, the chief inspector of the company, to accompany me on the journey. This was agreeable news to me, because Mr. Gary was not only a pleasant companion, but he was able and skillful in detective work, and possessed a large stock of patience, — an absolutely essential element in such a case as we had in charge.

On Wednesday evening, August 7th, we left Philadelphia and went direct to Chicago, arriving the next afternoon. In company wit Inspector Fitzpatrick, we went to the Harrison Street Station and had an interview with Mr. and Mrs. Patrick Quinlan, who were under arrest on suspicion of having been associated with Holmes in alleged crimes committed in the Sixty-third Street house, known as the "Castle." Our object was to ascertain if Holmes had taken the children to Chicago, after leaving the Circle House in Indianapolis on October 10th. Both Quinlan and his wife stoutly maintained their ignorance of any knowledge of the children, and I am bound to say I believed them.

On Sunday, August 11th, Mr. Gary and I left Chicago for Logansport. From Logansport we went to Peru, Indiana, thence on following days to Montpelier Junction, Ohio, and Adrian, Michigan. In each of these towns we spent days in searching among hotels and boarding houses and in interviewing real estate agents, but all to no purpose, and we finally concluded to return to Indianapolis and settle there and search until District Attorney Graham and his assistant, Mr. Barlow, told us to stop, or until we had found the boy. I must confess that I returned to Indianapolis in no cheerful frame of mind, and the large stock of hope which I had gathered up in the District Attorney's office in the Philadelphia City Hall was fast dwindling away. There was nothing to do, however, but to go at it again, so headquarters at the Spencer House was once more established. My confidence in our ultimate success, was sustained at all times by my continued faith in the Indianapolis theory. I believed the boy had been murdered in Indianapolis, or in some nearby town, but my ill success in locating the house, after so much effort and such wide publicity, greatly annoyed and puzzled me. The mystery seemed to be impenetrable.

The desire on the part of the police authorities of Indianapolis to assist me in the search, never wavered. On this, my third return to that city, I was greeted with the same kindness and unvarying courtesy I had enjoyed on the previous occasions. In fact, this can truthfully be said of the police authorities in all the citi'es embraced within the circuit, from Cincinnati to Toronto, where my mission had taken me. Everywhere I found kind hearts and willing hands, ready to assist me in running to earth one of the most accomplished villains of modern times, and if ancient times produced his equal, I have yet to read of him.

The Indianapolis newspapers, published announcements of the renewal of the search in that city, and reports from many kind and well disposed persons, of mysterious people who rented houses for a short time and then disappeared, came pouring in again. Not a single suggestion was unheeded and every report was carefully and patiently investigated. The advertisements of private houses for rent early in October of 1894 were listed and each one visited and examined. No less than nine hundred supposed clues were run out. We then commenced a search of the small towns just beyond the city of Indianapolis, and finally finished the work in all, except Irvington. About this time I wrote a letter to District Attorney Graham, repeating to him all that I had reported almost daily to Superintendent of Police Linden, and concluded by saying: "By Monday we will have searched every outlying town, except Irvington, and another day will conclude that. After Irvington, I scarcely know where we shall go." On Tuesday morning, August 27th, we took the trolley line for Irvington, a most beautiful town, about six miles from Indianapolis.

As there are no hotels in the town, we decided to look up the real estate agents. A short distance from wliere the cars stop, I noticed a sign of a real estate office, and in we went. Opening up a package of papers and photographs which I had carried, and which I had untied and tied over a thousand times, until it had become soiled and ragged from wear, I asked a pleasant faced old gentleman who greeted us as we entered the office, if he knew of a house in his town, which had been rented for a short time in October of 1894, by a man who said he wanted it for a widowed sister. I then handed him a photograph of H. H. Holmes. The old gentleman who proved to be Mr. Brown quietly listened, and then adjusting his glasses took a long look at the photograph.

"Yes," said he, "I remember a man who rented a house under such circumstances in October of 1894, and this picture looks like him very much. I did not have the renting of the house, but I had the keys, and one day last fall, this man came into my office and in a very abrupt way said, I want the keys for that house. I remember the man very well, because I did not like his manner, and I felt that he should have had more respect for my gray hairs."

While the good old man was talking, Mr. Gary and I stood still. When he had finished, we looked at each other and sat down. We had found the clue at last.

All the toil; all the weary days and weeks of travel, — toil and travel in the hottest months of the year, alternating between faith and hope, and discouragement and despair, all were recompensed in that one moment, when I saw the veil about to lift, and realized that we were soon to learn where the poor little boy had gone with Holmes, "when he came."

"Truth, like the sun, submits to be obscured but like the sun, only for a time."

CHAPTER XV.

"WHEN HE CAME."

A Warm Trail— The One and a Half Story Cottage— Searching the Cellar — Broken Trunk Under the Piazza — A Strip of Blue Calico — Amateur Detectives — Finding the Charred Remains — The Boy's Coat — Geyer Has a Good Night's Rest.

Mr. Gary and I did not remain seated very long. Mr. Brown offered to take us to Dr. Thompson, the former owner of the house, and we thankfully accepted his invitation. Dr. Thompson's office was near by and when we entered, Mr. Brown introduced us as two detectives from Philadelphia in search of one of the Pitezel children. The doctor at once recognized the photograph of Holmes and identified him as the man who had rented the house he formerly occupied. He said further that a boy in his employ, named Elvet Moorman, had seen Holmes and a little boy he had with him at the time. A messenger was dispatched for Elvet, and the instant he saw Holmes' photograph he said:

"Why that is the man who lived in our house, and who had the small boy with him."

He also recognized Howard's picture as that of the boy whom he had seen at the house with Holmes. Our anxiety to get to the house and to search the premises can be imagined. We asked the doctor to show us the way. On our arrival at the house, I found it to be a one and a half story cottage, standing some little distance from Union Avenue, in the extreme eastern part of the town. Across the street is a Methodist church and two hundred yards to the south are the Pennsylvania railroad tracks. The house stands in a secluded place, and there are no other houses in the immediate neighborhood. To the west is a small grove of young catalpa trees, and to the east is a large common. There are two roads leading to the street cars which run into Indianapolis.

On entering the house, we searched the cellar first. I found it divided into two apartments, — the rear having a cement floor and evidently intended for a wash room and the front having a clay floor, but as hard as flint. It was quite evident that there had been no disturbance of the floor in the cellar, and so we decided to make a search on the outside. To the right wing of the house is attached a small piazza, with open lattice work under the floor. In looking through this lattice work, I discovered the broken remains of a trunk. It took but a moment to remove the steps leading up to the piazza floor, and crawling under I brought out what proved to be a strong piece of evidence against the distinguished criminal who was sitting in his cell in the Philadelphia County prison, and wondering how near I had set my feet on his tracks. When I brought out the piece of the trunk, I discovered that a strip of blue calico had been pasted along the side seam and evidently intended to repair and cover it. The calico was about two inches wide, and had printed on it the figure of a white flower. I felt sure that I had found at least a portion of one of the trunks that had given me so much anxiety, and I was very careful to see that it was deposited in a safe place for future use as evidence. I observed, under the piazza, that the earth had been disturbed, and procuring a shovel dug very deeply to ascertain if a body had been buried there, but no evidence of that nature was discovered. We then turned our attention to the barn and other outhouses. In the barn I found a large coal stove, called the "Peninsular Oak," and some other articles of furniture.

The stove was three and a half feet high, and about twenty-two inches in diameter, — the entire top working upon a pivot. On the top I found what appeared to be blood stains. We then examined the floor of the barn and the grounds about the house, and wherever we discovered a soft spot in the earth, we dug deeply to see if a body was buried there.

By this time, several hundred people had gathered about the house, seriously interfering with our operations, but all expressing great sympathy with us in our work, and as it was almost evening I decided to defer a further search until the following day. I ascertained also that the house had been rented by an agent in Indianapolis by the name of J. S.

Grouse and I wanted to see him before the sun went down. Mr. Gary and I then took the trolley car into Indianapolis and called at once upon Mr. Grouse. I learned that the house had been rented to a man who wanted it for his widowed sister by the name of Mrs. A. E. Gook, who intended to open a boarding house. He paid one month's rent in advance, and was never seen again. When I produced the pliotograph of H. H. Holmes, it was promptly identified as that of the man who had rented the house.

As Holmes had registered at the Hotel Bristol in Cincinnati as A. E. Cook and three children, I felt certain that I was working in the right direction.

After leaving the real estate office, I sent the following telegram to Mrs. Pitezel, Galva, Illinois:

"Did missing trunk have a strip of blue calico, white figure over seam on the bottom."

To this telegram I received the following reply:

"Yes, missing trunk had a strip of blue calico white figure on the bottom."

While I was at the telegraph office, I received a telephone from the Indianapolis Evening News Office, requesting me to call there without delay. At the news office I met Mr. Brown, their city editor, who told me that Dr. Barnhill the partner of Dr. Thompson was on his way from Irvington and that he had something of importance to communicate to me, and that I should wait for him. The doctor arrived in a few moments and opened a small package containing several pieces of charred bone, which he declared were a portion of the femur and skull of a child between eight and twelve years old. The piece of the skull showed the sutures plainly. Dr. Barnhill then explained that after Mr. Gary and I had left the Irvington house, he and Dr. Thompson had continued the search.

THE SPADE WITH WHICH HOLMES BURIED ALICE AND NELLIE
IN THE BASEMENT

They were accompanied by two boys, Walter Jenny and Oscar Kettenbach. One of the boys suggested that they should play detective and they went together into the part of the cellar having a cemented floor, and in which there was a chimney which extended above the roof of the house. In the chimney was a pipe hole about three feet six inches from the floor. Young Jenny put his arm in the opening and pulled out a handful of ashes, among which was one of the pieces of bone, which Dr. Barnhill brought to me. The boys continued to bring out ashes and pieces of bone and then ran and called the doctors, who soon determined the character of the discovery.

This information induced me to return to the house that evening, and upon our arrival, we found the entire neighborhood assembled there. I requested the Marshall of Police who was present to clear the house, which he did in short order. The doctors and several members of the Press were then admitted, and we proceeded to the cellar, and with hammer and chisel I took down the lower part of the chimney. I then took an old fly screen which I found in the house, and used it as a sieve, and as the ashes and soot were taken from the chimney, I passed it through the screen and found an ahost complete set of teeth and a piece of the jaw, which I turned over to Dr. John Quincy Byram, a dentist, for examination. At the bottom of the chimney was found quite a large charred mass, which upon being cut, disclosed a portion of the stomach, liver and spleen, baked quite hard. The pelvis of the body Avas also found. All this was handed to Dr. Barnhill for examination.

In the chimney we also found some of the iron fastenings which belonged to the trunk, some buttons, a small scarf pin, and a crochet needle. Upon searching for outside evidence, we found a boy's coat in possession of a grocer in Irvington. The grocer said that early in October, of 1894 a man called at his store and left the coat with him, saying that a boy would call for it the next morning, but the boy never came. Thoroughly convinced that we had found all that remained of little Howard Pitezel, we returned to Indianapolis and at once repaired to the City Hall where we had a consultation with Superintendent of Police

Powell.

The superintendent advised us to see the coroner, Dr. Castor, a suggestion which we acted upon the next day.

That night I enjoyed the best night's sleep I had had in two months. I was sure that my work was complete, and as I fell into an easy slumber, I thought that after all, the business of searching for the truth was not the meanest occupation of man. It is the manner in which it is searched for that sometimes makes it ignoble.

CHAPTER XVI

THE CHAIN COMPLETE

A Coroner's Inquest Again — Mrs. Pitezel Summoned from Galva, Ill.— Identifies the Piece of Trunk— Identifies the Clothing and Toys — Moorman's Testimony — Other Pertinent Testimony— Surgical Instruments Sharpened— Thanks for Generous Aid — Return to Philadelphia — This Monster Must be Punished.

The day following our discoveries at the Irvington house, we were requested by the Sheriff of the county in which Irvington is situated, to appear before the Grand Jury. This request we complied with, and we recited the whole Holmes Pitezel story to that body.

The coroner, Dr. Hiram A. Castor, held an inquest. To this sad scene, Mrs. Pitezel was again summoned. She had hoped to the last that her little son had been placed in some institution, or in the care of some person in a secluded part of the country.

It will be remembered that Holmes declared this to be his purpose to Mr. Ackelow, the proprietor of the Circle House, and Mrs. Pitezel always clung to the hope that Howard would ultimately be found alive. The Irvington revelation came to her, therefore, with all the force of a dreadful shock and it was a great tax on her strength to leave Galva again and make another sad journey to Irvington.

She identified the overcoat found at the grocer's, as Howard's. She had repaired it in a number of places and sewed a new pocket in it, and had no difficulty in proving the identification. The piece of trunk was easily recognized, because of the strip of calico which her father had pasted along the bottom. A little spinning top and a tin man, which Pitezel had bought for Howard at the World's Fair and which I had found in the house, were also identified. Mrs. Pitezel had placed them in the trunk herself at the time of the departure of Holmes with Nellie and Howard from St. Louis. A little scarf-pin and a pair of shoes she also identified as Howard's, and a crochet needle that belonged to her daughter Alice. These had all been found in the Irvington house.

Elvet Moorman testified that he went over to the house one afternoon early in October of 1894 and saw a transfer wagon with furniture unloading, and a man and a boy assisting in transferring the articles to the house. Later in the afternoon of the same day he went over to milk a cow that was kept in the barn, connected with the house. While he was milking, the man who was with the boy, came to him and asked him to assist him in putting up a stove, which he did. Moorman asked the man why he did not make a gas connection (for natural gas) and use a gas stove, and the man said that he did not think gas was healthy for children. A photograph of Holmes was shown the witness and he identified it as the man whom he had assisted in putting up the stove. He also said that the photograph of Howard Pitezel shown him, was that of the boy he had seen with Holmes, and who was present when the stove was put up. He also said that after Holmes and the boy disappeared, he had examined the house and found a lot of corn rubbish on the floor that seemed to indicate that a fire had been made with corn cobs.

Dr. Byram, a dentist, identified the teeth and portion of the jaw as those of a child between the ages of eight and eleven years, and Dr. Barnhill declared the bones found to be portions of a skeleton of a child between the ages of seven and ten years. The large portion of charred remains found, contained the liver, the stomach and portions of the intestines.

Albert Schiffling testified that he keeps a repair shop at No. 48 Virginia Avenue, Indianapolis. On the 3d of October, a man, whom he identified as Holmes, came into his shop accompanied by a small boy. Holmes had two cases of surgical instruments, which he wanted sharpened. He returned for the instruments on October 8th, paid for the repairs and took them away. Other testimony and identifications of Holmes and Howard were heard, but all in corroboration of the evidence which I have briefly stated. Dr. Byram, the dentist, very cleverly and skillfully mounted the teeth on wax jaws, which exhibited their character and their age most admirably, and Doctors Barnlll and Thompson, made a very exhaustive and scientific report of the other contents of the chimney which had been found, and the coroner's jury had no difficulty in finding tjjat little Howard Pitezel had come to his death at the hands of H. H. Holmes.

Our work being done, we visited the City Hall and thanked Superintendent Powell and his assistants for their kind and courteous treatment during our stay in Indianapolis. In fact we were grateful to everybody, for we had received from all citizens the most generous and unselfish aid in the performance of our task, so bidding farewell to our many friends, we left for Philadelphia, arriving home Saturday, September 1st.

The District Attorney and his Assistant, Mr. Barlow and I had a happy meeting. They, like myself, had been giving to the case, the days and weeks of a summer of almost unprecedented heat and we all rejoiced over the success and end of the search.

Much remained, however, to be done. The greatest of criminals had yet to be brought to answer for his foul deeds. All that had been unearthed, would count for but little, if this wretch were permitted to elude the firm grasp of the law or to avoid a punishment, not such as he deserved, but that which is provided under the orderly forms of legal procedure, and we then and there fully and freely consecrated the best that was in us, to the consummation of that great end.

CHAPTER XIX

JUSTICE CRIED "AMEN"

The Trial — Desperate Fight for Postponement — Application for Postponement Refused — Holmes Dismisses his Counsel — Holmes Conducts His Own Case — Holmes' Shrewdness — Playing for Sympathy — Holmes' Lawyers Re-enter the Case — Mrs. Pitezel's Heart Breaking Narrative — The Murderer Unmoved — Testimony of Miss Yoke — Holmes Cross-examines the Woman He had Foully Wronged — Admissions of Prisoner's Counsel — Testimony of Physicians — The Worthless Note — How Holmes Deluded Mrs. Pitezel — All Doubts Dispelled — Murder in the First Degree — Press and People Congratulate Prosecutors and Detective.

Herman W. Mudgett, alias H. H. Holmes, was indicted on the day of September, 1895, by the grand jury of Philadelphia County, for the murder of Benjamin F. Pitezel on September 2, 1894. On September 1895, the prisoner was arraigned and entered a plea of "not guilty," and in answer to the question propounded to him by the crier of the court, "Pleading not guilty, — How will you be tried? "He answered, "By God and my country."

Upon this occasion he was represented by two young attorneys, who had been advising him since his incarceration in the county prison in November of 1894, and one of whom assisted in his trial for conspiracy in June of 1895. They had visited him in prison, scores of times and were familiar with every point and detail of his case. The officers of the commonwealth had been groping in the dark, following this clue and then that, but his own attorneys were, or should have been in the broad light of knowledge of all that Holmes knew concerning Pitezel and his fate, and the destruction of the children. After the entry of the plea of "not guilty "by the prisoner, and issue had been joined between him and the Commonwealth of Pennsylvania, the District Attorney asked the court to fix a day for the trial. He suggested that a time be set so remote, that ample opportunity should be given for the prisoner, as well as for the commonwealth to prepare for the great contest which should decide the guilt or innocence of the accused. The court then stated to all parties, that the trial should take place on Monday, October, 28th, five weeks distant, and gave notice to both sides to be prepared. In spite of this notice, when the day fixed arrived, October 28th, the prisoner and his counsel made one of the most desperate fights for postponement ever witnessed in a criminal trial.

One of the city newspapers said: "It was not that the struggle was long, or conducted with anyfine display of legal generalship, but it was fierce, painful and impressive while it lasted, suggesting the wild mad cries and writhings of a murderer, already condemned and battling with inexorable jailers on the way to the scaffold."

The application for a postponement was refused, thereupon counsel asked permission to withdraw from the case. This was also refused, — the Court reminding counsel, that they had represented the prisoner for many months, and had ample time for the preparation of the trial. Counsel then had a consultation with the prisoner, and returned to the bar of the court with the astounding statement that the prisoner had dismissed them from the case, and that he had declared it to be his purpose to conduct his own defense. The court then warned counsel not to leave the case, even in the face of a dismissal by the prisoner, and directed them to proceed and defend their client. This the attorneys refused to do, and they left the court room. The Hon. Michael Arnold, who presided at this trial, is not only a good lawyer and a wise judge, but lie is conspicuous for his abundant stock of good common sense, so notwithstanding the desertion of the attorneys for the defence, he directed the case to proceed. Then followed one of the most remarkable scenes ever witnessed in a court room. The prisoner, on trial for his life, crossquestioned each juror as he appeared for examination on his voire dire, and with an ability and shrewdness which astonished every person within hearing. It soon became quite evident, that the wily criminal was playing for sympathy, but he did it all too well, for not a few among the spectators in the court room quickly determined that Holmes was quite as able as his counsel, and that their absence was no loss to him. Apart from this, amid the examination and challenging of the jurors, both the Court and District Attorney were careful to see that a fair and impartial jury was empanelled, — not a man being accepted who exhibited any prejudice or bias against the prisoner. The American love of fair play, even to one so base and vile as Holmes, protected the prisoner in his rights, and nothing was permitted to enter the case which would justify the slightest criticism. When the examination of witnesses commenced, the Court repeatedly instructed the prisoner as to his rights, and when sustaining or overruling his objections, explained to him the reason for so doing.

On the second day of the trial, the young lawyers, who had departed with such dramatic effect the day before, returned, and the trial proceeded in an orderly manner to the end.

The trial was distinguished by a dignity and decorum, which was maintained at all times, despite the sensational and dramatic disclosures which came naturally from the testimony, or the characteristic behavior of the prisoner, as he squirmed in the net in which he was caught.

When the entire audience was dissolved in tears at the pitiful, lieartbreaking narrative of Mrs. Pitezel, the prisoner sat unmoved in the dock, scribbling notes and occasionally glancing at the woman, whose husband and children he had so cruelly murdered.

When Miss Yoke, the young woman whom he had so grievously wronged, appeared upon the stand, the prisoner suddenly began to weep, and industriously applied his handkerchief to the tears which came or appeared to come from his eyes.

At the close of her examination in chief, Holmes insisted upon conducting the cross-examination himself, in the face of the protest of his counsel and he did his best to catch her eye and to break the face of the terrible disclosures she had made.

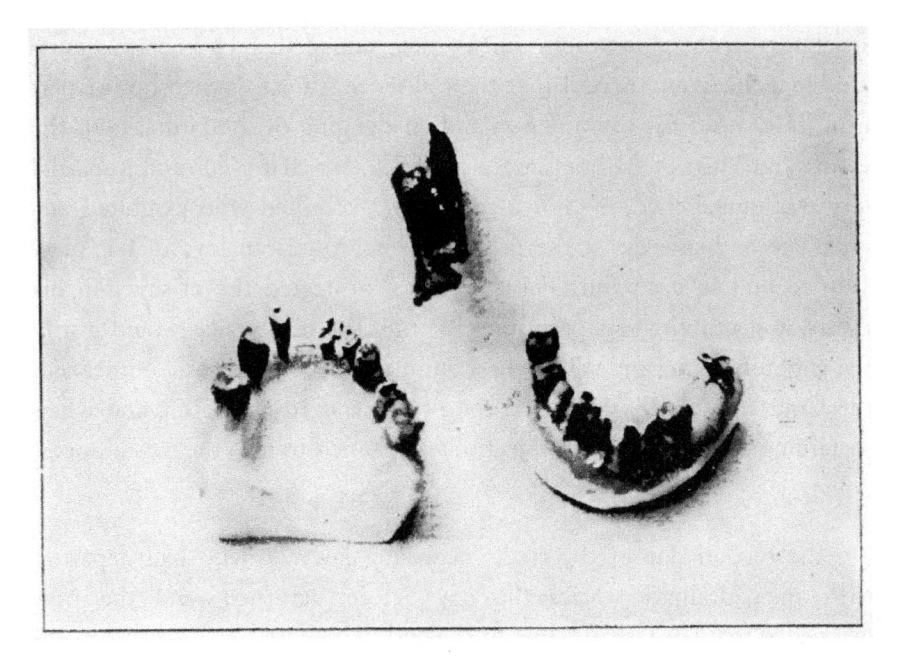

THE LITTLE TEETH OF HOWARD PITEZEL (found in the ashes)

The character of the prisoner's grief may be better understood, when a remark he made to his counsel, just before he arose to cross-examine Miss Yoke, is known. He was overheard to say: "I will now let loose the fount of emotion." Who has ever seen or heard of his equal?

The details of the trial have been widely published. Whatever doubt existed as to the death of Pitezel was dispelled by the admission of the prisoner's counsel at the trial, who said that the body found at No. 1316 Callowhill Street on the second day of September, 1894, was Benjamin F. Pitezel, and therefore the testimony of the more or less numerous citizen, who had declared that he had seen Pitezel alive in St. Louis, Mobile, Chicago and other places a week or so before the trial and who was so evidently drawing upon his imagination, was not required in evidence. Prisoner's counsel also admitted that Holmes was present at No. 1316 Callowhill Street on September 2d, but contended that Pitezel had been found dead, — that he had committed suicide. Three physicians, one of them an eminent expert in toxicology, Dr. Henry Leffman, all testified that the condition of the body wlien found excluded the possibility of suicide, and that the man had been killed by chloroform poisoning. His robbery of Mrs. Pitezel of the insurance money, his repeated assurances to her that her husbad was alive, the manner in which he had taken her from Galva to Detroit, "to meet Ben," then from Detroit to meet him "because Ben was followed by detectives," on to Toronto to meet him there, then upon her arrival in Toronto, his declaration that Ben had gone to Montreal, their subsequent trip to Burlington, Vermont, and his many, many lies to her were all recited in pitiful tones by the distressed and grief-stricken widow and mother.

One of the hardest blows received by the prisoner, was from the testimony of Sidney L. Samuels, Esq., a member of the bar of Fort Worth, Texas, an accomplished lawyer and gentleman, who when upon the stand referred to Holmes, (much to his disgust) as "the individual sitting in the cage." Mr. Samuels came all the way from ls home in Texas to Philadelphia, to prove that the note which Holmes gave to Mrs. Pitezel was worthless. Mr. Samuels had written the body of the note himself and gave it to Holmes to have it signed by Benton T. Lyman, who was no other than Pitezel himself, who in Jnuary and February of 1894 was in Fort Worth assisting Holmes in the perpetration of one of his Minnie Williams schemes. When Holmes returned, he produced another note, and told Mr. Samuels that he had lost the first note. This note he gave Mrs. Pitezel. It was not endorsed on the back, and had never been negotiated, and it Avas a worthless piece of paper. The note he alleged he had lost, he pahned off on the poor deluded woman, taking from hev all but five hundred dollars of the seventy-two hundred dollars she had received from Howe.

Miss Yoke was with Holmes in Philadelphia at the timie of the murder. She said that in the evening of September 1st, a man called at No. 1905 North 11th Street, where she and the man she supposed was her husband were stopping. The visitor, Holmes told her, was a messenger from an official of the Pennsylvania Railroad Coripany, who had advised him that this gentleman would meet him the next morning at Nicetown, a suburb of Philadelphia. (He afterwards admitted to her that this man who called, was Pitezel.) She said that Holmes left the house on the morning of September 2d at ten or ten-thirty o'clock, and returned about four o'clock. He then said he had seen the Pennsylvania Railroad man but had not completed the business matter with him and might return, and that he would like to leave for the West that evening. He told her to tell Dr. Alcorn, that they were going to Harrisburg, Pa., and not to let her know that their destination was Indianapolis. This was the time he said he went to No. 1316 Callowhill Street and found Pitezel dead in the third story of the house, discovering that he had committed suicide.

His presence at the house at the time of death, his concealment of the death both from the authorities and from Mrs. Pitezel, the proof that the man had not died from chloroform self-administered, his robbery of Mrs. Pitezel and the insurance swindle, mingled with his audacious fabrications, made up one of the strongest cases of circumstantial evidence ever presented in a criminal court, and when the jury returned a verdict of murder in the first degree, in the language of Mr. Samuels, Justice cried "Amen "to the verdict, and the people and press poured in their congratulations upon the District Attorney and his Assistant and the able and faithful detective, Mr. Geyer, whose noble work, revealed the bloody tracks of a human monster, whose like we hope never to see again.

CHAPTER XX

LOOKING BACKWARDS

The Motive For the Murders— Pitezel Knew too Much — The Entire Family in the Way of The Arch Plotter— The Insurance Fraud the Means to the End — Separating the Family — A Grave Dug for Alice and Nellie — Chloroform Found in the Burlington House — Mrs. Pitezel's Suspicious Aroused — The "Eye That Never Sleeps" — Holmes' Arrest Prevents Three More Murders.

What was the motive for these murders? Why did he kill Benjamin F. Pitezel? And after committing that foul deed, why was it necessary to remove Pitezel's family? That he fully intended to murder Mrs. Pitezel and Dessie and the baby, Wharton, is too evident for contradiction. Apart from his suspicious behavior at Burlington, recited by Mrs. Pitezel in her testimony at the trial, the commonwealth had further evidence on this point which it was not permitted to disclose.

The cellar of the Burlington house was never searched until the week of the murder trial in Philadelphia, when a thorough investigation of the premises was made by request of District Attorney Graham. Jerome Dumas, the Burlington clef of police ordered every part of the cellar to be carefully examined, with the result of finding in a little recess back of a joist in the cellar and under the first floor, a bottle containing eight or ten ounces of chloroform. As every step of Mephistopheles is marked by a track of fire, so do the devious paths of Herman Webster Mudgett, alias Holmes, bear the scent of the deadly chloroform. Holmes found that it was a more difficult task to dispose of Mrs. Pitezel and her eighteen months' old baby and her daughter Dessie, a vigorous girl of sixteen years, than it had been to destroy the younger children, so he deferred that part of his scheme until it was too late, and hence the discovery of the bottle of chloroform just where he had placed it. He was arrested before he was able to return to Burlington, Vermont, after his visit to Gilmanton, New Hampshire. In fact he knew he was being shadowed by detectives while he was visiting Gilmanton, and journeyed to Boston, where he believed his chances for escape were greater.

But we have asked what was the motive for these murders? The reader will remember a statement Holmes makes in ls letter to Mrs. Pitezel just before she was released from the Philadelphia county prison. He said "We never quarreled," alluding to the relations which had existed between Pitezel and himself. This was a base falsehood; — they had quarrelled. They had a dispute in Chicago in June or July of 1894. The subject of the dispute was the interest wlch Pitezel claimed to own in the Castle property in Chicago, and the Williams real estate in Fort Worth, Texas. He told Holmes that he was tired of scheming and wanted to return to his home, (which was in St. Louis) and lead a quiet and peaceful life with his family. He declared that he was part owner of the Chicago real estate, and that the title to the Fort Worth property was in his alias, Benton T. Lyman, and he wanted to be paid the value of his interest and play quits.

Pitezel drank heavily and while under the influence of liquor, talked a good deal. It is impossible to say just how much of the past life of Holmes, Pitezel knew; what secrets of the Castle he carried in his breast and whether if he opened his lips he could have sent Holmes to prison or the scaffold. He certainly knew enough to make him in his cups a dangerous associate.

Holmes quieted Pitezel, by suggesting that they should work out one more scheme together and that should end their relations. That scheme was to cheat and defraud the Fidelity Mutual Life Association of Philadelphia, in the perpetration of which, Holmes saw the opportunity to rid himself of every person, Pitezel, his wife and his clhlren, who could lay claim to a dollar of the value of the real estate. Incidentally he proposed to reap every dollar of benefit from the insurance swindle.

Proceeding to carry out his scheme, he directed Pitezel to lease a house in Philadelphia, to which he said he would bring the body which was to be substituted for Pitezel's. Pitezel advertised himself as a dealer in patents, but Holmes showed him a splendid recipe for a solution for cleaning clothes, containing chloroform, benzine, and ammonia and which they should manufacture and sell. Thus chloroform was introduced into the house in an unspicious manner. While poor Pitezel was waiting for the cadaver which Holmes assured him he was arranging to obtain. Holmes murdered him. He went to St. Louis and saw Mrs. Pitezel. He did not dare to tell her that her husband was dead. No tale of suicide would have been accepted by Mrs. Pitezel, who had been receiving cheerful letters from her husband., and mureover he wanted to dispose of her eventually and the opportunity to do that would present itself, when he led her from city to city to meet her husband. He told her that Ben was alive, and suggested that some member of the family should return with him to Philadelphia to identify the body. This was the first move he made in separating the family. Alice Pitezel went to Philadelphia and after identifying the body as that of her father, he took her to Indianapolis where he left her in the Hotel English. Holmes went back to St. Louis again. By this time the insurance money was paid. He then robbed the poor woman of most of the $7,200 she had received from her attorney Howe, and holding up to her the horror of discovery of her husband by detectives, said the family should separate. "The Insurance Company knows that you have five children, and you must separate," said Holmes. Nellie and Howard were then handed over to his tender care and they went with him to Cincinnati, "where Alice was under the care of such a good woman, and where they could go to school until all the clouds had rolled by."

He moved the tliree children October 1st, 1894, to Indianapolis and on the 10th of that month killed Huward in the house at Irvington. Thus two of his victims had been disposed of, the father and the son.

He now moved Alice and Nellie to Detroit and hired the Forest Avenue house where he intended to kill them and bury them in the hole he had dug. To Detroit he also invited Mrs. Pitezel and Dessie and the baby, "where Ben was Avaiting to see her."

Some hitch occurred in Detroit, and he moved his three parties to Toronto, where on October 25th, two other members of this obnoxious family were disposed of. He was getting along very well. He had killed four people in three different places, and without arousing the interest or any inquiry from anyone. The promise to see Benin Toronto was not fulfilled. Ben was in Montreal, so he removed the remainder of his company to Burlington, Vermont, where he thought he would be able to clean up the job, by removing Mrs. Pitezel and her youngest and eldest child.

He found the task a hard one. Mrs. Pitezel's suspicions, which had been dormant so long, were now aroused and she was on the alert. To give himself an opportunity to think over the matter more carefully, he concluded to visit his old home in Gilmanton, New Hampshire, where for the first time the "eye that never sleeps" rested upon him. No one more quickly discovered this than Holmes himself, and he went hurriedly to Boston, but only to walk into the cell of the felon. His scheme had failed after all. He was quite content to stand the punishment of imprisonment for the insurance fraud, but he was awfully afraid of the gallows. He used all the cunning for which he lias become famous, in avoiding an issue which might end in death to him. He who had dealt destruction to others, was afraid of it himself, and so followed his confessions and statements and counter statements as he squirmed and struggled in the net.

The destruction of Pitezel and his family without detection, would have left Holmes the sole and undisputed owner of the real estate, they jointly held, as well as of the money received from the Insurance Company.

CHAPTER XXI

A TRIPLE ALLIANCE

Holmes' Desperate Fight to Exclude Miss Yoke's Testimony — Declared Her to Be His Lawful Wife — His Unexampled Duplicity With Women — Mrs. Herman Webster Mudgett — Mrs. Harry Howard Holmes — Mrs. Henry Mansfield Howard — He Lies About His Parents When the Truth Would Have Done as Well— He Tells to His Sister the Greatest Lies He Ever Told.

There is just one clean, bright spot in the career of Mudgett, alias Holmes, alias Howard, alias etc., etc., for which he should have some credit, and that is, the care he exercised in keeping from the women whom he had deceived, his various schemes and crimes, and especially is this true of Miss Yoke. He told her that his name was Holmes, but that his uncle, Henry Mansfield Howard, of Denver, Colorado, had devised property to him, provided he would assume his name and thus he married Miss Yoke in Denver under the name of Howard.

From the time of their meeting, during their engagement, and after the marriage ceremony that followed, Miss Yoke was taught to believe that her supposed husband was engaged principally in the business of selling or leasing a new and improved patent copier, and had acquired considerable property by devise from his Denver uncle. Their journey to Texas was made for the alleged purpose of taking possession of a ranch, which his uncle had willed to him. Upon arriving at Fort Worth, he told her, that squatters were in possession of the ranch and as squatters' rights received more seous recognition in the South than in the North, and as he was afraid he might be in personal danger if he announced himself or ajipeared as the owner of the ranch, Henry Mansfield Howard, they had better, for the time being, take the name of Pratt. Thus he appeared in Fort Worth with Pitezel as D. T. Pratt, and Pitezel, who was also there at the time, took the name of Benton T. Lyman.

Miss Yoke never knew that Lyman was Pitezel, until Holmes was arrested in Boston. Although she had accompanied Holmes on the tour from Detroit to Burlington, she never knew that Mrs. Pitezel and her children were travelling from city to city, under the care of her supposed husband; nor had she the slightest knowledge of the scheme to defraud the insurance company, or of the fictitious names lie was giving, or of the hideous crimes Holmes had committed on the way. Nor did Mrs. Pitezel know that Holmes was travelling with Miss Yoke, nor had she ever heard of her and never knew of her until the arrest in Boston. Upon the trial, Judge Arnold in charging the jury said: "Truth is stranger than fiction, and if Mrs. Pitezel's story is true it is the most wonderful exhibition of the power of mind over mind I have ever seen and stranger than any novel I ever read."

The claim made by Holmes at the trial, that Miss Yoke was his lawful wife, is entirely in keeping with his record for deceit and audacity. He was married to Clara A. Lovering on July 4th, 1878, and this woman is now living in Tilton, New Hampshire. He was married to Myrta Z. Belknap on January 28th, 1887, under the name of Hariy Howard Holmes.

On February 14th, 1887, a little over two weeks after his marriage to Miss Belknap, he filed in the Supreme Court of Cook County, Illinois, in the city of Chicago, a petition praying for a divorce from Clara A. Mudgett nee Lovering on the ground of infidelity. On June 4th, 1891, this petition was dismissed for failure of prosecution and hence it clearly appears that his lawful wife is Mrs. Clara A. Mudgett, who now resides at Tilton, New Hampshire.

On September 19th, 1893, he made application to the Fidelity Mutual Life Association for a $10,000 policy of insurance and named therein in his own handwriting as beneficiary, "My wife, Myrta Z. Holmes." At this very time, September, 1893, he was engaged to be married to Miss Yoke and in fact married her in Denver in the following January, 1894.

It need cause no surprise therefore, to learn that when Miss Yoke was called to the witness stand at the trial, she gave her maiden name. She had become familiar with the marriage record of her supposed husband, and was fully convinced that she was not his lawful wife and had been grossly and cruel deceived.

When arrested in Boston, Miss Yoke met the sister and brother of Holmes, and her eyes were opened and her real position made clear. Holmes had told her that he was the last of his race and that his parents and brothers and sisters had long since departed this life. This lie he had evidently told also to Miss Belknap, for in his application for insurance in September, 1893, he declared that his mother had died at the age of fifty-eight years of a disease he did not remember, and his father at the age of sixty-two from injury to his foot.

One may readily imagine Miss Yoke's amazement when she learned of the existence of Mrs. Mudgett, at Tilton, New Hampshire, and of the further shock she experienced when she learned that upon leaving her at Burlington, New Hampshire, "to go on a business trip," he had revisited his real wife at Tilton, resumed his relations with her, took her to the house of his parents who were living and in good health at Gilmanton, and remained with her and them at the homestead for two or three days, and upon leaving promised his wife to return the following April, and never desert her again.

This is the position in which Holmes found himself at the homestead: — a wdfe at Wilmette, Illinois, another waiting for his return at Burlington, New Hampshire, and his real wife, taking him back and receiving him with a loving and forgiving spirit,— notwithstanding his petition for divorce for alleged infidelity, a charge which was doubtless as false and as wicked as his own depraved heart.

His situation was one fraught with peril, so he concluded to open up a line of retreat. He told one or more members of his family, that he had had a remarkable experience. (His introduction to this story was certainly true.) He said he had been in a railroad collision in the West and had teen severely injured. When he awakened out of the unconscious condition caused by the injury, he found he was in a hospital. He further discovered to his amazement that all memory of his former self had been blotted out. Who he was, his name, his occupation, his home, his parents, his friends, — the memory of all had fled. On tha night of the accident a curtain had dropped between him and his past, and all idea or knowledge of his former self had been swept into oblivion. To the hospital in which he was treated, came a beautiful woman, who brought flowers to the sick and read to them from good books, and with her gentle voice sought to bring cheer into the dull hospital wards. This sweet woman brought flowers and read to him, and finally fell in love with him and he with her. Upon his convalescence they were married. This good woman was very rich and was deeply touched when she observed the suffering he constantly endured, as he in vain endeavored to regain the threads of memory of his past. Finally, through her influence and wealth, she secured the assistance of a great surgeon who performed a wonderful operation upon his head. When he came out of ether, to his amazement his memory had like a flood come back upon him and to his unspeakable horror he realized what a wrong he had committed in marrying the sweet woman who had administered to him as lie lay helpless and sick in the hospital. Pie remembered then that he was a married man and that his real wife, Carrie Mudgett, was living.

He further said to his family that he had not told this lovely woman that she was not his wife, and betrayed to them the deep grief and distress from which he was suffering in the unusual situation in which he found himself and for which he was really not responsible.

This alleged patroness of the hospital and reader to the sick was Miss Yoke, for this he told his sister.

It is scarcely necessary to say that there was not a word of truth in this story, from beginning to end. Miss Yoke was not the patroness of a hospital, nor had she visited or read to the sick, nor had she met him in such an institution, nor was she wealthy.

What a wonderful meeting it would be, between these three women, —

Mrs. Mudgett, Mrs. Holmes, and Mrs. Howard. If each would tell the other the tales he had told, what an "infinite and endless liar" they would prove him to be.

CHAPTER XX

A FRIEND IN NEED

Geyer Receives a Cipher Letter, with the Key Attached — Was It an Efifort to Divert the Detective from His Pursuit? — Letters from the Insane — Holmes Taught Ciphers to His Friends.

Holmes was never so much in need of his friends as he was in the summer of 1895. The hunt for the missing children, was known to the uttermost ends of the country, and if the District Attorney's office received suggestions of all sorts and kinds, anonymous and otherwise, so did Mr. Holmes. That he had sympathizing friends outside, friends who would have been helpful to him had opportunity offered, cannot be questioned.

These friends were aware that all mail sent to Holmes to the Philadelphia County prison was inspected before delivery to the prisoner, and some of it for proper public reasons, never reached the prisoner. One of these friends undertook by a device to divert Detective Geyer from the pursuit of the track of Holmes, just as he was leaving Indianapolis after his second visit. The detective received at the Spencer House an anonymous letter in cipher, with the key attached, advising him that an important letter had been sent to Holmes to Philadelphia; that the writer was advising the detective at great personal risk and that the letter should be opened and inspected before delivery to the prisoner. The letter came in due course and a copy of it is given elsewhere.

This letter tells Holmes not "to worry about the boy; he is safe and sound," and at first it gave the impression, that Holmes had in some way conveyed to an outside party the place where the remains of the boy had been buried, and that the boy's remains had been removed from the place of concealment.

After careful deliberation, the District Attorney's office concluded that it was a trick or device for a purpose not very clear and it was totally disregarded, and the search subsequently continued with the result already narrated. This is one of the many letters, some in cipher which were received and are now among the great mass of manuscript which have accumulated in the case. Newspapers evidently make their way into lunatic asylums, for letters from the insane came in by the score. The name of Holmes also seemed to become as common as Brown or Smith, for many letters referring to this person and that person by the name of Holmes and requesting information as to comparisons of points of identity with the prisoner were received.

One of the letters received in cipher is given below. This letter is very easily read by dropping every other sentence, separated by commas.

Chicago, Aug. 2d, 1895.

Friend H. H. H:

I, and Jim, will not, saw and, split, the wood. They, can't and, don't, want to, know, whether there is, anything, around or, about, the, conservatory or, green house, I, think, will leave, the dog, for, Mrs. John, Cleveland, at Bleak House, to-morrow. Will, join him under, cover, and fix, all, circus board, signs, there. Same, time I will, sigh for, Ponto's fate and yours in his misfortune. R. I. T. U. A. L. Friend,

L. S. Page.

" Friend H. H. H:—

I will not split. They don't know anything about conservatory. I will leave for Cleveland to-morrow. Will cover all signs. Same cipher."

```
                                        Chicago, Aug. 2nd. '95
Friend H.H.H.
          I, and Jim, will not, saw and, split, the wood. They, can't and,
don't, want to, know, whether there is, anything, around or, about, the, con-
servatory or, green-house.,     I, think, will leave, the dog, for, Mrs. John,
Cleveland, at Bleak House, tomorrow. Will, join him under, cover, and fix,
all, circus board, signs, there.  Same, time I will, sighfor, Ponto's fate
and yours in his misfortune.
                                Friend,
                                  L S. Page.

R.I.T.U.A.L.
```

This letter was apparently written by some one familiar with the famous Chicago "Castle," and referred to a place, a "conservatory" not known to the police. As it had no relevancy to the Philadelphia case, it created little or no comment and is given simply to illustrate how the habit of writing ciphers into which this great criminal had drifted, had been taught to his friends and was made a method of communication between them.

CHAPTER XXI

THE EXCLUDED TESTIMONY

Witnesses from Six States and the Dominion of Canada — Thirty-five Witnesses Positively Identify Holmes — Holmes Grows a Beard — "The Individual in the Cage "— The District Attorney Thanks Officials and Witnesses — Devoted Services of the Officers of the Insurance Company.

Thirty-five witnesses, who were not citizens of the state of Pennsylvania and who were not subject to the subpoena or process of the Philadelphia court, responded to the request of the District Attorney to appear at the trial. These witnesses were from Cincinnati, Indianapolis, Irvington, Detroit, Toronto, Burlington (Vermont), Boston and Fort Worth, Texas.

At the proper time after Mrs. Pitezel had told her sad story, District Attorney Graham offered to prove that Holmes had murdered Howard Pitezel at Irvington, Indiana, and Alice and Nellie Pitezel at Toronto, Canada. This offer was made to show what the prisoner had done during his flight from Philadelphia around the circuit of the cities he made until he reached Boston, where he was arrested. That the murder of Pitezel and the murder of the children were really parts of one transaction, with one design, to wit, the extermination of the Pitezel family, and the evidence was admissible in proving the motive and purpose of the prisoner. The Trial Judge sustained the objection of the defence to this offer and the case went to the jury on the testimony produced by the commonwealth, which related simply and solely to the murder of Pitezel at No. 1316 Callowhill Street.

The witnesses, produced with so much labor and expense, were, in consequence of this decision of the Court, not called, and what they would have said on the witness stand was not given to the public.

It will be, therefore, of much interest to note that they each and all identified the prisoner. Holmes had permitted his beard to grow during his confinement, but his active participation in the examination of jurors and witnesses as the trial proceeded, together with large and finely executed photographs of the prisoner as he appeared without a beard at the time of his arrest, enabled every witness to identify him at once and beyond a question or shadow of doubt. He was identified by W. L. Bain, clerk of the Hotel Bristol, Cincinnati, as the man who brought the three Pitezel children to that hotel on Saturday, September 29th, and registered as "A. E. Cook and three children "; by J. C. Thomas as the person who rented No. 305 Poplar Street, Cincinnati, under the name of "A. C. Hayes "; by Miss Etta Hill as the person whom she saw take a large stove into the Poplar Street house and who the following day came to her, said he had concluded not to keep the house, presented her with the stove and departed.

Of the Indianapolis witnesses, Wm. Sherman Welch, of the Stubbins House, said Holmes whom he saw in court, was the man who brought Alice Pitezel to that hotel on September 24th, registered her as "Etta Pitsel," and took her away four days later. He was also identified by Herman Ackelow, proprietor of the Circle House, as the person who brought the three children, Alice, Nellie and Howard, to his hotel on October 1st and took them away on the 10th; also by J. C. Wands as the man who rented the Irvington house "for his sister, Mrs. A. E. Cook;" by Dr. J. L. Thompson, who saw him at the house at Irvington, after he had taken possession, and by Elvet Moorman who assisted him in putting up the stove, while Howard Pitezel, the little boy, stood by looking on.

The Detroit witnesses were equally positive as to the identification.

Peter Cotter, of the New Western Hotel, identified the prisoner as the man who brought Alice and Nellie to his hotel and registered them as "Etta and Nellie Canning." Mrs. Lucinda Burns was positive he was the man who brought Alice and Nellie to her boarding house. No. 91 Congress Street. It was from this house that Alice wrote her last letter, in which she complained of "almost freezing in that thin jacket," and said,

"Howard is not with us now." No one can read that letter without the conviction that Holmes had cautioned the children about speaking of when and where Howard had left them. It is inconceivable that Alice would have written a letter to the home folks, simply saying that Howard was no longer with them, and no more, unless she had been following the instructions of the archfiend who was waiting for his opportunity to put them to death, and who had already made an end of the boy.

George Dennis, runner for the Albion Hotel, Toronto, said Holmes was the man who placed Alice and Nellie in his care on the evening of October 19th, and instructed him to take them to his hotel. Herbert Jones, clerk of the Albion, identified Holmes as the man who called for the little girls every morning, returning them every evening, until the morning of October 25th, when he paid their board in full, and took them away. They never returned.

Mrs. Nudel and her daughter, Miss Minnie, said Holmes was the man who rented the house No. 16 St. Vincent Street, for "his widowed sister."

Thomas W. Ryves of No. 18 St. Vincent Street, identified the prisoner as the man who on October 24th, borrowed his spade, "to dig a pit for potatoes," in the cellar of No. 16 St. Vincent Street, and who returned it the next day, the 25th. He told Mr. Ryves that his widowed sister and her children were to occupy the house.

W. B. McKillip, said Holmes was the man who rented the house in Burlington, Vermont, gave his name as Judson and said he wanted the house "for his widowed sister, Mrs. A. E. Cook."

Sydney L. Samuels Esq., a lawyer of Fort Worth, Texas, at the request of District Attorney Graham, journeyed all the way from his home to the city of Philadelphia, to testify as to his knowledge of the fraudulent and bogus note which Holmes used in robbing Mrs. Pitezel. Mr. Samuels came North on this long and tiresome journey, to assist the law officers of the Commonwealth in administering public justice, and. refused the compensation which he could have properly claimed for such a protracted absence from his professional duties and business at home. His identification of the prisoner. Holmes, as "the individual in the cage," (meaning the prisoner's dock) will never be forgotten by those who witnessed it. The tone of contempt with which Mr. Samuels used the expression, drew the hot blood to the prisoner's cheek, and he threw a quick glance at the lawyer-witness, full of malevolence and which boded ill for him, had the prisoner been free, and a bottle of chloroform handy.

The reader will not fail to observe how plainly marked was the track of the prisoner, once it was discovered. He used the same names repeatedly and rented a house in each of the cities, Cincinnati, Indianapolis, Detroit, Toronto and Burlington, and told practically the same falsehood in each instance.

The detection of this great criminal and the preparations for the trial, was a work of great labor, but the burden was made easier by officials and citizens in all the cities and towns where Holmes and his victims had been traced.

After the trial had ended, District Attorney Graham sent to each of the police officials of Cincinnati, Indianapolis, Detroit, Toronto, Burlington and Boston, and to all the witnesses who had attended the trial from distant parts, the following official communication:

Nov. 6th, 1895.

I desire to express to you my warm appreciation of the manner in which you so kindly aided the Commonwealth of Pennsylvania, in the recent trial of Hermann W. Mudgett, alias H. H. Holmes charged with Homicide.

Your loyalty and fidelity, and your willingness to so cheerfully assist in dispensing justice, deserve my highest commendation.

The result of the trial will be of benefit, not only to Pennsylvania, but to all communities wherever justice is vigorously and impartially administered through the orderly procedure and under the forms and protection of Law.

Sincerely Yours,

George S. Graham.

In this connection and as a conclusion to this story of unparalleled crime, it is proper to speak of the unselfish and devoted services of the officers of the Fidelity Mutual Life Association. Mr. L. G. Fouse, the distinguished President of the Company and his associates furnished the officials of the county, charged with the prosecution, with every possible aid and assistance, measured neither by what it cost in money nor in effort, and prompted by the highest considerations of humanity and the demands of public justice.

CHAPTER XXIV

CHRONOLOGY

1860 May 16	Herman Webster Mudgett born at Gilmanton, New Hampshire.
1878 July 4	He is married to Clara A. Lovering at Alton, New Hampshire, by John W. Caurrier, Justice of the Peace.
1887 January 28	He is married to Myrta Z. Belknap under the name of Harry Howard Holmes.
1887 February 14	He files in the Superior Court of Cook county, Illinois, a libel in divorce against his wife, Clara A. Levering Mudgett, praying that their marriage may be dissolved.
1891 June 4	The said court orders this suit to be dismissed for default of appearance of complainant.

1893 March	He meets Miss Georgiana Yoke in March Chicago.
1893 September 19	He makes application for a twenty year optional insurance for $10,000 in the Fidelity Mutual Life Association in which he avers: "Mother died at 58, don't remember the disease, no acute disease. Father died at 62 from injury foot."
1893 November 9	Fidelity Mutual Life Association insures Benjamin F. Pitezel in the sum of $10,000.
Same month	Holmes is engaged to be married to Miss Yoke under the name of Henry Mansfield Howard.
1894 January 12	He is married to Miss Yoke in Denver, Colorado, by the Rev. Mr. Wilcox, and they journey on their honeymoon to Fort Worth, Texas.

1894 January February March April	Mudgett and Pitezel, (the former under the name of D. T. Pratt and the latter under the name of Benton T. Lyman) in Fort Worth, Texas, where they engage in building a store property on land formerly owned by Minnie Williams.
April	Pitezel leaves Fort Worth and goes to Chicago.
May	Mudgett and Miss Yoke leave Fort Worth and journey to Denver, Colorado.
May 21	They make their appearance in St. Louis. About this date Holmes (Mudgett) and Pitezel go to Memphis, Tennessee. In this vicinity they first consider the location of the place where they propose to execute the insurance fraud.
June 8	Holmes and wife return to St. Louis.

June 15	Holmes purchases a drug store in St. Louis, Missouri, under the name of Howard, upon which he gave a mortgage.
July 19	Holmes is arrested in St. Louis by the Merrill Drug Company and sent to prison under a charge of fraud and for selling mortgaged property. The man "Brown," to whom he sold it is supposed to have been Pitezel. During his imprisonment in the St. Louis jail, he meets Marion C. Hedgepeth.
July 28	He is released on bail.
July 29	He is rearrested and again committed to prison.
July 31	He is again released on bail furnished by Miss Yoke.
August 2, 3, 4	He is in New York and Philadelphia
	Miss Yoke (Mrs. Howard) leaves Lake Bluff, Illinois, where she was visiting,

and journeys to Philadelphia.

August 5 — Sunday. Holmes meets Miss Yoke at Broad Street Station, Philadelphia, and takes her to a boarding house, 1905 N. 11th Street (Mrs. Dr. Alcorn's.) He tells Miss Yoke he is selling a patent letter copier.

August 9 — Holmes telegraphs $157.50, (the half yearly premium on the Pitezel policy), to the Chicago office of the Fidelity Mutual Life Association.

August 17 — Pitezel, under the name of B. F. Perry, rents 1316 Callowhill Street and pays $10 on account of the rent to Walter W. Shedaker, Agent.

Holmes and Pitezel purchase second hand furniture of John F. Hughes, 1037 Buttonwood Street, which was sent to 1316 Callowhill Street.

August 18 — Pitezel calls at the furniture store alone

	and purchases a cot and some old matting.
August 22	Eugene Smith calls upon Pitezel and sees Holmes pass into the house and go upstairs.
August 22 to September 1	Pitezel is seen in and about 1316 Callowhill Street by a large number of persons.
September 1	Evening. Pitezel calls upon Holmes at 1905 North Eleventh Street.
September 2	Holmes leaves 1905 N. 11th Street at about 10.80 AM He returns about 4 PM He tells his wife (Miss Yoke) that the man who called the evening before, was a messenger from the Pennsylvania Railroad Company and that he could have an interview with a Pennsylvania Railroad official the next day at Nicetown. This Sunday morning he said he was going out to Nicetown to see the official and that if he was successful, and

	as their week was up, they would probably start West that night.
September 2	Evening. Holmes and Miss Yoke leave Philadelphia on the 10.25 train and went direct to Indianapolis.
September 3	They arrive in Indianapolis and register at the Stubbins House.
September 4	They take boarding at 488 North Illinois Street, Indianapolis.
September 4	Pitezel's body found at No. 1316 Callowhill Street by Eugene Smith.
September 5	Coroner holds first inquest.
September 5	Holmes goes to St. Louis, calls upon Mrs. Pitezel and tells her to go to Howe with the papers, meaning insurance policy, etc. She takes papers to Howe. Holmes told her that a body had been substituted for her husband and that

"Ben was alive and all right," and not to worry.

September 8	Fidelity Mutual receives a telegraphic dispatch from George B. Stadden, Manager for Missouri, at St. Louis, stating that "B. F. Perry, found dead in Philadelphia, is claimed to be B. F. Pitezel, who is insured on 044145. Investigate before remains leave there." |//

About this time Howe writes to the company in Philadelphia, stating that he was counsel for Mrs. Pitezel, the beneficiary under the policy and would come on with a member of the family to identify the body, etc.

September 13	Pitezel's body buried as B. F. Perry in Potters Field, Philadelphia.
September 5 to September 19	Holmes was with Miss Yoke at her mother's home in Franklin, Indiana, leaving her he said to go to St. Louis again or to Cincinnati, and then to Indianapolis. At this time Holmes was

occasionally with his other wife at Wilmette, Illinois. He was likely with her on September 11th. At Indianapolis he tells Miss Yoke that he had heard from the Pennsylvania Railroad official in Philadelphia about the copier and they were ready to pay over the money, and they had directed him to come on at once. He left her at the Circle Park Hotel, Indianapolis, and went to Philadelphia.

September 17   He writes a letter to Mr. Cass, Chicago Cashier of the Fidelity, stating that his wife (Wilmette wife) had told him that information was wanted of B. F. Pitezel, who was found in Chicago as B. F. Perry.

September 18   He writes another letter to Cass, saying that he overhears the body was in Philadelphia and not in Chicago, and that he would go to Philadelphia if his expenses were paid.

September 19   Holmes leaves Indianapolis for Philadelphia. He again stops at No.

1905 North 11th Street; Mrs. Alcorn's.

September 20   He calls at the office of the company in Philadelphia, No. 914, Walnut Street. He tells Mr. Fouse, President of the Company that he had corresponded with Cass. He asks Fouse about the circumstances of the death, which Fouse relates briefly. Holmes said it was a very peculiar case, and asked Mr. Fouse the cause of death, etc.

September 20   Alice writes her first letter to the home folks.

PHILADELPHIA, PA.,

Cor. Filbert & 11th sts., Sept. 20, 1894.

DEAR MAMMA AND THE REST:

Just arrived in Philadelphia this morning and I wrote you yesterday of this. Mr. Howe and I have each a room at the above address. I am going to the Morgue after awhile. We stopped off at Washington, Md., this morning, and that made it six times that we transferred to different cars. Yesterday we got on the C. and O. Pullman car and it was crowded so I had to sit with some one Mr. Howe sit with some man we sit there quite awhile and pretty soon some one came and shook hands with me. I looked up and here it was Mr. Howard. He did not know my jacket, but he said he thought it was his girl's face so he went to see and it was me. I don't like him to call me babe and child and dear and all such trash. When I got on the car Tuesday night Mr. Howe ask me if I had any money and I told him 5 cents so he gave me a dollar How I wish I could see you all and hug the baby. I hope you are better. Mr. H. says that I will have a ride on the ocean. I wish you could see what I have seen. I have seen more scenery than I have seen since I was born I don't know what I saw before. This is all the paper I have so I will have to close & write again. You had better not write to me here for Mr. H. says that I may be off to-morrow.

If you are worse wire me good-bye kisses to all and two big ones for you and babe. Love to all.

E. ALICE PITEZEL.

September 21	Howe and Alice Pitezel called at Insurance Office. Holmes calls same time. They meet as strangers, although they had travelled together from some point in Ohio to Washington, D. C. Howe and Alice got off at Washington and Holmes took train for Philadelphia. Howe and Alice came to Philadelphia on later train. That day Holmes took Alice out to see the sights of the city and then to Mrs. Alcorn's that night, stating that she (Alice) was his little sister. Alice slept in the 3d story next to Holmes' room which communicated with it. Alice had stopped with Howe at the Imperial Hotel, 11th and Filbert Streets, from which place she wrote two letters. Following are copies:

Imperial Hotel,

Eleventh, above Market Street,

Hendricks & Scott, Propr's.,

PHILADELPHIA, PA., Sept. 21, 1894.

DEAR MAMMA AND BABE:

I have to write all the time to pass away

the time.

Mr. Howe has been away all morning. Mamma have you ever seen or tasted a red banana? I have had three. They are so big that I can just reach around it and have my thumb and next finger just tutch. I have not got any shoes yet and I have to go a hobbling around all the time. Have you gotten 4 letters from me besides this? Are you sick in bed yet or are you up? I wish that I could hear from you but I don't know whether I would get it or not. Mr. Howe telegraphed to Mr. Beckert and he said that he would write to you tonight. I have not got but two clean garments and that is a shirt and my white skirt. I saw some of the largest solid rocks that I bet you never saw. I crossed the Patomac River. I guess that I have told all the news; So good bye Kisses to you and babe.

Yours loving daughter,

MISS E. A. PITEZEL.

If you are worse telegraph to the above address. Imperial Hotel, Eleventh above Market Street.

September 21   Howe and Alice Pitezel called at Insurance Office. Holmes calls same time. They meet as strangers, although they had travelled together from some point in Ohio to Washington, D. C. Howe and Alice got off at Washington and Holmes took train for Philadelphia. Howe and Alice came to Philadelphia on later train. That day Holmes took Alice out to see the sights of the city and then to Mrs. Alcorn's that night, stating that she (Alice) was his little sister. Alice slept in the 3d story next to Holmes' room which communicated with it. Alice had stopped with Howe at the Imperial Hotel, 11th and Filbert Streets, from which place she wrote two letters. Following are copies:

Imperial Hotel,

Eleventh, above Market Street,

Hendricks & Scott, Propr's.,

PHILADELPHIA, PA., Sept. 21, 1894.

DEAR MAMMA AND BABE:

I have to write all the time to pass away

the time.

Mr. Howe has been away all morning. Mamma have you ever seen or tasted a red banana? I have had three. They are so big that I can just reach around it and have my thumb and next finger just tutch. I have not got any shoes yet and I have to go a hobbling around all the time. Have you gotten 4 letters from me besides this? Are you sick in bed yet or are you up? I wish that I could hear from you but I don't know whether I would get it or not. Mr. Howe telegraphed to Mr. Beckert and he said that he would write to you tonight. I have not got but two clean garments and that is a shirt and my white skirt. I saw some of the largest solid rocks that I bet you never saw. I crossed the Patomac River. I guess that I have told all the news; So good bye Kisses to you and babe.

Yours loving daughter,

MISS E. A. PITEZEL.

If you are worse telegraph to the above address. Imperial Hotel, Eleventh above Market Street.

Imperial Hotel,

Eleventh above Market Street,

Hendricks & Scott, Propr's.,

Philadelphia, 189-.

DEAR DESSA:

I thought T would write you a little letter and when I get to Mass. you must all write to me. Well this is a warm day here how is it there. Did you get your big washing done if I was there you would have a bigger one for I have a whole satchel full of dirty clothes. I bet that I have more fruit than all of you. Dessa I guess you are without shoes for I guess they don't intend to get me any. H. has come now so I guess I have to go to dinner.

Dessa take good care of mama. I will close your letter and write a little to Nell and Howard next time so good bye love to you with a kiss.

DEAR MAMA:

I was over to the insurance office this afternoon and Mr. Howe thinks there will be no trouble about getting it. They asked me almost a thousand questions, of course not quite so many. Is his nose broken or has he a Roman nose. I said it was broken. I will have to close and write more tomorrow so good bye love to all with kisses to all.

Your loving daughter,

E. ALICE PITEZEL.

September 21st   At the conference at the company's office on this day, the marks of identification were agreed upon.

September 22   Pitezel's body exhumed at Potters Field. Holmes finds wart on neck and other marks of identification, and says the body is that of B. F. Pitezel. Alice recognizes teeth of her father. He takes Alice to No. 1904 North 11th Street.

September 23   Holmes and Alice make affidavits before Coroner Ashbridge that the body found as B. F. Perry at 1316 Callowhill Street was that of Benjamin F. Pitezel. That evening Holmes and Alice leave for Indianapolis.

September 24   They arrive in Indianapolis. He registers Alice as Etta Pitsel in his handwriting.

September 24   Insurance Company pays Howe <f9715.85, face of insurance policy, less expenses.

September 24   Alice writes another letter home. The person alluded to in these letters as 4, 18, 8, is the children's cipher for Holmes.

Stubbins' European Hotel,

One square north of Union Depot on Illinois Street.

INDIANAPOLIS, IND.,

Sep. 24, 1894.

DEAR ONES AT HOME,

I am glad to hear that you are all well and that you are up. I guess you will not have any trouble in getting the money. 4, 18, 8 is going to get two of you and fetch you here with me and then I won't be so lonesome at the above address. I am not going to Miss Williams until I see where you are going to live and then see you all again because 4, 18, 8 is afraid that I will get two lonesome then he will send me on and go to school. I have a pair of shoes now if I could see you I would have a nough to talk to you all day but I cannot very well write it 1 will see you all before long though don't you worry. This is a cool day. Mr. Perry said that if you did not get the insurance all right through the lawyers to rite to Mr. Foust or Mr. Perry. I wish I had a silk dress. I have seen more since I have been away than I ever saw before in my life. I have another picture for your album. I will have to close for this time now so good bye love and kisses and squesses to all.

Yours daughter,

ETTA PITEZEL.

P. O. I go by Etta here 4, 18, 8 told me to O

Howard O Dessa, O Nell O Mamma, O Baby. Nell you & Howard will come with 4, 18, 8, & Mamma and Dessa later on won't you or as Mamma says.

ETTA PITEZEL.

September 25	Holmes goes to St. Louis and remained there until the 28th.
September 27	Holmes gets $6,700 of the insurance money out of the $7,200 received by Mrs. Pitezel from Howe. He gives her the bogus note
September 28	Holmes takes Nellie and Howard from Mrs. Pitezel at St. Louis. Alice joins them at Indianapolis and she goes with Holmes, Nellie and Howard to Cincinnati, where Holmes registers at the Atlantic House under the name of Alexander E. Cook and three children.
September 29	He rents 305 Poplar Street from Mr. J. C. Thomas and takes a large stove to this house.
	Over night of 28th he remains at Atlantic House and on the 29th he takes them to Hotel Bristol, registers there as A. E. Cook and three children, and remains there until Sunday, September

30th when he left with the children for Indianapolis and registers them at Hotel English as "Three Canning children."

October 1   Mrs. Pitezel left St. Louis for Galva, Illinois with Dessie and the baby. Galva was the home of her parents. Holmes takes the children to the Circle House, Indianapolis (registers as "Three Canning children") where they remained until October 10th. oet. 1st. Alice and Nellie write letters as follows:

INDIANAPOLIS, IND.,

Oct. 1st, 1894.

DEAR MAMMA.

We was in Cincinnati yesterday and we got here last night getting that telegram from Mr. Howe yesterday afternoon.

Mr. H. is going to-night for you and he will take this letter. We went us three over to the Zoological Garden in Cincinnati yesterday afternoon and we saw all the different kinds of animals. We saw the ostrich it is about a head taller than I am so you know about how high it is. And the giraffe you have to look up in the sky to see it. I like it lots better here than in Cincinnati. It is such a dirty town Cin.

There is a monument right in front of the hotel where we are at and I should judge that it is about 3 times the hight of a five story building. I guess I have told all the news so good bye love to all & kisses. Hope you are all well.

Your loving daughter,

ETTA PITEZEL.

INDIANAPOLIS, IND.,

Oct. 1st, 1894.

DEAR MAMMA, BABY AND D.

We are all well here. Mr. H. is going on a late train to-night. He is not here now I just saw him go by the Hotel He went some place I don't know where I think he went to get his ticket.

We are staying in another hotel in Indianapolis it is a pretty nice one we came here last night from C.

I like it here lots better than in C. It is quite warm here and I have to wear this warm dress becaus my close an't ironet. We ate dinner over to the Stibbins Hotel where Alice staid and they knew her to. We are not staying there we are at the English H.

We have a room right in front of a monument and I think it was A. Lincolns. Come as soon as you can because I want to see you and baby to. It is awful nice place where we are staying I don't think you would like it in Cincinnati either but Mr. H. sais he likes it there.

Good bye your dau.

NELLIE PITEZEL.

October 5	Holmes rents the house at Irvington from Mr. Crouse (J. C. Wand's clerk.) He said he wanted it for his sister, Mrs. A. E. Cook and her children, and that she intended using it as a boarding house
October 6, 7, 8	Children write letters home.
October 10	Howard disappears on this day. Same day. Holmes takes Alice and Nellie from the Circle House.
October 12	Evening. Holmes arrives in Detroit. Himself and Miss Yoke in one party; Alice and Nellie in another. He registers the children at the New Western Hotel as Etta and Nellie Canning, St. Louis, Mo. He registers himself and Miss Yoke at the Hotel Normandie "G. Howell

and wife, Adrian."

October 13	Mrs. Pitezel, Dessie and the baby leave Galva, Illinois for Detroit, stopping in Chicago. Holmes has written to her that "Ben "was waiting to see her in Detroit.
October 13	Holmes and Miss Yoke remove from Hotel Normandie to 54 Park Place. He gave their names as Mr. and Mrs. Holmes.
October 14	Mrs. Pitezel, Dessie and the baby arrive in Detroit, and register as C. A. Adams and daughter at Geis's Hotel.
October 14	Alice writes her last letter.
October 15	Holmes takes Alice and Nellie to boarding house of Lucinda Burns at No. 91 Congress Street.
October 15	About this date, Holmes rents of Mr. Boninghausen the house No. 241 E.

	Forest Avenue. Mr. Boninghausen does not remember name Holmes gave. In the rear of cellar under porch of the house, Holmes digs a hole four feet long, three and a half feet wide, three feet six inches deep.
October 18	Holmes and Miss Yoke leave Detroit for Toronto, Canada. He tells Mrs. Pitezel that Ben had gone to Toronto.
	At Toronto, Holmes registers at Walker House as Geo. H. Howell and wife, Columbus. Some day Mrs. Pitezel, Dessie and the baby left Geis's Hotel, Detroit for Toronto; were met at Grand Trunk depot by Holmes and taken to the Union House, where they register under the name of C. A. Adams and daughter.
October 19	Alice and Nellie leave Detroit for Toronto; arrive in the evening about 8 o'clock; were met by Holmes who turned them over to George Dennis, a hotel porter, for the Albion Hotel, and they were registered as Etta and Nellie Canning, Detroit.

October 20	Holmes rented house No. 16 St. Vincent Street of Mrs. Nudel. Said his name was Howard and that he wanted it for his sister. Same day Holmes and Miss Yoke went to Niagara Falls.
October 21	They returned and registered at the Palmer House under the name of Howell.
October 24	Holmes borrows a spade from Mr. Ryves, 18 St. Vincent Street to dig a hole in the cellar, "for the storage of potatoes." While in Toronto, Holmes called at Albion Hotel for Alice and Nellie every morning, returning them in the evening.
October 25	On the morning of this day, he takes Alice and Nellie from the Albion Hotel, paying their account for board in full. The children disappear.
October 25	He requests Mrs. Pitezel to go to Ogdensberg. He tells her Ben is in

Montreal. He said that he had rented a house in Toronto, but that two detectives on bicycles were watching it, and it would not be safe for Ben to visit her there

October 26 Holmes and Miss Yoke leave Toronto and go to Prescott, Canada; remained there over night.

October 31 He is found at Burlington at the Burlington House; registered as G. D. Hale, Columbus, Ohio. He moved to rooms at Mr. Aherns, where he gave the names of himself and Miss Yoke as "Mr. Hall and wife."

November 1 He rents a house No. 26 Winooski Avenue of W. B. McKillip under the name of J. A. Judson, for his sister Mrs. Cook.

November 1
to
November 16

Between these dates visited his parents at his old home in Gilmanton, New Hampshire; resumes his relations with his real wife, Mrs. Mudgett. He tells a

	romantic story accounting for his absence from home.
November 17	He is arrested in Boston.
November 18	He makes his first confession. He says Pitezel is alive in South America, or on his way there, and that the children were with him. He said Pitezel was bound for San Salvador. That their means of communication was to be in the personal column of the *New York Herald*.
	Mrs. Pitezel is arrested on the same day.
November 20	Holmes and Mrs. Pitezel brought to Philadelphia; committed to county prison.
December 6	Mrs. Pitezel makes a full statement to Mr. Fouse and Mr. Perry of the Fidelity Mutual Life Association.
December 15	Holmes now says Pitezel is dead, and that the children were given to Miss

	Williams, who took them to Europe.
December 17	Makes another confession, declaring that Pitezel was dead and that he had committed suicide.
1895 June 3	Holmes is tried for conspiracy to cheat and defraud the Insurance Company, and on the second day of the trial, pleads guilty.
June 27	Detective Geyer leaves Philadelphia and commences his search for the children.
July 15	Geyer finds the bodies of Alice and Nellie in the cellar of the Toronto House, No. 16 St. Vincent Street.
August 27	Geyer finds the remains of Howard in the house at Irvington, a few miles from Indianapolis.
September 12	Holmes is indicted in Philadelphia for

the murder of Benjamin F. Pitezel.

September 23	He pleads not guilty. The Court fixes the day of the trial to be October 28th.
October 28 to November 2	Motion for continuance denied. Trial commences, and continues until November 2d. Jury render a verdict: "Guilty of murder in the first degree."
November 18	Motion for a new trial argued.
November 30	Motion for new trial overruled. Holmes sentenced to be hanged.
1896 January 30	Sends a copy of his memoir *Holmes' Own Story* from his cell in Moyamensing, Philadelphia County Prison, to the Honorable Samuel Pennypacker at the Court of Appeals. He writes "I take pleasure in addressing to your Honor these lines to which I append my, at present, very memorable signature. I am, Sir, Very Respectfully Yours,

HW Mudgett MD

alias

HH Holmes

April 9	Writes cover letter for the manuscript of his confession to the Philadelphia Inquirer. It reads
	"The following statement was written by me in Philadelphia County Jail for the Philadelphia Inquirer as a true and accurate confession in all particulars. It is the only confession of my fearful crimes I have made or will make. I make it fully apprehending all the horrors it contains and how it condemns me before the world.
	<div style="text-align:center">Signed H H Holmes</div>
	April 9th 1896
April 12	Sunday. The Philadelphia Inquirer runs the 10,000 word confession with Holmes's cover letter on the front cover.
May 7	Is hanged in the basement of the Philadelphia County Jail at Moyamensing, and taken five miles to

Holy Cross Cemetery at Yeadon.

May 8   Buried in an unmarked vault in Section 15 of Holy Cross Cemetery, Yeadon, Pennsylvania.

THE COTTAGE AT IRVINTOWN, IND., WHERE HOLMES MURDERED HOWARD

APPENDIX I.

SPEECH OF HON. GEO. S. GRAHAM, DISTRICT ATTORNEY.

With submission to your Honor; Gentlemen of the Jury: I am quite sure that it is with a feeling of relief that you see the end of this trial rapidly approaching, and that you, who have been taken from your homes, your places of business, and practically imprisoned during the whole length of these proceedings, are now to be released and permitted to return and resume your usual places and duties in society. I know, also, that you feel relieved, because the speaking at the conclusion of the case is to be somewhat limited. Instead of the three speeches that were contemplated yesterday afternoon, in view of the illness of Mr. Shoemaker, T have voluntarily waived that which is the right of the Commonwealth— to close; the right of the Commonwealth is not only to open or sum up, but to close the argument in this case.

I propose, therefore, to ask you now, to join with me in reasoning for a little while about the evidence which you have heard — the testimony in this case. I am going to ask you to give me your best attention, and your best thought, while I try to refresh your recollection, and aid your reason in reaching right conclusions from the evidence. After which I propose to leave the final argument to my young friend who represents the prisoner at the Bar. I ask you to listen to him, and the reasons he may assign, and if they are consistent with the evidence in the case, and in your judgment more nearly accord with the truth, as you see it, adopt them; and if the firm finger of duty points you in that direction, acquit this prisoner and set him free.

The Commonwealth of Pennsylvania is the prosecutor in this case. You will take up this Bill of Indictment and read, "The Commonwealth of Pennsylvania, against Herman W. Mudgett, alias H. H. Holmes." The Commonwealth of Pennsylvania wants no victim. The Commonwealth of Pennsylvania does not ask for the conviction of this man, though he may be covered with the evidences of guilt in other matters, unless in this specific case now on trial, the testimony that you have heard points indubitably to his guilt and authorizes his conviction. I ask your attention to the evidence, because I propose to say to you that, after a careful perusal of it, my mind is forced to the conclusion that I must press upon you the discharge of a great, and perhaps to you, a trying duty. I believe that I can take up the testimony in this case just as it stands to-day, and lead you through it by a straight path to but one conclusion, and that conclusion absolutely inconsistent with the innocence of the prisoner at the Bar. If it were not so, it would be my duty to abandon this case. If it were not so, or if, in that review, my mind would hesitate in reaching a conclusion, because of the weakness of the evidence or any defect in the proof, then it would be my duty to say that there is a doubt of this prisoner's guilt and he is entitled to the benefit of that doubt, and upon that doubt he ought to be acquitted.

The task laid before me is this: I must point out from this evidence the facts which prove conclusively that this prisoner at the Bar murdered Benjamin F. Pitezel, at No. 1316 Callowhill Street, on the 2d day of September, 1894, — so conclusively that there will not be a single doubt left lurking in your minds — so positively that you will feel under your oaths as jurors that there is but one course left open for you, and that is to find the verdict pointed out to you in the opening of this case — the highest known to the law — a verdict of murder in the first degree.

It is true, as my friend on the other side has said, this case has consumed five days. It is true that a large amount of testimony has been produced; that a great number of witnesses have been called to the stand for the purpose of establishing the Commonwealth's case; but that ought not to be a subject of complaint from the defendant — that care has been taken; that the testimony has been carefully selected; that it has been marshalled in court; that it has been presented to you, with all the time necessary for its inspection and consideration — that ought not to be a subject of complaint from the prisoner; for the Commonwealth is bound to prove its case from the initial step, down to the very last syllable of testimony requisite to make it complete.

The Commonwealth has done so in this case. The Commonwealth has proved by testimony every step in this important proceeding, out of the lips of thirty-five witnesses who have been examined before you. We have endeavored to establish it link by link, one by one, each one separate and distinct from the others, but together making the chain complete and perfect.

May I recall to your attention, without attempting to read this mass of testimony, but with a word here and a suggestion there, what we have listened to during these past five days?

I am sure there is not a man in that jury-box, but will be grateful to me for redirecting his attention to that which must be the basis of his action — to wit, the evidence in the case. I am sure you want to know it; I am sure you want to remember it; I am sure you want to act intelligently upon it: and I am firmly convinced that you wish to reach a right conclusion from it.

The testimony began with the calling of Miss Jeannette Pitezel to the stand. You remember her. That was her first appearance in the case. She has been called quite a number of times since. She was called then but for one single purpose. This picture holding up picture of Benjamin F. Pitezel) was shown to her, and she was asked the question, "Whose picture is that?" That witness identified this picture, used so frequently during the trial — the picture of the dead man. "That's the picture of my father, Benjamin F. Pitezel." That was her identification.

The next witness called was a young man from the Detective Bureau, who established the identity of two other pictures that you and I have used so often in this case. These are the pictures of the prisoner (holding up two pictures of Holmes). We feared, since the prisoner during his imprisonment had chosen to cultivate a beard upon his face, that when the witnesses would be called into this court room during the trial, there might be difficulty in identifying him, and the Commonwealth's case might be imperiled for lack of identification, and so, as a precautionary measure, we procured these pictures of him as he was when these witnesses saw him, in order that we might have them here, in this enlarged form, for the use of the witnesses in identifying him, and so that they might not be puzzled in so doing by his changed appearance. When he entered the prison cell, his face was like that (holding up the picture of the prisoner without a beard). He has not shaved since that time and this beard has grown. Why? Of course, I do not know; but it was my duty — and that of my colleague, Mr. Barlow, who attended to these arrangements — it was our duty to see that no injury should come to the Commonwealth's case by reason of any change in his appearance while in the prison cell, and that our witnesses might be aided in their identification by this counterfeit presentment of what he was at the time of these occurrences.

The next witness you listened to was Mr. Eugene Smith. I am not going to read the testimony he gave you, but simply ask your attention to it again. He came in here and told you the story of the finding of the body. He knew No. 1316 Callowhill Street. He had visited the place on business several times. He went into the store or office on this Monday afternoon, the 3d of September, and he saw no sign of Pitezel, everything was in place there, but no man was there; the door closed, but not locked. He found articles of clothing hanging in the room. After waiting some time and unable to wait any longer, he passed out, but returned again the next morning. He found the room precisely as he had seen it on Monday afternoon — no change in appearance; even the articles of clothing that were hanging in the room were in the same place. It looked suspicious to him; it immediately excited his attention, and he commenced to look through the house. He tells you how he went through that office or store part of the building, back to the entrance to the stairway, and passed on up to the head of the stairs, or the landing on the second floor. He tells you how the door to his left on this landing opened into the back room, and that along the entry way in front of him there was another door leading into the front room. Hastily glancing from where he stood into that front room, he saw a cot, but it was empty; no one seemed to be there. Then turning, he looked into the open door at his side, when, lo! there upon the floor he discovered the body of a man. Looking in hastily, and supposing that the man had probably been killed or shot, he did not enter. Instantly descending the stairs, he summoned two police officers; and they, in turn, summoned Dr. Scott, who lived in the neighborhood. All of them returned to the house, and he tells you what they saw; the position of the body lying perfectly straight on its back on the floor, the right arm laid across the breast, the left hand down at the side, the limbs straight out from the body, the heels together, the feet in position, the whole indicating all absence of struggle and a condition of perfect tranquility and repose.

Smith was examined and questioned on this matter with a wonderful amount of insistence, where it was wholly unnecessary, about a little incident which occurred and which he related of the prisoner. Of course, the Commonwealth wanted to show that the prisoner had been there; that he knew this house; that he was in the habit of visiting it; that he was not a stranger to Pitezel. This was one of the steps in that direction, and therefore Mr. Smith was asked to relate what occurred on the occasion of one of his visits to this store. He had visited this store before the Monday and Tuesday to which I have called your attention. He says, "I went in there; I had some business with Mr. Pitezel. While I was there, this prisoner came into the room and, with some sign or motion, that called Pitezel's attention, he passed directly on." He seemed to be familiar with the place — to be no stranger there. He knew where to go; that house was no unknown place to him. Pitezel was his tool, his creature, and with a wink, or a nod, or a beck, or whatever it might be called, he silently summoned him to attend him, and then passed, as the witness said, through this door (indicating on the plan of the house) up the stairs. He was asked by the prisoner, "Well, did you see me pass up the stairs?" Of course he did not. The witness said what any witness would say under those circumstances, — "I saw him — that door being open, and the stairs being there and starting at the door, and my chair being down near the front of the room with a direct view to the door — I saw him pass and turn in that direction." Of course, that meant, speaking about such an event as you or I or any other person would, that he saw him pass upstairs. That is what he meant. There was no other exit in that direction, but to go upstairs. But the prisoner, with insistence, thought he had made a point upon Mr. Smith that might affect his credibility and said, "Did you see me go upstairs? How could you see me go upstairs when the stairs are not in view from where you sat?" Why it was perfectly plain. He saw him turn in that direction, and possibly step upon the first step; that would be within the line of his vision, and therefore he would say, I saw you going upstairs to the upper story.

But, gentlemen, that is only a little incident in the case, and is of very minor importance; whether or not they went up in the second story, or whether they went out into the back yard, does not matter at all, so far as the Commonwealth's case is concerned. The fact that this man Holmes was there — the fact that he was on terms of intimate acquaintance with the proprietor of that place, and had knowledge of the place itself as shown in his leading the way after beckoning the deceased to follow — these are the facts that rise out of this little circumstance, and are important as showing how completely he was at home in Pitezel's house. That was the testimony of Smith.

Then you will remember that the prisoner, who had been conducting his own case, interrupted the examination of Smith and said that he would like to have a plan of the house. We complied with his request and called Marshall Pugh, who was employed in the Board of Surveys, one of the City Departments, and proved the making of this plan, and that it had been correctly made. The examination of Mr. Smith was then proceeded with to its end.

Our next step was to call Mr. Ran, the photographer, who presented for our better understanding of the situation, two pictures, one picture of the front of the house No. 1316 Callowhill Street, where the body was found, and the other a picture showing the rear of the same house and for our information the double window, in the second story room, with its large white shutters. These photographs were then offered in evidence.

We then proceeded with the facts of the case, and called Dr. Scott, whom you will all remember — a clear, bright, intelligent witness; crisp, plain, and strong in his talk. He came to the stand and told you what he saw when he went into No. 1316 Callowhill Street, when summoned by the officers. We have the advantage in Dr. Scott of not simply an ordinary witness. We have an intelligent physician; an observing man, who looks closely and scans everything in that room; who takes particular note of the body, who pays particular attention to everything there. He corroborates Smith in all the details with relation to the position of the body, and the position of the man's arm, and the burning of the body, the singeing of the moustache, the singeing of the hair on his head, and how the skin was taken off his hands, how the clothing over the chest was burned through to the flesh, and the flesh underneath burned; how, in the position in which the arm was placed, the under side of the arm being against the body, it was absolutely protected from the flame, so that not one particle of fire touched the under side of that arm; and demonstrating that it was burned while lying in that position upon the body, and also described the skin hanging off the hand where the fire and flame had blistered it. He tells you about these points. He goes into minute description of the clothing — how it was tucked down into the trousers, with nothing disturbed — everything as a man fixes his own clothing when about to start out upon the highway, or go about his business. He gives you all these details, and tells you how reposefully and how tranquilly the body was arranged. There it lay. I want you to remember in this connection, gentlemen, another circumstance that may be of some importance to you in arriving at the truth. When we take up the story of this prisoner, as told in his confession, it may be important to remember another thing stated by the Doctor. There was a discharge from the mouth. There was a fecal discharge, and the bladder also was empty. These were the results of a condition that comes on when death is imminent — the relaxation of the involuntary muscles of the body, so that what a man could do in health to prevent these discharges could not be done in that condition, and the contents of his bowels and bladder flowed from him. That, gentlemen of the jury, was the condition of this body on the second floor of this house — the flow from the mouth, and the other discharges from his person, occurred on that floor. The dead man died there. There was no trace of any discharge on the third-story floor.

Dr. Scott not only testified to what took place at No. 1316 Callowhill Street, but he also testified to what took place at the post mortem examination. You will remember his testimony. You will recall that he covered two points — what was found in the room No. 1316 Callowhill Street and what Dr. Mattern found in the body at the time he made the post mortem examination of it. He told you about the congested condition of the lungs. He told you about the empty condition of the heart, indicating speedy death — paralysis of the heart — that the man died instantly, quickly. He told you about the condition of the stomach, the kidneys, and the liver, these all denoting an alcoholic condition, showing that the man was a heavy drinker of alcoholic stimulants, and that irritation of the stomach due to alcohol was also present, but that there was no irritation there due to the action of chloroform, although he told you another thing, — that there were about two ounces of chloroform found in the stomach. The doctors both told you the smell was strong, and could not be mistaken. Otherwise the stomach was what they call an empty stomach. That does not mean literally void of every particle of food, but practically an empty stomach. There was mucus there, but remember he testified that that chloroform in the stomach had not produced any irritation of the membrane or lining of the stomach — not a particle. That chloroform in the stomach had never produced the slightest effect upon the dead man. That was Dr. Scott's testimony.

Maintaining the order of proof, we next call Dr. Mattern: Dr. Mattern told you very much the same things that Dr. Scott did. He repeated to you the story of the post mortem examination of the body of Pitezel. He told you of the congested condition of the lungs. He told you of the condition of the heart, the condition of the stomach, the liver, the kidneys, and all the viscera. The result of the examination of the body of this man was to enable these doctors to say to you, as a positive fact in this case, and one that is not disputed, for there is no one to contradict the statements that they make, (and that is one of the things it is important for you to remember) — that this man died from chloroform poisoning.

That you have an undisputed fact in this case. He was poisoned with chloroform; there is no doubt about the cause of his death. That is a fact that stands before you undisputed. This man died from the effects of chloroform. It was chloroform poisoning that took away his life, so that, although you may find in the description given by Dr. Scott, and by Mr. Smith, that there was an attempt to create an appearance in the room where the body was found which would lead one into the belief that an explosion had taken place in that building, you are freed from the further consideration of all idea of an explosion having taken place. Indeed it is admitted that no explosion killed this man. While it is true that the flames touched his clothing, and partially consumed it, and burned and blistered his flesh, — yet they did not kill him. While the broken jar, and the other evidences of that explosion were present, they were artificially produced by somebody with the intention to mislead and deceive. There was no explosion. Holmes now admits that he himself broke this jar, and Doctor Scott demonstrated the fact that it had not exploded. Even the smartest, even the brightest, even the keenest criminal will make mistakes, and when Holmes broke that jar, he broke it leaving the glass particles or fragments lying inside the bottle, whereas an explosion would have scattered them all about the room. I want you to remember, therefore, gentlemen, at this stage of the argument, that the Commonwealth has established one fact beyond contradiction, which is that this dead man was killed by the use of chloroform poisoning. Two witnesses have sworn to this fact — no one has contradicted them — and the defence admits that this was the cause of death.

The next witness was a very important witness in this case. I will now simply call your attention to what he testified to, and to the subject upon which he testified, for I do not propose to discuss the effect of his testimony at this point. I refer to the testimony of Dr. Henry Leffman, one of the most distinguished analytical chemists perhaps in this country

— a man of fine scientific attainments, of splendid intelligence and culture. He comes upon the stand and gives to you his story as an expert upon the subject of chloroform, and states certain facts to you, to which I will advert in a short time, and by the help of which I will discover to you, not only that this man was poisoned with chloroform poison, but that that chloroform poison was not self-administered. In other words that the deceased did not commit suicide.

After Dr. Leffman, comes Samuel H. Ashbridge, the Coroner. You will remember, of course, that he did not testify to any facts from his own knowledge. That was not the object in calling him. The Commonwealth was talking a second step in the progress of this case. It had produced the evidence of the finding of a dead man, and that this dead man had been poisoned. It had shown by the aid of Dr. Leffman, and the circumstances of the finding of the body and the post mortem examination, that he was not self poisoned. Now the Commonwealth must proceed to show you, for we can assume nothing, that that dead man was Benjamin F. Pitezel, the man named in this indictment as the subject of this murder. We called Coroner Ashbridge; why? We could not call Alice Pitezel, the child who identified him before the Coroner; we could not call her to prove that that stiff and disfigured corpse, upon which her young eyes gazed at the Potter's field, was the body of her dead father. We could not produce her for that purpose, for the mother had told us that the last she saw of her was her dead body in the morgue in the city of Toronto, in a foreign jurisdiction. No, that piece of evidence the Commonwealth could not produce, but the Commonwealth proceeds formally, and in an orderly manner, to establish to your satisfaction that this body was the body of Benjamin F. Pitezel. Is it not strong proof to take the prisoner's own statement for it? Is it not beginning at a good point to ask the Coroner to identify the prisoner's own affidavit, in which he swore that that was the body of Benjamin F. Pitezel that lay in that upper room? Fortunately for us, for the prisoner was the man who handed it to the Coroner, and so made it evidence against him, we were able to get Alice Pitezel's affidavit on that point, as delivered by him to the Coroner. By Coroner Ashbridge we begin to establish the second point, and take the second important step by proving the identity of this corpse.

But, gentlemen, we did not stop with the two affidavits, one made by this prisoner, and the other by Alice Pitezel. The Commonwealth had abundant evidence, I think, to prove that this was Benjamin F. Pitezel. We determined to do it thoroughly, for we did not know how much of an attack would be made by the defence upon the question of identity. We had no knowledge where the attack might be made, and as this seemed to be one of the points threatened, we marshalled one bit of evidence after another, until there can be no doubt in the mind of anyone about the body of Benjamin F. Pitezel. That it was his body cannot be gainsaid. Let me say to you once more gentlemen, and let it be said so as to set at rest this question forever, the man who was sent from time into eternity in that second-story room at No. 1316 Callowhill Street was Benjamin F. Pitezel, the companion, the friend, the colleague of the prisoner who sits in the dock, and he knows it as well as I, for he identified him to the Coroner, and he took the dead man's little daughter there to swear that it was her father's body.

We next went into the neighborhood; we produced William Moebins, a bar tender in Mr. Richards' saloon. He waited upon Perry, as Pitezel was called while living in Callowhill Street, the Saturday night before his body was found. He had seen him before. He had seen him in there, talking with Mr. Richards, the saloon keeper, and he knew Mr. Perry — Mr. B. F. Perry. Now, of course, it would have done us very little good to have simply stopped there, and proved that this was B. F. Perry, who lived in that house, but we go a step further, and we hand this picture to him, and ask him, "Is this the picture of the man that you knew as B. F. Perry?" (handing to the witness the picture of Pitezel.) He said, "Yes, that is the picture of the man I knew as B. F. Perry." So we established clearly that that man who lived in No. 1316 Callowhill Street as B. F. Perry was B. F. Pitezel.

We called the last witness's employer, the saloon keeper himself, Mr. Richards. Mr. Richards had changed two ten dollar bills for him that day, the Saturday before the murder, the Saturday before this body was found, and he says he knew Benjamin F. Perry. He was asked, "Is that the picture of the man you knew as Benjamin F. Perry?" and he replied, "It is." That is Pitezel's picture. Another witness says Pitezel and Perry are one.

We also called Mr. Hubbard and Mr. Lampen, and they established that this picture was the picture of Perry. Well, now, all that, gentlemen, is persuasive, but it only goes part of the way in establishing the identity of the corpse, for I want to discuss this testimony with you frankly, and as I would with my own self, trying to ascertain only the truth. We prove but a single fact, to wit, that B. F. Perry and B. F. Pitezel are the same. You understand that that proves the identity of one person under these two names, which is corroborative only, of the identity of the body that was found there. But we went further, and now, abandoning for an instant the order of proof, I wish to call your attention to this fact. Not only were these five or six neighbors called to prove that Perry was Pitezel, but we produced the patrol sergeant of police. And here came in a new kind of testimony. The other witnesses had looked on the living man called B. F. Perry, and then they had looked upon this picture, and said, "The man who was living was the same man whose picture you present to us." But Police Sergeant Sauer comes upon the stand, and he is asked the question, "Were you in that room that day? "He says, "Yes." He was asked, "Did you see the man that lay stretched out on the floor? "He says, "Yes, the body was beginning to decompose; it was considerably discolored," and all that. He was asked further, "But are you able to identify that picture?" Why, you remember gentlemen how that man told you he was standing or sitting over there in this court room among the witnesses for the Commonwealth, when he happened to see this picture, as it was handled before you and identified by the witnesses, and subsequently placed by me standing upright on that desk and facing where he sat, and identified it as the likeness of the dead man from that distant point. "Why, that is a picture of the man I saw lying on the floor at No. 1316 Callowhill Street," he stated to you when placed on the witness stand. That is identification. That picture of B. F. Pitezel is the picture of the man who was killed by the use of chloroform poison in No. 1316 Callowhill Street.

But, gentlemen, we did not stop even there in our efforts at identification. Not only has Holmes or Mudgett identified him; not only has Alice Pitezel identified him; not only have these half dozen people said Perry and Pitezel were the same; not only has the police sergeant told you that that picture was the picture of the man who was poisoned; but we go out to the grave itself, and from its dark recesses, we bring forth silent but persuasive testimony on the question of identity. Pieces of the clothing that was around the dead body were taken from it by the Doctor.

Here is a piece of the shirt that this man wore; poor Mrs. Pitezel was called back again to that stand, and you may remember the broken sobs with which she exclaimed, "Oh, that's Benny's shirt that he took with him when he left St. Louis for Philadelphia." That burned fragment is part of the clothing that the wife identifies as that of her husband's, buried with the body, deep down in that dark grave, it comes forth to the living light to proclaim that the body resting there was not the "stiff "gotten from New York, but was the body of Holmes' friend, Benjamin F. Pitezel.

Look at this necktie; the necktie of a poor man. This has been disfigured by being in the grave, for it was taken from his dead body. Mrs. Pitezel said it was Benny's. Dessie, the daughter, comes upon the stand, and tells you a little incident that must have impressed you with its truthfulness. One part of the necktie is better than the rest, you observe, and she says, "I asked papa before he left, one day, if he wouldn't let me take that lower portion to put into a crazy quilt." What more natural than for a girl to do that very thing? That piece of silk that was fresh and clean, because it had been covered by the vest

and the coat when worn and was thus protected and preserved — she wanted to cut off that portion to make up into a crazy quilt, just as girls will do. She says, "That's my father's necktie." Does anyone doubt it?

The trousers were identified in the same way.

> Indianapolis
> July 21/95
>
> Dear old try—
>
> For God's sake don't worry about the boy any more — he is safe and sound, and everything will turn out all OK in the end.
>
> As ever yours
> Jim.
>
> P.S. Don't write any more but just keep cool.

FAC-SIMILE OF LETTER FROM "JIM" TO HOLMES.

So that, gentlemen of the jury, out of the very tomb comes the voice of identification, confirming what all these living witnesses have said, and what the police sergeant has so emphatically said "This is Pitezel." Pitezel's identification is complete.

So the Commonwealth has taken the second step in this trial. It has reached another point of advance. It has proved to your satisfaction that this man was killed by chloroform poison. It has proved, in addition, that the man who was thus killed was Benjamin F. Pitezel, the friend of this prisoner. Before finally leaving the question of identity, I simply, in a word, call your attention to what took place in the Potter's Field; you will remember that the body was exhumed in the presence of Dr. Mattern, Mr. Fouse, Mr. Perry, the prisoner, Jeptha D. Howe, of St. Louis, and Alice Pitezel, whom, the prisoner had taken from her mother, and sent in company with Howe to Philadelphia, and whom he had with him up at No. 1905 N. 11th Street at that boarding house. He had taken her out to the Potter's Field. This body was identified by the marks upon it, the wart upon the back of the neck, the mark across the bone below the knee, the bruised finger, the color of the hair and of the mustache. It was there identified as the body of Pitezel again.

Now after this testimony had been offered, the next witness was Dr. Alcorn. You will recall Mrs. Alcorn; she kept a boarding house at No. 1905 N. 11th Street, at which Holmes boarded with Miss Yoke, under the name of Mr. and Mrs. Howell. She came upon the stand to prove that he was there, and to prove that Miss Yoke was there as Mrs. Howell, as she honestly believed herself to be; to prove the length of time that he was there, from the beginning of August — about the first week in August — down to that fateful second day of September, and to prove that he left this city hurriedly, quickly, on that second day of September 1894, although his wife was sick, and part of the time confined to bed, unable to be up and about — not in a fit condition to take a long journey — yet on that Sunday night, that fateful Sunday night, when this man was killed in No. 1316 Callowhill Street, Holmes in company with his wife practically fled from the city of Philadelphia, and went out to the West. Think of the circumstances under which he left! Not those of an honest man, travelling in the ordinary way. You or I would have said to Mrs. Alcorn, "It's none of your business, Madam, if we did not wish to tell her where we were going"; but that is not the characteristic of this man; wherever a lie could serve the purpose, he preferred it to the truth. But he had a reason for concealing, if possible, where he was going, fearing subsequent inquiry as to what his destination would be, so he told Miss Yoke to say so, and he himself told Mrs. Alcorn, "We are going to Harrisburg," when in point of fact, they were not, but took the 10:25 train for Indianapolis.

Why did he go away hastily? Why did he conceal the place of his destination? Was it because all that transpired on that Sunday in No. 1316 Callowhill Street was haunting him and pursuing him? As lie tells you, he came into Miss Yoke in an excited condition; he helped to pack her trunk; he hastened to catch the 10:25 train, and left Philadelphia leaving a lie behind him at the boarding house, as to where he was going. That was Mrs. Alcorn's testimony.

The next witness called was John Grammar. You will remember that he lived in the same house; that he was one of the boarders in Mrs. Alcorn's house, and he corroborates what she says as to their residence there, and their time of leaving.

Then came three witnesses upon the question of identification. I have already adverted to what their testimony was. One witness procured Perry or Pitezel his boarding house. Mrs. Harley, with whom he boarded, identified his picture. Miss Alice Pierce, who kept the cigar store, testified as to how he came in to buy cigars, identifying him.

We then took up another branch of the case — the insurance conspiracy. Mr. Perry was called. He began to tell the story of the insurance conspiracy; the policy of insurance was identified; a policy issued on the life of B. F. Pitezel; the receipt was also identified, showing the settlement that was made, and how, by reason of this conspiracy, nearly $10,000 were taken out of the treasury of that company. This is only an incident. The insurance matter, except as it plays the part of being the beginning of these occurrences, each connected with the death of Pitezel, and sheds light on the motive of the prisoner, is practically unimportant. The insurance company itself is not a factor in this case. The Commonwealth of Pennsylvania is the prosecutor. The insurance company has nothing whatever to do with it, beyond having been the victim of the conspiracy and having paid its money upon the policy of insurance, on Pitezel's life.

The money was paid. The conspiracy had been successful apparently. Holmes was profiting by the result. Pitezel was dead, and out of the way, and very soon his widow and children were taken on a curious journey, and the effort is made by the prisoner to conceal everything pertaining to the family.

Mr. Gary comes upon the stand, and gives us an inkling as to how the conspiracy was first discovered away out in the St. Louis jail. Hedgepeth, a fellow prisoner with this man, to whom part of the proceeds had been promised, tells the Chief of Police of St. Louis that he and Pitezel and others had perpetrated a fraud upon the insurance company. Gary interviews him. What was said in that interview is not given in evidence to you, but in consequence of that interview, search is made for this man, the prisoner, and an earnest effort was made to find him, only, at that time, because it was supposed that he was guilty of a fraud and a cheat, and that he had succeeded in cheating the insurance company out of money. The search for him led through the States, up into Canada, back into the States again, and finally on to Boston, where he was arrested and brought back to Philadelphia. Then it was that we proved that part of our case to which Mr. Hanscorn, the Deputy Superintendent, from Boston, has testified. Holmes was not arrested in Boston upon this charge of cheating the insurance company, but was arrested upon another charge — that of being a horse thief. He was accused of being a horse thief, who was wanted in Texas. He was wanted in Texas to be dealt with according to their law, upon the information that he was a horse thief. He was arrested in Boston, held there until he voluntarily said to the Chief, fearing the kind of Southern justice that is meted out to horse thieves, for they do not stand in high favor in the South, or among the rural populations, the prisoner bethought himself, "Well, all they have got on me in Philadelphia is the charge of conspiracy, for which I will get two years' imprisonment at the outside; I will be comfortably housed and fed and taken care of, and at the end of two years, I'll get out again, and probably escape this pending accusation down at Fort Worth, Texas," and so — shrewd, skillful fellow that he is, he says to the Chief of Police, "I'll volunteer to go to Philadelphia." It speaks well for the hospitality of our City. He preferred it to Texas. He was willing to go to Philadelphia. It did not need any warrant to bring him here. He was not waiting for any requisition from the Governor of Pennsylvania upon the Governor of Massachusetts, asking for the return of Hermann W. Mudgett, alias H. H. Holmes. These formalities were dispensed with. He said, "I'll go to Philadelphia," and Detective Crawford brought him to Philadelphia. Before he left the city of Boston, he made a statement to Mr. Perry. He confessed the fraud that had been perpetrated upon the insurance company, and voluntarily and of his own free will and accord, told Mr. Perry about this cheat and this fraud. You remember, I am sure, what Mr. Perry related as his statement to him. It was to the effect that himself and Pitezel, and Jeptha Howe, of St. Louis, and Hedgepeth, who was in jail, had joined in a conspiracy to cheat the insurance company, and he said that they had sent to New York to procure a dead body that would look as much like Pitezel as possible, and that they were going to use that dead body, and that they did use it, and that Pitezel himself, you will remember, was living and in South America at that time, and had the boy, little Howard, with him. That is his first story. I want you to listen to these statements. They are marvellous productions in the line of fiction; they are wonderful statements, with scarcely an element of truth in them. The facility with which this man could utter one falsehood after another must be apparent to you in your observation of this testimony, and from the statements that you have heard, not only from the officials, but from the lips of this pure, good woman, whom he called his wife, Miss Yoke. Think of it! Think of it! Think of the deception and the falsehood! Think of his deceit to her I He meets her in St. Louis. He is going to engage her as his wife. He then tells her the story of a fictitious uncle, with his millions, or whatever the estate may have been, and who had requested that he, H. H. Holmes, should take the name of Henry Mansfield Howard, and thenceforth be known as his heir. He enters into one of the most sacred relations in life with deception and deceit upon him. He marries her as Henry Mansfield Howard. Then he goes down to Fort Worth masquerading as Pratt. "Why," said he to this confiding woman, "I have been out to one of the ranches that my uncle left; "— one of those ranches of this fictitious uncle — a fictitious ranch, — "and found squatters down there, and you know the people of the South favor squatters more than the people of the North do; so it wouldn't be safe for me to be known as Mr. Henry Mansfield Howard, the heir of my uncle, and the claimant of this ranch; oh, no!" Then he masquerades as Pratt. In the line of this story, during all his journeys, he never once places his own name upon the register of a hotel, and never once places upon the register the real name of anyone that is with him. Lies supply the place of the truth at every point, and false registry is the order of his journey at every hotel. Upon every step, from point to point, as we go through this evidence, we find Mudgett, alias Holmes, a fabricator and a falsifier.

But this is a digression, so I ask your attention to his statement again. He tells you that a body was substituted. Was there a body substituted? Don't you believe with me that that man (pointing to Pitezel's picture) was the man who was buried in Potter's Field? Don't you think with me that that man was the man whose body was found in that second story room? Lie No. 1. But he says, "B. F. Pitezel is down in South America, and he has little Howard with him." Oh, gentlemen, that is an awful, a frightful statement. What fearful twisting and destruction of the truth! Pitezel in South America! He had seen his body taken up out of the Potter's Field, and made little Alice testify that it was the body of her father — down in South America! It is a wonder that the lie did not scorch his lips, as the flames scorched the dead body of Pitezel and consumed the flesh. Little Howard with his father in South America! Gentlemen, think of it, and then recall in that connection the broken utterances of that poor woman, Mrs. Pitezel, as she was about to leave the stand, when she said, in answer to the question where did you see Howard last? "I last saw little Howard's belongings in the coroner's office in Indianapolis." Little Howard in South America with his father! God help such a liar!

But he is not done yet. I now call attention to his statement to Mr. Hanscom. I am not going to repeat all this statement of his to Mr. Hanscom. I do not want to weary you, but I do feel obliged to go over the testimony at some length in the performance of what I conceive to be a solemn duty. Therefore I ask you patiently to listen to me while I call your attention to a few more of the things which this man has said.

A statement was made by him in Boston, and was taken down at that city. Mr. Hanscom, the police official, who came upon this stand, told you how it was taken by Miss Annie Robbins, a stenographer, word for word. We do not depend upon the frailty of human memory to recall what this man said in this instance. It comes to us with all the strength and power of a written statement, taken down question and answer, just as it transpired in that office in Boston, where he poured out new fabrications for the purpose of misleading and deceiving. He was examined as follows: By Mr. Hanscom:

"Q. What is Pitezel's name?

A. B. F., I think — Benjamin Fuller.

Q. When did you last see him?

A. I can't give you the day I'll leave a blank and fill it in."

Oh, how sly and sharp he is — how skillful in fencing in his answers! Mr. Hanscom says: "State it in your own way. A. Well, I saw him last in Detroit. It was in the neighborhood of three weeks ago, but I can give you the exact date by consulting my wife." The alleged wife who was with him then was Mrs. Howard. She has been on the stand. Did he consult her as to that date, when he had seen Mr. Pitezel alive in the city of Detroit? Did he make any effort to find out the date? Not a single one. Why, gentlemen, no effort was made solely because he knew that Pitezel was then rotting in his grave, and was not in Detroit. He could gain nothing by consulting or questioning this woman. She had not seen him in Detroit. He had never seen him in Detroit; that was a falsehood told to mislead the authorities. He was then asked,

"Do you know where he was stopping in Detroit? "

A. No, I don't know; he had been there several days waiting for me to come there."

Would he not have known where he was stopping? Why did he not name some hotel and thus seem candid in his answer? He was afraid the officers might send to the hotel to find out. He is covering it up.

"Q. When was the last time before that that you saw him?"

A. Well, I had not seen him but once since this Philadelphia occurrence." (Quoting further from the statements made in Boston.)

He told Mr. Hanscom that he had seen Pitezel in Philadelphia, and having procured a corpse in New York, had packed it in a trunk, and that he put that trunk on the express, and had given the check for it to Pitezel. Of course, he made it near the first Sunday in September. He was telling a falsehood for the purpose of misleading the officer, and yet it was with relation to the frauds that he had confessed.

Gentlemen, there is one point in this connection that has always been a subject of thought with me, and I conceive it to be a strong argument against this man and his defence in this case. Will you follow me a moment, while I point it out. Remember that he had confessed to the story about the fraudulent insurance. There was nothing in that to be concealed, because he had confessed that he was guilty. He had cheated this company. He had confessed, and he was going back to go into prison for it. Why, under those circumstances, was it necessary for him to lie? The truth would have been sufficient then. It cannot be said that it was to get the money from the insurance company, for that was already secured, and was in his pockets. It was not for that purpose. Why did he lie? What was his motive? What was he concealing by these falsehoods about Pitezel living? The insurance fraud was exploded; he had confessed his guilt in cheating the company. The money had been received; nothing was to be gained either in the way of money or freedom from imprisonment, for he had admitted his crime, and he was going back to Philadelphia to go to jail. Gentlemen, there is only one thing that explains that falsehood, uttered by the prisoner to Mr. Hanscom. When he said he saw Pitezel alive, he knew that Pitezel was dead, murdered by him. He feared prosecution for that murder. There is no other explanation — no other reason. The cheating of the insurance company had been confessed; the money secured upon the policy had been divided, yet he lied about Pitezel and about the children. To Perry, he said, "Pitezel is in South America, and Howard is with him." To Mr. Hanscom, he said, "Pitezel was in Detroit three weeks ago," and then subsequently he said, "I saw him in Cincinnati." Then he tells about the use of a dead body. That it was not Pitezel, but merely some corpse that was used to stand for his body, and goes through the long story of the cheat and fraud upon the insurance company, with which you are familiar and with which I will not now weary you.

While we were on the line of proving these confessions of his, we proved another, which was taken after he came to Philadelphia. The first confession was simply taken by question and answer. This one is in a more solemn form. We now come to an oath bound statement. I wonder if, when he has taken the solemn obligation of an oath, he will tell the truth. I wonder if now, when he is sworn, he will tell us really what has taken place; let us see. Being first duly sworn, he says, "That while incarcerated in jail in St. Louis, Missouri, he met one Hedgepeth." — Well, then, it was true that Hedgepeth was with this man out in the St. Louis jail, and was his companion in the conspiracy — "who said that for $400, he could secure his release from imprisonment." (Quoting further therefrom.)

Think of the audacity of the man, afterwards, in Mr. Fouse's office, after these occurrences that he is speaking about, but before this confession was made. After the insurance was claimed by Jeptha D. Howe. When Jeptha D. Howe came into the office, Mr. Holmes was announced. Mr. Holmes was in waiting outside. Mr. Holmes walked in. Mr. Howe was sitting there. He pretended he did not know Mr. Howe — not he. Another deception; another fraud! He does not know Mr. Howe! Mr. Fouse has to turn and say, "Why, Mr. Howe, let me present Mr. Holmes," and Mr. Holmes bows and shakes hands with Mr. Howe, and makes a new acquaintance. Think of it, and remember he has known him out there in St. Louis for some time. Howe had been sent for by

Hedgepeth, and as Miss Yoke said, was brought to the jail to act as this prisoner's counsel, and saw him in the jail and talked with him in the jail. Oh, how deceit and deception and fraud run all through every statement, from beginning to end!

Then he goes on telling about the relation of Howe to the conspiracy; that Howe was in it How he got word while in Philadelphia, that they had a body which could not be used, and that he sent to New York and got another body which had a small wart on the neck; that he then concluded not to take any more chances to carry out the scheme, and that he brought that body to Philadelphia and left it in the care of Pitezel. This "stiff" that he procured in New York, and brought to Philadelphia, he left with Pitezel, who was to carry out the details of the scheme at that place. He then left Philadelphia at 10:30, in company with his wife, and she was taken sick, as lie says. But no, that is not true for she was sick when he took her away. The truth is that he hurried her away while she was sick. Then he stopped off at Indianapolis, and stayed there one night, reaching St. Louis on Tuesday night, when he went directly to the office of McDonald & Howe; that he afterwards went to Pitezel's house, in St. Louis, and found his wife and children very much excited about the news which they had seen in the paper; that he then went about 9 o'clock the next morning to Howe's office, and asked him to help out in the matter, etc. He then goes on with the story of the identification, and tells the story of the fraud. He then tells about the meeting in St. Louis, when they met to divide the plunder at McDonald & Howe's office. Mrs. Pitezel was there present. The spoils were divided; Mrs. Pitezel got her little share out of the proceeds of the money from her husband's death. Ten thousand dollars were paid, but how much of it went to poor Mrs. Pitezel? She was a party to the conspiracy, as they say, but she was in the hands of a sharper. Five thousand dollars were taken on one pretext, and with reference to how it was taken, departing again, slightly, from the order of testimony, I ask that you will remember Mrs. Pitezel's testimony on that subject. She tells you that Holmes said, "Now, we'll go to the bank and pay a note there that your husband owes," and he took her to the bank. They went inside, and there

Holmes obtains from this woman, out of her satchel, $15,000. He then walks around in the bank to another window, and pretends to be paying this note. I say "pretends," because the evidence in this case shows conclusively the falsity and deception of the man beyond question, and that he was literally and absolutely deceiving her in what he said and did. Fortunately, we have this note. Here it is, and we have also a picture of it, which we can handle with more safety. You will notice that the note is for $16,000, dated May 16th, 1894, and due September 16th, 1894, drawn to the order of Mr. Samuels. You will notice on the original note that it bears no endorsement. Mr. Samuels never endorsed that note. You can see, therefore, that it was not negotiable. It could not pass from one man to another. That simply says that Mr. Lyman owes Mr. Samuels this money. If it had been deposited in Lank for collection, upon the back would have been found the words "deposited for collection," and the signature of Mr. Samuels, and his signature would have given the bank the right to collect it. But no, this note has never been negotiated. In point of fact, no note was at that bank. There was nothing to be paid there, and a fraud was being perpetrated upon Mrs. Pitezel.

But if we had any doubt before, I am sure that doubt is absolutely removed when we hear Mr. Samuels on the stand. You remember him, the lawyer from Fort Worth — his clear-cut, plain, and frank answers. He had no trouble in telling you the story of that false note. "Why," says he, "the body of that note is in my handwriting, I filled that in for this man," or "for that individual there," for that is the way he designated him, if you may remember "I filled it in for that individual; he came to negotiate a loan from my brother; the note was drawn for $16,000, and he took the note away to get it signed by his partner, Benton F. Lyman," that being the name used by Pitezel. He was to take the note away and get Pitezel to sign it, and then bring it back. What did he do? He came back to Mr. Samuels, and he said, "Oh, I mislaid that note or lost it; I don't know where it is, but I have had this new note made to take its place," and the new note is handed over to Mr. Samuels, and upon it he loans this man $2,500, and that new note — that real note is in the hands of these gentlemen in Fort Worth, Texas, and this dead man stands debtor to them upon it to-day, unpaid, uncancelled, while this note written by Mr. Samuels in his own handwriting is fraudulently concealed by Holmes, and fraudulently produced to Mrs. Pitezel as if it were a living debt, though it is nothing more than a piece of paper, and does not stand for a single dollar. So the story goes. The money is divided and Holmes gets this $5,000. He has made his profit by the transaction. He is the man who received the proceeds from the insurance on the life of Pitezel, and he starts away.

Then comes the story of Mrs. Pitezel. Gentlemen, you remember that story; I am not going to weary you by its repetition. In all the fifteen years of my service in this office, I do not remember a story that stirred my heart or moved my sensibilities like the broken sentences of that woman, when, with evident suffering in every line and mark upon her face, in the supreme effort that she made to control herself, and to avoid breaking down, she told that pitiful, yet marvellous story, of how this man led her from place to place in the pursuit of her husband. I do not see, for the life of me, how he could sit there in the dock unmoved and look her in the face, conscious, as lie must be, of the awful wrong that he has perpetrated upon her — how he could sit there and look her in the face, and listen to the harrowing tale of suffering and agony, without wincing, without changing a muscle — he is a man of steel with a heart of stone, and remains utterly unmoved.

Gentlemen, there was once during the course of this trial that tears seemed to come to his eyes, and he appeared to be moved when Miss Yoke came upon the witness stand the first day. But it was a subject of such universal comment that you must have noticed it as well as I, and others that when she was recalled to the stand the second day, no tear dimmed his eye. The questions of his lawyers showed that the tears of the first day were summoned to influence her, to excite her pity for him so that in telling her story she might be induced to favor him. But on the second day, when his lawyer's shafts were dipped in malice, and question upon question was thrust at her regardless of how they placed her before the world or the community, he sat as stony, as immovable, as when Mrs. Pitezel told her pitiful story from the witness box.

That was a strange story, gentlemen; if you and I had read it in fiction, we would say perhaps that the novelist had overdrawn or overstated the facts; that he had overdrawn the story, and made it stronger than our imagination or fancy could tolerate.

Now, let us return to that story. After Alice was taken to Philadelphia to identify the father, she was taken back to Indianapolis. He went to St. Louis, and saw the mother, and took from her the other two children. There are now three children started upon the journey in one group. In a few days, he starts the mother upon her travels, and with her are Dessa and the baby, forming a second group. In a little while after that, Miss Yoke proceeds with him. They are travelling in three detachments, each utterly ignorant of the location and proximity of the other. Mrs. Pitezel does not know where the three children are located: Miss Yoke does not know that Mrs. Pitezel is travelling with Dessa and the baby, and that the three children are also under his control. Another exhibition of the marvellous ingenuity, craft, cunning, and power of this man. Travelling in three separate detachments, and in the city of Detroit, stopping within a few blocks of each other. The hotels have been named at which they stopped, within a few blocks,— the mother yearning to see her children, and yet ignorant of their whereabouts, and kept from communicating with them; the children pleading to communicate with their mother, and yet, kept from communication with her; within four blocks of each other in the same city, and kept apart. Poor Mrs. Pitezel! The will o'the wisp, the hope of meeting Benny, held out, and held out to her day after day! "Oh," said he, "Benny will be in Detroit." She is at Galva, Illinois, with her parents. He tells her to come in the middle of the week, but no, her eagerness to meet her husband prompts her to start early, and she leaves for Detroit from her home on the 13th of October. "Where is Ben?" "Well, we'll find Ben in Toronto." They go to Toronto. You remember the days they spent there. "Oh, he'll come over here and see you when I get a house; he wanted to come and see you without the children being present; it'll never do to permit the children to know that lie is living; he can't show himself in the presence of the children." That is Holmes' story. Gentlemen, right in that connection, let me call your attention to something he said to Mr. Hanscom. In that statement to Mr. Hanscom, he tells this remarkable story. Said he, "Pitezel was in Detroit, and of course I was keeping him out of the sight of the children, but one day he got to drinking while in Detroit, and before I knew it, he walked right in to the children, where the three children were, and they all saw him, and they all knew him, and he was there with the children, and I permitted him then to take the children away with him." That is what he told Hanscom. Let us now see how that fits with what he told Mrs. Pitezel. "Oh," says he to Mrs. Pitezel, "wait until I get a house; it will never do to have Mr. Pitezel come and visit you, and have your children see him." Why he told Hanscom that he had called on those three children in. that hotel in Detroit, and that the children knew all about his being alive. — "Oh, wait until I can get a house for you, and then with the children away, he can come into the house and see you, and the children will not know it." A man has to be a good liar, with a strong memory if he wants to make all the stories that he tells fit each other. His story told to Hanscom is vitally different from his story told to Mrs. Pitezel. Poor Mrs. Pitezel, however, was lured on and on and on, and finally is taken to Prescott, in Canada, thence to Ogdensburg, New York; thence to Burlington, Vermont, and at last to Boston to be arrested. He brings her to Boston to be arrested. What talent he displays! Here are the three detachments travelling separately, each kept in ignorance of the existence of the others, with this prisoner the postmaster for Mrs. Pitezel and the children; with orders to collect her letters at every post-office upon their route; this postmaster for these innocent little children, who wanted to write letters to Dear Mamma — every letter intercepted, and those letters found in his tin box, identified in broken sentences by Mrs. Pitezel on the witness stand when she exclaimed in anguish; "Oh, that's Alice's" ; "That's Nellie's" ; "That was done by Alice" ; "That's my letter." Was ever power over a family more complete than this man's power over these people? Every letter intercepted — no communication between them. Not one syllable from child to mother; not one syllable from mother to child. Did I speak wrongfully, gentlemen, or was I cruel in making the statement when I said that this man was a man of steel, with a heart of stone? Anyone that would take these children's letters addressed to their mother, and hide and conceal them, may justly be charged with being heartless, and with being cruel beyond comparison. He is the jailor of the family. He suppresses and destroys their mail. No, lie does not destroy it; for in almost every case of villainy, and criminality, somehow or other, whether it be Providential for the detection and punishment of the rascal or not, I cannot tell, but somehow the villain overreaches himself in his efforts at concealment, and here and there a telltale fact comes to light and points the unerring finger of accusation at him, saying "That's the guilty man." Yes, this is a marvellous story, and the conclusion of it is not less marvellous than the rest.

Mrs. Pitezel and Dessa have appeared before you. Mrs. Pitezel was asked, "When did you see those children again?" and her heartrending answer some of us may remember for many, many years to come; it was pitiful, it was infinitely sad coming from a heart broken with grief — "Oh, I didn't see them again until I saw Alice and Nellie in the morgue in Toronto, and the last belongings of little Howard in the Coroner's office in Indianapolis." What a tale of horror and of woe is unfolded in that harrowing sentence. How this woman's pitiable plight should have moved every man of us to treat her with the utmost consideration and kindness, yet I say to you, gentlemen, that my blood boiled with indignation yesterday when counsel, with mistaken zeal, attempted to harrow up that poor woman's soul, and attempted to press her with questions under disguise, for the purpose of making her appear a party to the conspiracy in this case. Why, of course, she knew what her husband was going to do; she was particeps criminis to the extent that she concealed that fact to protect her husband, and that is all that they can charge against her. The counsel for the prisoner was compelled to probe with questions, and he said, "Weren't you arrested in Boston?" "Weren't you brought back under arrest?" "Weren't you put in the county prison?" "Weren't you indicted for conspiracy?" In the name of justice, has there not been enough done? Yes, they think this is necessary. One more burden must be added. This man wants to make her appear to have been as black as he in the conspiracy. That was the object — to argue against her credibility — to make her appear to be a co-conspirator with him, and therefore not worthy of belief. But every step of that journey was corroborated practically by Dessa; everything that occurred in it was corroborated by her. Think of the cipher letters that he prepared! What a disingenuous, uncandid, and villainous man it is who would prepare a cipher letter to bring into that mother's presence, and read to her as if coming from her little children. Those children whose voices she could never hear again were to be misrepresented by that cipher letter as if speaking to her. Think also of the other cipher letter, purporting to have come from her husband. Well might they be in cipher! Well might he attempt to disguise them in some form, pretending that one came from the children, (then dead,) and that one came from Benjamin F. Pitezel, (who was mouldering in his grave,) telling her of his whereabouts in Montreal. Was there ever a case of more wicked and inexcusable deceit than this? Why did he adopt all this duplicity? Why was he guilty of all this subterfuge? Why was it that he deceived everybody with these stories? Gentlemen, there is but one answer, and it is that in the room on the second story of No. 1316 Callowhill Street, he took the life of Benjamin F. Pitezel. Now why do I say that? I say it because this evidence shows it, and I am going to demonstrate to you that fact out of this testimony — demonstrate to you the fact that this man did destroy Benjamin Pitezel in No. 1316 Callowhill Street. He was telling these malicious lies to cover up a horrible murder. In the first place, there is no doubt that it was Pitezel, whose body was found as described. There is no doubt that he came to his death from chloroform poisoning. That is an unquestioned, uncontradicted fact in this case. There is no doubt that he was seen alive up until about ten o'clock on Saturday night, out buying his whiskey to take his drink — buying his cigars at the cigar store to smoke. He had written to his wife a few days before that he expected to go home and see her, and he had told her that if he could succeed, he was going to bring her and the children on to Philadelphia.

Nothing in the whole case, from beginning to end, to indicate a suicidal intent or purpose on his part — not a particle of evidence produced for the purpose of showing that he ever attempted to commit suicide. Not one word from the wife; not one word from his letters; not one word from his neighbors, but what indicated a hopeful outlook on the future — a building up of plans a« to what he was going to do in that future. He says, "I am going to visit St. Louis; but if I can succeed in establishing a business here, I'm going to bring you and the children on to Philadelphia." That was the outlook of the man. He was buying his whiskey; — he was a free drinker; he was buying his cigars; he was a smoker, laying in a stock for that Sunday — not laying in death for himself — he was going to live; he was going to drink his whiskey, and since he could not, under the Excise laws, get it on Sunday, he was laying in a stock on the Saturday night before, so that everything indicated a purpose of life, and not a purpose of suicide.

Now, then, we see him alive and well, and apparently all right at that time. There is no doubt, gentlemen, in this case, for it is proved out of this man's own lips, (pointing to the prisoner) and out of the lips of Miss Yoke, that on that fateful Sunday, he, the prisoner, spent the greater part of the day at No. 1316 Callowhill Street; in other words the day that Pitezel was done to death, Holmes was in that house; he is fixed in that house by his own statements made more than once, and by the testimony of his alleged wife, Miss Yoke. Remember that what she says is very significant.

" Somebody came on Saturday night to his house, and sent a message upstairs; the man, whoever it was, would not come upstairs, so Holmes went down to see him, and came back and told her"— and there again comes in the old deception — "it is a man from the Pennsylvania Railroad Company, with whom I am about to close a deal, and I am going out to Nicetown tomorrow to see him." This was not true for afterwards in Philadelphia, he told Miss Yoke that the man who called on that Saturday night was Benjamin F. Pitezel. Benjamin F. Pitezel called on that Saturday night. The man with whom he had an engagement the next day was Benjamin F. Pitezel; and I asked Miss Yoke the question whether Holmes was at home the next day. The answer was: "No, he went out about ten or half past ten in the morning, and did not come back until the afternoon, about half past three or four o'clock." All of those intervening hours he spent in No. 1316 Callowhill Street, on the day of the murder. Here, then, we find Pitezel was alive and well on Saturday night, at Ox about ten o'clock. His body is found on Tuesday morning in a state indicating that he had been dead fur probably two days. On Monday, no living person was about there; Smith came in on Tuesday and found the deceased. On Sunday, Pitezel was killed; on Sunday Holmes was in the house with him; on Sunday he spent several hours in that house. He is the man who was present when Pitezel died. Benjamin F. Pitezel and Herman H. Mudgett, in No. 1316 Callowhill Street met on that Sunday. Now we can understand why he tells these stories about Pitezel being alive. If this was a substituted corpse, then he cannot be convicted of murder. He has confessed the insurance fraud. He has got the money for the insurance. No motive or inducement to lie on that account; but because back of that is the crime of murder, therefore he denies these stories, explaining that Pitezel lives, and that a substituted body has been put in that place, and he tells you himself that he was there. He tells you, by his questions to the witnesses on the stand, that he was there. You remember what he said to Miss Yoke. He did it with one purpose, but I argue to you a totally different effect. He said, "Miss Yoke, did you notice my appearance when I came in on that Sunday afternoon, between half past three and four?" She said "Yes." He asked, "Wasn't I excited?" Now this man, with his story of Pitezel's suicide discovered by him, wants to make us believe that he came in excited, because of that discovery, but I will tell you the secret of his excitement. Miss Yoke said to him, " No, you looked worried, and you were hot," Why, of course, lie was worried, and had reason to be worried, because those hours were spent in doing a fellow-being to death — worried — yes. It was worriment that made him start for the West that night with his wife; it was fear that made him get away from this city before the body was discovered. He had cause to be worried that night; there is no doubt of that. He was excited. I suppose such a thing would make him excited. I do not know of much else that would. You have seen him; you have a right to observe him, not only as he sits here now, but as he stood there and conducted his own case. You observed him as he addressed physicians, as a physician, a skillful man, addressing them upon scientific subjects. You observed him, the man whose very life is at stake, in this awful ordeal, displaying more calmness than even I could, conducting the examination of the witnesses, one after the other, and manifesting an absolute want of all fear, nervousness, or fright. Yet I think there is one thing that would make him nervous; I think there is one thing that would make him worried, and that was what took place at No. 1316 Callowhill Street on that day, not the discovery of a suicide, but the recollection of a murder.

Now let us consider all his stories of what took place there. We have put in evidence his confession or statement to Captain Linden. Months have elapsed since the murder before this statement is made. These stories that he has told about the substitute body — about Pitezel living and the children have been discounted and disbelieved; everybody who has come in contact with him has told him that they did not believe them. He thinks it is necessary to frame a new story, as he sits down in Moyamensing Prison, with nothing else to do but to coin narratives to exculpate himself. He fashions a new statement which is to be palmed off upon the authorities, and upon the public. Now, what is that statement? That statement admits that it is Pitezel who is dead; no longer are we sent roaming into South America, or off to Detroit or up to Montreal, in Canada, to find Pitezel. He now admits that Pitezel is dead, and that this was Pitezel. It has become evident that the story of a substituted corpse has been so much discredited and is so generally disbelieved that it is now necessary to bow to the inevitable and admit the body to be that of Pitezel. "Oh," he says, "but I did not kill him; he died from suicide." This man who was out the night before, apparently happy, and making provision for his comfort for the next day, not intending to die, but intending to live, and intending to have some of those things that he considered necessary for his comfort the next day — Holmes claims has committed suicide — that this man who was writing to his wife, "I am coming out to see you, and if I can make arrangements to conduct business in Philadelphia, I am going to bring you and the children and the baby "— and that baby seemed to be very dear to him — "I am going to bring you to Philadelphia, and we'll live here" — this man, Holmes says, committed suicide. All the surroundings in this case deny that he thought of suicide; the evidence springing from the finding of the body denies that he committed suicide, and the story that Holmes tells of how the suicide which lie alleges was committed is absolutely impossible and is rebutted by the testimony in this case, and I will show you, I believe, as clearly as mathematical demonstration, that Pitezel was not self-destroyed, but that he was destroyed by a second person in that house, and in that room. Why do I say that? I say it because the evidence warrants it. Holmes tells you that when he went in there, and I want to direct your attention specially to this remarkable story — "When I went into that room, I found Pitezel lying on the floor dead." Then lie constructs a remarkable story telling of a wonderful arrangement, all coined in the mint of his own fancy, intended to explain how Pitezel had committed suicide, which you can readily see is worthy of his keen mind and thought, and which never came from the mind, or from the thought of Pitezel, — an ignorant man, as he calls him in one of his confessions. Why, up there on the till id floor, he says, Pitezel had arranged a mechanical contrivance that would do justice to the ingenuity of a Holmes — to the skill of a Mudgett. On a chair, according to his story, is a gallon bottle — a bottle that would hold a gallon of chloroform — an enormous quantity — put on a chair; underneath the bottle on the seat of the chair on each side is a block holding up the bottom of the bottle so that as the bottle reclines on the chair, the bottom is higher than the neck. There is carefully inserted through the cork, which cork is fastened tightly into the mouth of the bottle, — a quill, and then over the quill is fixed a rubber tube, which leads down from the chair, down to a towel that is spread over the face of the deceased, the rubber tube, using his own language, being "constricted at the center." The tube was tied at the center so as to prevent the fluid from flowing rapidly down, and he says that, in that condition, this man came to his death. That he found him there — that he found him there in that third-story room, and that he took those things away from this man, and took this man himself — this slight, slim built, thin man, Holmes, took Pitezel, weighing 175 or 180 pounds, who must have been then a stiff, rigid corpse, and dragged him—he did not attempt to carry him across — but dragged him down the stairs from the third-story room to the second-story room, and there placed him in the position of repose in which he was found lying, and he tells you that that condition of repose in which he was found on the second-story floor was precisely the same as that in which he was found on the third-story floor, describing him in precisely the same position down there.

Was he describing a real scene or a fancied one? Where is that gallon bottle? Where is that tube? Where is any part of this strange suicidal device! Nothing of it found, not a trace of it anywhere. Why has it so mysteriously disappeared? Gentlemen, it never had an existence except in the fabricated story of this prisoner. The first question I ask is why, in the name of common sense, did he not leave him on the third-story floor? What necessity was there for bringing him down to the second-story? Could he not just as well have burned and disfigured him up there on the third-story floor, as he could on the second-story, and would not his deception have been as successfully practiced on the third floor as on the second floor?

Gentlemen, that body was never on the third-story floor. The relaxation of the involuntary muscles, and the involuntary discharges from the person took place at or immediately before dissolution. These discharges were found on the second-story floor, not on the third-story floor, clearly indicating that death took place where the body was found. This is a very significant fact.

The next thing to which I ask your attention is this. When that body was found down on the second-story floor, it was in perfect order. The perfect order in which everything was showed that it had never been dragged down those stairs by a second person. The clothing was not disarranged. Dr. Scott is careful to tell you that the shirt and underwear were carefully tucked down into the trousers, with everything in their perfect place, just as a man would fix himself, and just as no one else could do it for him, and anybody who knows anything about the preparation of a corpse for burial, will readily understand why. A corpse is not dressed in clothing, as a rule, but covered, because of the difficulty of dressing the corpse, and a second person not being able to adjust the clothing in nice order all over the person. This man's body showed that he had never been dragged down those stairs. It was not disordered.

Now gentlemen, unless he had found him before rigor mortis set in — that is, the stiffening of the corpse — he could not have fixed him in that position on the second floor; he could not have done it; it would have been perfectly impossible for him. Yet the very period that he fixes — the very time that he fixes as the time of his visit to that place — is after that corpse is stiff and cold; after it is dead and rigor mortis has set in.

I now ask your attention to another thing. He said that the body was lying upon its back and flat. I wish one of you would try, when you go to your room — I do not want to do it here, for it might appear like an effort after theatrical effect — to lie down upon the flat of your back, with your head on the floor, and the head turned to one side, and see whether any fluid, in order to go through that tube called the oesophagus, into the stomach, would not have to run up hill. Put yourself in that position, and see if it is not so. According to the prisoner's story the chloroform passed from the bottle down the tube to the towel, thence into the mouth and then into the stomach. Gentlemen that chloroform did not run up hill.

Now, the prisoner must account for this fluid or chloroform in the stomach. Do you remember what Detective Geyer said he told him? He said he told him that, as part of what lie had informed Pitezel to do — he had told Pitezel to take this stiff, as they called it — this dead body that was to be substituted and to put chloroform in its stomach. He said to put it in the mouth of the dead corpse, and then work the body like a bellows, so as to force it down into the stomach. That is what he said. And I argue to you that that is the way he passed the chloroform into Pitezel's stomach. This man who told Pitezel how to do it knew how to do it himself, and the chloroform which was found in that body, that had never irritated the walls and surface or lining of the stomach, was put in there after death, and the testimony of two physicians positively shows that it never flowed into that stomach, as Holmes says.

Now let me call your attention to another point. In his questions to Dr. Leffman, and to Dr. Scott, he tried to create the impression that if this bottle was eighth-tenths full, would not chloroform flow down that pipe, and on to the towel, into the man's throat, filling up the throat and forcing itself through into the stomach. Now there are two difficulties about that theory that he did not anticipate, and I could see when Dr. Leffman made his answer to him, what the effect was. It was like a stunning blow in the face. When Dr. Leffman answered him, "Why," said he, "it couldn't flow hardly faster than it would evaporate in the condition in which you put it." Now think of that. Here is a bottle corked tightly, a quill drawn through the cork, a pipe leading from that quill down to the towel; not one particle of air can get into that bottle, and unless the air can get into the bottle, the fluid will not flow out. The fluid will not flow faster than the air can pass it in the passage way of that pipe, and that pipe was tied in the center so as to constrict it. You and I have seen it illustrated. When a barrel of liquid of any kind is opened, they knock the bung out in the top or bore a hole through to let the air in, or the contents will not flow out freely at the spigot. They bore a hole in a barrel, when they put the spigot in, so that the air may get in and cause the liquid to flow out. Dr. Leffman says, in speaking of this, "It would not flow out faster than it would evaporate." Gentlemen, if it would not flow out faster than it would evaporate, how in the name of common sense could it collect in the throat in such quantity that it would force itself down into the stomach after death? Again, another difficulty. The Doctor has said to you, and that is uncontradicted here, that a dead oesophagus will not pass any liquid. With the beginning of every act of swallowing, there is a voluntary act on your part. The will transfers food beyond the point of the tongue, and you start it upon its way down to the stomach. After that, it is involuntary, by the closing of the oesophagus behind, and the opening of it in front, pressing the food down to its place. A dead oesophagus or a dead tube leading to the stomach will not pass any liquid in that way. There must be artificial aid, or there must be a second person. A second person standing in his position could do it. He would take the body and make a bellows of it, and create a vacuum, and draw the liquid down. That is what he would do, and that is what he did do. But the dead oesophagus is another difficulty in the way of his story.

Now gentlemen, you are to try this case according to the evidence — not according to anything else, but according to the evidence. It is the duty of the Commonwealth of Pennsylvania to make out this case beyond a reasonable doubt. It is to be decided according to the evidence that you have heard, the testimony that is before you, and the only testimony before you is the testimony of these witnesses to whom I have referred. It is from their testimony, standing uncontradicted, that this man's fate must be determined.

Let me now read you a few important answers from Dr. Leffman's testimony. This is very important, and it is testimony to which I ask your careful attention. He testified as follows:

" Q. You are a graduate of what school?

A Jefferson Medical College.

Q. Are you an analytical chemist?

A. Yes, sir.

Q. You have taught chemistry, I believe?

A. Yes, sir.

Q. You are a professor of that branch?

A. Yes, sir.

Q. Are you connected with any institutions? (He then goes on and tells what institutions he is connected with.)

" Q. Are you familiar with the effects and use of chloroform?

A. I have seen chloroform administered a great many times in the course of my attendance in college, and I have administered it a great many times to small animals. I have never seen a death from chloroform in my experience.

Q. What are the immediate effects of the inhalation of chloroform?

A. The first effect of the inhalation of chloroform is some excitement and stimulation, which varies a great deal in different individuals, and also varies with regard to the administrator. Expert operators can administer chloroform so as to produce very little disturbance. It is not exactly a spasmodic condition; it is rather one of intoxicating excitement, which is soon followed by a condition of relaxation and insensibility. In animals the effect is usually violent, in the nature of a fright, but the effect soon becomes that of insensibility."

So that the tendency of a person under the influence of chloroform would be to move restlessly, there being an inclination to motion, and a man could not compose himself and lie down, saying, "I will put this towel over my face, and I'll have this tube come down and feed the towel with chloroform, and I'll just go to sleep." He couldn't do it. It is physically impossible for him to do so. There would be a spasm; there would be contortion; there would be motion of the body that would displace that pre-arranged condition. And why? Because he cannot control himself in approaching unconsciousness. I think a man at the beginning might say, "I'll do this," yet the chloroform takes away his thought and his reason, so that he is unable to do it, and becomes unconscious in the very act of struggling. If any of you gentlemen have ever taken any anesthetic preparatory to having a tooth extracted, you may remember that while you breathed the gas, you found it grew harder, and that suddenly, with a gasp and a struggle, you passed into unconsciousness. Well, you could not arrange yourself after that, because the next thing you know is when the dentist taps you on the chin or on the head, and says, "Sit up; it's all right." You have been unconscious all that time, absolutely ignorant of what was done to you, with no power to place yourself in any position. Now Dr. Leffman was further examined:

"Q. Is there any struggle before insensibility takes place?

A. There very often is a struggle by the patient being apparently not exactly aware of the character of the struggle. It is rather an involuntary struggle, or at least, a semi-conscious condition.

Q. An effort of nature, is it not, to resist the effects?

A. To resist the effects. Also it is probably connected with the direct intoxicating effect of the drug.

Q. The description given us in this case by those who found the body describe it as being found lying upon the back with one arm placed thus (indicating) across the body, the right arm, and the left arm close to the side, the feet stretched out, heels together, in a composed condition, lying on the back. I want to ask you whether or not it is possible for a man to administer chloroform to himself and then compose himself into such a position as that?

A. I think not."

Now this is the only testimony you have on that subject, and his answer is, "I think not." That is his opinion as an expert — that it cannot be done.

" Q. Why?

A. No one is aware of the time when consciousness ceases. Judging from my own experience, I have been four times under the influence of anesthetics, there is a condition of confusion before true insensibility comes on, and it would be, I think, impossible for anyone to arrange the body in a perfectly composed condition like that entirely by the person's own act. It would not, I think, be a natural position into which the body would come by a person administering chloroform to himself."

A man would be apt, if he had had it put to his lace, to have fallen forward on the floor, or caused a struggle, and have thrown down and displaced that tube. He could not have been found as this man describes him, in that composed condition, if the chloroform was self-administered. Dr. Leffman said that it could be administered in sleep without awaking a person. This man Holmes did not have to ring the doorbell to enter this house. He had a key. The testimony has shown you that, and he could enter it when he pleased. If the man happened to be in a drunken sleep, if he had a pint of whiskey, and was in an intoxicated sleep, then how easy the task to administer chloroform to him, and then compose him, while the body was still fresh and warm, and put him in this position — how easily that could be done! Holmes could enter with his key; he had access to the house — access to the man — knowledge of the condition around the house — ability to use the chloroform — everything in his favor; it was no trouble to him.

Dr. Leffman was further examined as follows;

" Q. Is chloroform easy to swallow?

A. It is rather objectionable; the taste. It is an irritable substance, and its taste is of a disagreeable sweet character, so that it is even difficult for persons to swallow it in small amounts."

He illustrated by a few drops in water.

This question was then put to him:

" Q. If a person was lying on his back, flat on the floor, with a tube leading from a bottle containing chloroform to the mouth, could there be any of that pass into the stomach in that position? "

Now this is the testimony of a competent expert on the subject, a man of keen, clear judgment; it is the uncontradicted testimony in the case, and there has been no effort to contradict it — not one word said against it by anybody. It is the absolutely uncontradicted testimony, and counsel accepted it on the other side as a true statement. The answer was:

"A. If it ran into the mouth in considerable quantity it would produce a choking effect which would cause the prisoner to move about and disturb the condition. I do not think it could flow quietly without disturbing the individual, from the tube down into the stomach.

Q. State whether or not the direction would be rather up hill than down hill, to flow into the stomach through the oesophagus?

A. Yes, sir.

Q. If lying on the back, it would have to flow uphill?

A. Rather up hill, a little higher level.

Q. How about the bronch and the lung cavity connecting with it in that position?

A. They are always distended. The bronch are stiff walled and there would be some possibility of the chloroform, probably of some of it getting into the bronch. It is a volatile vapor, and some of the vapor would pass in there also. At the temperature of the body it is decidedly volatile.

Q. The absence of chloroform in the bronch would indicate what, under those circumstances?"

You will remember that there was none found in the bronch. His answer was:

"A. It would indicate that there was no very great quantity in the mouth."

So that the physical conditions in this dead man's case deny the prisoner's theory. His theory and his story is that it flowed down in such quantities that it forced itself down into the stomach, but none was found in the bronch; none was found to have penetrated there, and I said to him,

"Doctor, What does the absence of it there indicate?"

He said,

"It indicates that there was never very much in the mouth."

There could not have been. Therefore, there was not this quantity that would have forced it into the stomach, and the very physical condition of this corpse denies the story of the other side, that was artfully palmed off upon the officials, to explain the death of Benjamin F. Pitezel.

Dr. Leffman further testified:

" Q. Could the chloroform pass a dead oesophagus without outside aid of a living person?

A. I think not. The oesophagus is collapsed in its active condition, and I do not think a dead oesophagus could swallow any appreciable amount of chloroform.

Q. Explain to the jury what the oesophagus is?

A. It is the tube leading from the mouth to the stomach. It is the tube through which the food passes. It is a muscular tube which the food is passed down by a sort of contraction, the tube contracting after the food and expanding before it, so that the food is quickly passed on into the stomach. The bronch, or trachea, which are the bronchial divisions of trachea, are the tubes leading to the lungs. They are stiff walled, always open, and rather larger than the oesophagus. At the upper part, at least. They divide and sub-divide, becoming very small, penetrating all parts of the lungs.

Q. Does or does not the act of swallowing require an effort of the will?

A. It requires an effort of certain muscles. Not exactly of the will.

Q. A voluntary act?

A. It requires 'the act of certain muscles, of living tissue. It is really involuntary in the sense that when the food once starts we cannot control it. After it starts we cannot control it. The first part of the act is voluntary, but back of the back part of the tongue the food goes without our control. It requires the action of living tissue. It is a reflex effect; that is, it requires an irritation of the surface of the mouth and swallowing tube, which is returned by a nerve current back to the muscles that perform the act.

Q. Would there be any effect upon the lining of the stomach visible in a post mortem examination due to the taking of chloroform in the stomach in life?

A. I would expect to see the stomach irritated — the lining membrane irritated as by an ordinary irritant.

Q. Would the absence of that irritation indicate that the chloroform had been inserted in life or after death?

A. The absence of the irritation would indicate that the chloroform had not been in the stomach long enough to produce any of its effects. It would indicate at least an introduction of the chloroform very near to death.

Q. After death would it produce an irritation?

A. It would produce no irritation after death.

Q. So that if it were inserted after death, you would not find the irritation?

A. No, sir."

Now both doctors are positive that an examination upon the post mortem disclosed no irritation of the walls of the stomach due to chloroform.

Q. So that if it were inserted after death, you would not find the irritation?

A. No, sir.

Q. If it were inserted in life, you would expect to find that as one of the natural consequences?

A. Yes, sir."

Now I ask your attention to this question:

" Q. Taking the history of this case as I have given it to you, could you say whether or not, in your opinion as an expert, the chloroform in this case was self-administered or administered by a second person?

"THE PRISONER: I object to that question, for this reason, that I think it should be stated distinctly as to What the District Attorney means by 'as this case has been stated.' "

The District Attorney then stated:

"I will repeat it, I have stated to you. Doctor, that this body was found lying upon its back upon the floor, with one hand laid across the body in this wise (illustrating), and the other lying close to the side, both limbs stretched out, heels together, and the whole body in a condition or pose of repose, and there was congestion of the lungs, and empty heart, and while there was an alcoholic condition of the stomach, there was no irritation of the lining, but there was chloroform in the stomach, a pipe filled with tobacco lying at the side, a burned match beside it. Those are the conditions as I intended to describe them."

That is the answer to the statement of this man; the very condition physically and otherwise of this body indicate that it could not have been self-administered. That man did not die by his own hand. If he did not die by his own hand then it was by the defendant's hand, for he was the only person who was with him at the time.

"Q. It could not have been self-administered under those conditions?

A. No, sir."

Now you are to try this case according to the evidence, and that is the uncontradicted evidence in this case; the evidence that this could not have been self-administered, the finding of that body, the place where it was, the surrounding conditions all clearly indicate that this man was not self-poisoned, but was poisoned by a second person.

See how far in our progress we have come. We have established that this is Benjamin F. Pitezel, we have established that he has died of chloroform poisoning, we have established that that was not self-administered, but administered by a second person; we have shown that he was there in that house on that fateful Sunday alone with the dead man , we have shown that every story told by him to explain his presence was false , we have shown that his theory and therefore his allegation of suicide was false; we have shown the effort at concealment when there was no other object unless it be that the defendant knew he had committed a murder and was telling these falsehoods one after the other to conceal it. Upon no other hypothesis can his conduct be explained than that lie was concealing the crime of murder. That is what made him flee from city to city, that is what made him take this wife with him upon this wonderful journey, that is what made him take even the children along, that is what made him conceal the letters and that is what made him shut off communication between the different members of that household. This man was fleeing from the shadow of murder; that was the crime he was seeking to avoid, that was what he was fleeing from. It was the menace of pursuit and detection that made him take this journey which, if it had not been interrupted at Boston, would only have terminated when he reached Berlin with his alleged wife. Miss Yoke.

I have now occupied your time a great deal longer than I expected, and I trust you will attribute it only to the desire I have to fully aid you by every thought I can present on this testimony.

You are to listen to counsel upon the other side. I do not know what they will say, I do not know what their line of defence will be. You must remember that the Commonwealth is obliged to grope in the dark; we have not the aid of an opening speech from my friend to indicate the line of defence, so I am left completely in the dark as to what course the argument on the other side is going to take. But I want to call your attention to the limitation put upon it by the evidence. Under this evidence there is only one thing the counsel can argue to you, which is that Pitezel committed suicide and was not murdered. There is nothing else in this case but that narrow question, and it is in the line of that thought I have called your attention to the facts and circumstances, and the testimony of the experts which exclude the theory of suicide. It is in that connection I have called your attention to Pitezel's own declaration and what he said and did, indicating his hopeful outlook on the future, and shown that there is not a scintilla of evidence here to indicate any intention upon his part to commit suicide, and I ask you if it is possible upon the statements of this man concerning the mechanical contrivance of a bottle, a tube and a towel; the condition in which the deceased was placed and the circumstances under which the body was found, you are going to set aside the weight of this mass of testimony pointing to a guilty crime and say that this subterfuge, this tricky statement shall work an acquittal of the prisoner, when the charge is so thoroughly and completely brought home to him by the evidence in this case; such evidence as that of Dr. Leffman, who says it would be impossible for the chloroform to be self-administered, the untenable description of the contrivance for the alleged selfadminstration in which, the Doctor says, there is no provision made for an air vent so that the air might enter and the liquid flow out of the bottle. The story of the explanation of how suicide was committed will not stand the test of criticism, and how the defence of suicide is going to be supported by any reasonable argument I am at a loss to understand. I ask you to confine yourselves to the testimony concerning the facts in this case: not the statements of counsel, not the things outside of the case, but to the evidence as you have heard it and as I have endeavored to review it and recall it to your memory so that you may be able to be guided by it in reaching a proper result.

Now this strange trial is drawing rapidly tu a close. It has been dramatic in its incidents, but those incidents have nothing to do with the case. The fact that this man appears without counsel and then with counsel has nothing to do with the question of his guilt or innocence. The simple question is, Has the Commonwealth of Pennsylvania, as it is bound to do, made out its case beyond a fair and reasonable doubt? If you believe it has, then your duty is to find a verdict of murder of the first degree against this man.

I told you in the opening that, while in this bill of indictment there were several degrees of guilt which you might find in your verdict, and that you might also find a verdict of not guilty, yet the evidence would point indubitably to one result; this man is either innocent and ought to be acquitted, or is guilty of murder in the first degree. There is no middle ground in this case. It is the highest crime known to the law under the circumstances surrounding the deceased, fur he was poisoned to death, and the poisoning itself indicates a clear intent to kill. If this man were poisoned then there was the purpose to kill, and it was a willful, premeditated and deliberate murder, and his prisoner is responsible in the highest form of verdict you can render.

I know it is not a pleasant or agreeable duty to be called upon as you are, taken from your ordinary pursuits and selected to sit here and as part of the administration of criminal justice, to sit in judgment upon the life of a fellow man. You doubtless find it repugnant and disagreeable, and I can readily understand how you might shrink from finding such a verdict as the one I ask involving the consequences it does; so as my concluding thought I appeal to your manhood and sense of right and ask you to do what the crier of the court has asked you to do, "Stand together, good men and true."

You have hearkened to the evidence. I ask you to complete the work which the law has cast upon you by fearlessly, manfully and honestly declaring your judgment upon this evidence, no matter what that judgment may involve to this man; no matter what its consequences may be to the Commonwealth. It requires courage to discharge one's duty in times of peace; in the temple of justice, as part of the administration of the criminal law, just as it does upon the field of battle in its flame and smoke. The man who faces the cannon's month, the man who faces the charging regiment, has no greater or higher courage than the man who sits calmly in the place of a juror, rising in his majesty, might and strength as an individual man to discharge fearlessly a great and solemn duty. I ask you to stand as men, and if you believe this man is guilty, aye, though it consign him to punishment that involves death, he true to your conscience, be true to your oaths, discharge that duty fearlessly in the sight of God and man, and remember you are not responsible for his fate. That was sealed in the silence of that Sunday in No. 1316 Callowhill Street. He wrought the facts and fashioned the circumstances that brought him here. You are not responsible for his being here or for his trial upon this charge; you are only responsible as good men and true for the finding of a righteous, an honest, and a just verdict.

I ask you, therefore, while guarding against prejudice, while guarding against any false appeal, not to be afraid to do your duty like men and not to cower in the presence of that duty though it involves things upon your part which are repugnant, things that are repellant, things that you would far rather shift away from you and avoid encountering. I ask you to face the duty and acquit yourselves like men. I know that great stress will be laid upon "A reasonable doubt." "If you have a doubt this man is entitled to the benefit of it." So he is, but it must not be a doubt suggested by the desire to avoid the performance of an unpleasant duty. If the evidence fails to make the case out he is entitled to his acquittal, but you are asked to perform no higher function here than in your own home or office or place of business. If this evidence would convince you as men outside of this Court of this man's guilt it ought to convince you equally in the jury box.

There are no two standards of judgment, there are no two standards by which to reach the result. Your minds must operate simply and only as plain honest men. Because you are sworn as jurors; you are given no higher power of discrimination, no greater judgment; you are asked simply to acquit yourselves as in the everyday affairs of life. If this testimony convinces you of his guilt you must say so; if it convinces you of his innocence honestly then you should acquit.

I ask you to remember this testimony, I ask you to remember that it is uncontradicted, that there is not one scintilla of evidence to attack the statement of Dr. Leffnian, that there is not one scintilla of evidence to attack the statement of Dr. Scott or of Dr. Mattern; those statements stand before you unchallenged. Nay, I go further and say they stand before you admitted. They are admitted in this case. In the face of this evidence and his statements; in the face of his flight far away, there can be but one conclusion in your minds I am sure, and that is that the man in the dock is guilty in the manner and form in which lie stands indicted of this crime.

I thank you for your patience and earnest attention. I have been talking to you for nearly two hours and a half, very much longer than I expected, and although perhaps uninteresting and rather prosaic and full of detail, you have given me your earnest attention from beginning to end. I ask you to give it now to my adversary and then to the Court and to the end, and with your verdict whatever it may be conscientiously reached I will be satisfied.

APPENDIX.

COMMONWEALTH	Court of Oyer & Terminer
vs.	Philadelphia County.
HERMAN W. MUDGETT, alias	Sept. Sessions, 1895.
H. H. HOLMES.	No. 466.

MOTION FOR NEW TRIAL,

Arnold, J. The first three reasons assigned for a new trial, to wit, that the verdict is against the evidence and the law, render necessary a statement of the facts, as they were developed by the evidence at the trial.

The defendant and Benjamin F. Pitezel, the deceased, were engaged in a conspiracy to cheat and defraud the Fidelity Mutual Life Insurance Company of Philadelphia. In pursuance of their scheme, Pitezel obtained a policy of insurance on his life, dated November 9th, 1893, for $10,000, payable to Carrie A. Pitezel, his wife. Pitezel lived in St. Louis, and the defendant at Wilmette, a town about fourteen miles from Chicago. Pitezel left St. Louis to come to Philadelphia on July 29th, 1894, rented and occupied the house No. 1316 Callowhill Street, assumed the name of B. F. Perry, and held himself out as a dealer in patents. The defendant appears to have come to Philadelphia shortly thereafter, and took board for himself and putative wife on August 5th, 1894, at No. 1905 N. 11th Street, a distance of nearly two miles from the house in which Pitezel lived. On Tuesday, September 4th, 1894, Pitezel was found dead in his house; his body was lying on the floor, composed in position, but decomposed in condition; his right arm was laid across his breast; his left arm was lying by his side; his breast was burned, except that part of it which was covered by his arm; his face was black from decomposition, and there was a stench arising from his body, which indicated that he had been dead for several days. Beside him was a pipe, filled with tobacco, but not smoked; also a burnt match. There was also a broken bottle, containing a mixture of benzene, chloroform and probably ammonia, near to his side, so that the appearance of things indicated that there had been an explosion. Pieces of the bottle, however, were not scattered about the floor, nor sticking in the side of Pitezel, as might have been expected in case of an explosion, but they were all on the inside of the bottle.

Pitezel was last seen alive by several witnesses on Saturday, September 1st, 1894, on the evening of which day he purchased a pint of whiskey, and took it home with him. Subsequent developments proved that Pitezel came to his death on Sunday, September 2d, 1894, and that his body lay unseen by any witness, so far as known, until Tuesday, September 4th, 1894, when it was discovered by a man named Eugene Smith, who had called to see Pitezel on the day before, but not finding Pitezel, and getting no response to his call for Pitezel, went away and returned the following day, Tuesday, and upon going to the second story, saw Pitezel's body lying on the floor. Smith went immediately to the police station, obtained two officers, and also a neighboring doctor, with all of whom he returned to the house, and found the body in the condition above described. The coroner's physician was also sent for, and upon an examination of the organs and vital parts of the deceased, the conclusion of the coroner's physician, and Dr. Scott, who took part in the examination, was that Pitezel had been killed by chloroform poisoning, and that the chloroform was not self-administered.

His lungs were congested; his heart was empty, which indicated sudden death; there was very little food in his stomach; his kidneys were alcoholic and so was his stomach. The doctors found half an ounce or more of chloroform in the stomach, but as the stomach was not irritated, their conclusion was that the chloroform was put in after death. On the night of September 2d, 1894, the defendant suddenly and hurriedly left Philadelphia, giving a false destination to his landlady. He had been away from his boarding house from 10:30 AM to 4 PM that day, and when he returned he was excited, nervous and worried, and his underclothing was wet with perspiration. Pitezel was buried, under the name of Perry, as a pauper in the Potter's Field. Several days thereafter, the officers of the life insurance company received word from the defendant that the man who was buried under the name of B. F. Perry, was the person who was insured in their company under the name of Benjamin F. Pitezel, and he offered to furnish proof of identification of the body. The agent of the company went to see the defendant at his house at Wilmette, but did not find him. He found, however, a lady who said she was the defendant's wife. Shortly thereafter, a letter was received from the defendant, stating that he had heard, through his wife, that he was wanted, and in due course the defendant came to Philadelphia after having arranged that Alice Pitezel, the daughter of the dead man, should also come here for the purpose of identifying the body. Accordingly the body was exhumed on September 22d, 1894, and was fully identified by the defendant and by Alice Pitezel as the body of B. F. Pitezel. On that identification, the insurance company paid the amount of the policy, on September 24th, 1894, to one Jeptha D. Howe, attorney in fact for Carrie A. Pitezel After the money was obtained, it was taken to St. Louis, where Howe retained $2,500 for a fee; $5,000 was obtained from Mrs. Pitezel by the defendant, upon his statement that her husband owed that amount on a note; and the balance was used in paying sundry expenses, Mrs. Pitezel retaining only $500 of the money. The note which the defendant stated he paid with the $5,000 was not a valid note; nothing had ever been advanced on it; nothing was due upon it; and nothing was actually paid upon it, the defendant, in fact, keeping the money. After the money was received, the defendant deceived Mrs. Pitezel by telling her that her husband was not dead; that he would return to her as soon as possible, coming to her by way of Puget Sound. He also obtained from her the custody of her two children, Howard and Nellie, taking them to Indianapolis, as he said, to meet their sister Alice, where the family were to be reunited. He also induced Mrs. Pitezel to leave her home, taking her remaining daughter and a babe with her, and going to Detroit, upon the promise of the defendant that he would produce her husband in that city. There he registered her under a false name, kept her two or three weeks without producing her husband, giving her, among his excuses for not doing so, his assertion that Pitezel was being watched by detectives. From Detroit, he led her to Toronto; thence to Prescott, Canada; thence to Ogdensburg, New York; and thence to Burlington, Vermont, all the while promising to produce her husband to her, and her children also. In some of these places, he rented furnished houses for her to live in, and set her to housekeeping. In Burlington, Vermont, he put dynamite in the cellar among the potatoes, telling her to take the dynamite from the cellar and carry it to the top of the house. She did take it from the cellar, but did not take it to the top of the house, for the reason, as she said, that it might explode, and do damage to the things stored there. From Burlington, Vermont, Mrs. Pitezel, and the two children she had with her, went with a messenger sent by the defendant, to Boston, where the defendant and Mrs. Pitezel were arrested about November 19th, 1894, and held to await requisition. The defendant was wanted by the authorities in Texas upon a charge of horse stealing, and also by the authorities in Pennsylvania to answer for cheating and defrauding the life insurance company, or any offense which might be alleged against him During all the journey in search of her husband and children, the defendant told Mrs. Pitezel that ho was in correspondence with her children, and had seen her husband, and would produce him and them at the various places to which he took her; but all this was a deception and a falsehood, for she never saw her husband, and all she saw of her children were the dead bodies of two of them at the morgue in Indianapolis. After the defendant was brought to Philadelphia, he was indicted upon the charge of conspiracy to cheat and defraud the life insurance company, by palming off a spurious body as that of Pitezel, and on that indictment, pleaded guilty, and sentence was suspended awaiting further investigation by the authorities. Mrs. Pitezel was confined in prison seven months and then discharged. In consequence of further investigation, an indictment was found by the Grand Jury on September 12th, 1895, charging the defendant with the murder of B. F. Pitezel on September 2d, 1894. At the trial, it was proved by several witnesses, and admitted by the defendant's counsel, that B. F. Pitezel was dead. It was also proved by the statement of the defendant to the superintendent of police, and one of the detectives of Philadelphia, as well as admitted by defendant's counsel, that the defendant was in Pitezel's house on Sunday September 2d, 1894, the day on which, according to the evidence, Pitezel was killed. The theory of the defendant's counsel, for no evidence was offered by him to substantiate the theory, was that it was a case of selfmurder; and that the defendant, fearing that the policy of insurance would be vitiated by the suicide of Pitezel arranged the body in the manner in which it was found, set fire to and burned it, and placed the broken bottles alongside of it, for the purpose of making it appear that Pitezel had died an accidental death, caused by the explosion.

Three questions were submitted to the jury to determine. First, was Benjamin F. Pitezel dead. Second, did he die a violent death; and third, if he died a violent death, did he commit suicide or did the defendant kill him. An answer to either one of these questions in favor of the defendant would have entitled him to an acquittal. The jury resolved them all against the defendant, and found him guilty of murder of the first degree. Upon the hearing of the motion for a new trial, I had the valuable aid of my colleagues, Judges Thayer and Willson. The evidence was rehearsed and it is our unanimous opinion that the verdict of guilty of murder of the first degree is fully justified by the evidence, and upon the facts of the case, there is no ground shown for a new trial.

The fourth reason assigned is new matter discovered since the trial. At the argument it was developed that this so-called after-discovered evidence was manufactured for the purpose and is utterly unworthy of belief, and we will not notice it farther.

The fifth and sixth reasons assigned are that the District Attorney, in his opening speech, made statements which were not proven, and which related to other crimes which could not be part of the evidence; and that the Court erred in not allowing an affidavit to be filed, and an exception to the statements made in the District Attorney's opening speech. These reasons, no doubt, are based upon a recent ruling of the Supreme Court, in Holden vs. The Penna. E. E. Co., 1G9 Pa., 1, in which that Court granted a new trial because of the remarks of counsel in summing up the evidence; abuse of witnesses, and other outrageous misconduct, which the Supreme Court properly rebuked, by granting a new trial. A similar decision was made in Waldron vs. Waldron, 156 U. S. 360 and cases cited, "t is manifest that there is a difference between opening speeches and summing up. In summing up a case, counsel can be and should be kept strictly within the evidence given at the trial, and abuse of witnesses without cause, and without decency, should be promptly checked, and if repeated, should militate against a verdict obtained by such means. In the opening, however, counsel often state matters which they expect to prove, but fail to prove, either from want of witnesses, or by reason of the evidence being excluded by the Judge, who cannot be expected to know in advance whether the case outlined by counsel will be permitted to be proven. As to the exception, it must be noticed that an exception is always preceded by an objection, and the exception is then taken to the act of the Judge in sustaining or overruling the objection. In this case, no objection whatever was made, and consequently an exception has nothing upon which it can be based. An exception, like an objection, must be taken at the time the objectionable act is done, either in offering evidence; or in remarks to the jury. The District Attorney's opening speech was made on Monday, October 28th, and no exception thereto was asked for until November 1st, or four days thereafter.

The remarks of Judge Dean in Commonwealth vs. Weber, 167 Penna., 164, are so apropos in this connection, that we quote them verbatim: "The attitude of defendant's counsel, as exhibited by the record, is in substance this: Counsel for the Commonwealth erred in the matter of his addressing the jury. I erred by remaining silent when I should have promptly brought his error to the notice of the Court by objection; the Court committed no error, but its judgment should be reversed because I did not perform my duty." This illustrates the dilemma in which counsel are placed by their own conduct. According to all law and reason, the exception was asked fur too late, even if it had been preceded by an objection made in time.

If it be said that the defendant was at this time without counsel, the answer is that it was his voluntary and deliberate choice. He was indicted September 12th, 1895. On September 23d, he was arraigned. The record shows that his two counsel were present with him at the arraignment. October 28th, or five weeks thereafter, was fixed for his trial. Counsel stated at the arraignment that they would not be ready, and when the case was called for trial moved for a continuance, which being refused, they first threatened to withdraw from the case, and on being told that they could not withdraw without leave of the Court, they entered upon the trial by questioning the talesmen, as they were called to serve as jurors.

After being thus engaged for some time they held a consultation with their client, and the defendant then announced that he had dismissed his counsel and would thereafter conduct the case himself. Other counsel were assigned him, but he rejected their services.

The Constitution of Pennsylvania as well as of the United States, secures to persons accused the right to have counsel to assist them at their trial, but it does not attempt to force counsel upon them. The right of every man to plead his own cause is a natural inherent right. The right to have counsel is given by the Constitution, and no man can be deprived of the right to defend himself or be compelled to have the services of counsel.

The Constitution also secures to the defendant the right to a speedy public trial. This was given in return for the right which the Commonwealth possesses to a like speedy public trial, and it is not within the power of persons accused to say when they will be willing to be tried, or to defeat a trial by dilatory motions and practices such as were resorted to in this case. Nor was the defendant without counsel, for during the recesses of Court and in the morning before the opening of Court he was in consultation with the same counsel whom he had discharged, and on the evening of the second day the counsel determined to return and take part in the trial, but permitted the defendant to make another dilatory motion, which was overruled, and the counsel immediately returned to the conduct of the case.

The opening speech of the District Attorney contained no statement not induced and justified by the remarks of the counsel for the defendant at the very beginning of the trial, when they asked for a continuance, because, as they said, there were to be three cases of murder tried, two of which were alleged t<j have been committed out of the jurisdiction of this Court.

In Commonwealth vs. Hanlon, 8 Philadelphia Reports, 423, it was decided by Judge Ludlow, that reference in opening by the prosecuting attorney to the fact that the prisoner had been guilty of other crimes is not a reason for a new trial. The Court very properly considered an opening speech like an offer of evidence which is rejected. An offer of evidence, which is rejected, does not furnish a reason for the release of a prisoner charged with murder or to annul the verdict and require a new trial. Com. vs. Crossmire, 156 Pa., 310.

In the summing up of the District Attorney, no allusion was made to these extra-territorial murders, evidence of which had been excluded, for the reason that no such connection between them was shown, as was required in Shaffner vs. The Commonwealth, 72 Pa. 60, another case of murder by poisoning in order to obtain insurance money; although there are cases in which evidence of two murders at the same time may be given on the trial of one, as in Brown vs. The Commonwealth, 76 Pa. 319; or cases in which an inheritance is secured by the killing of two persons at different times, as in Goerson vs. The Commonwealth, 99 Pa. 388, and 106 Pa. 477.

In charging the jury I was careful to instruct them that it was their duty to lay aside all impressions, and not be influenced by anything which they heard of other cases than the one on trial and decide the case only on the evidence given at the trial. Here I am tempted to say that the offer by the District Attorney of evidence of the murder of other members of Pitezel's family might well have been admitted to show the defendant's purpose to kill them all in order to rid himself of their claims for the money he had illegally obtained horn Mrs. Pitezel, and therefore the opening speech of the District Attorney was not open to objection. The violent death of at least four members of the family after they were within the defendant's toils, would justify the belief that they were murdered by the defendant, and that the murders were all part of one common design, and included the entire Pitezel household. The dynamite placed in the Burlington house by the defendant with his directions to Mrs. Pitezel to remove it, looks as if he intended to take her off by an explosion.

The seventh reason is that the District Attorney, in his closing speech, mentioned the death of the children, and the finding of their dead bodies in the morgue. In all cases of crime, especially cases of alleged murder, we naturally want to know what was the motive for the killing, although absence of proof of motive is not fatal to the prosecution. Commonwealth vs. Buccieni, 153 Pa. 525. The motive alleged for the killing in this case was a desire to obtain the insurance upon the life of Pitezel. The insurance money was payable to his wife. When she received the money, the defendant obtained from her at least $5,000 of it, in payment of an alleged debt which Pitezel did not owe. It became necessary for him to induce Mrs. Pitezel to believe that the money was obtained by fraud, and therefore did not belong to her; that her husband was still alive, and the defendant promised to produce Pitezel to his wife in the several cities to which he took her. He also obtained possession of three of her children, and lured her through the several cities in the vain search for her children, as well as her husband. As his motive was thus to obtain her money by deceiving her, it was necessary to receive her evidence of the deception practiced upon her in the several cities to which he took her, and having entered upon the story of her travels with him it was impossible, as well as improper, to receive only part of that story, and not hear all of it to its conclusion, which was that she did not find her husband, and that she never saw her children until she saw their dead bodies in the morgue. No evidence was received as to the manner of the death of the children, or who caused their death, if they had been killed, but a simple statement completing the story of his deception and falsehood practiced upon her, without in any way whatever incriminating him in their murder, if they were killed.

Eighth, ninth, and tenth reasons. Much of what has been said under the seventh reason applies to these reasons. As Mrs. Pitezel's story was clearly competent evidence in the case, it could not be broken up into pieces and only part of it given. The effort of the defendant to drag into the case troubles which Pitezel had in Terre Haute, Indiana, had nothing whatever to do with the case, and we think the evidence was properly rejected.

Eleventh reason, (a) Puling that defendant's wife was a competent witness. A lady named Georgiana Yoke, who was married to the defendant under the name of Howard, on January 17th 1894, was called as a witness to testify against the defendant. It was alleged that, at that time, he had a wife living at Wilmette, Illinois, to whom the agent of the insurance Company went when he was looking for the defendant. The agent of the company obtained from the lady who answered to the name of Mrs. Holmes a photograph of herself, with a babe in her arms, which ai)pears to be from three to six months old. Shortly thereafter, the agent of the company received a letter from the defendant, stating that he wrote it in consequence of the message left with his wife. In another letter from the defendant he alluded to his marriage to this lady in Illinois. Upon these statements made by the defendant in writing, it was considered that the marriage with Miss Yoke was null and void; that she was not his wife; and consequently she was permitted to testify against him. When the testimony was offered, I was inclined to believe that the jury were to pass upon the question of his previous marriage, in order to determine the competency of the witness, but subsequent reflection, led me to the opinion that, as the Judge is the trier of the competency of the witnesses (Lyon vs. Daniels, 12 Pa. 197) the matter should not be referred to the jury, and consequently it was not in my charge; but I quoted her testimony to the jury and treated it as competent, upon my judgment that the marriage between the defendant and Miss Yoke was absolutely null and void. Second marriages, where there is a former husband or wife living, are not only voidable, but they are absolutely void ah initio. Thomas vs. Thomas, 124 Pa. 646. Divorces are not granted in such cases, but decrees of nullity of marriage may be obtained, according to the forms of procedure followed in divorce cases. But a decree of nullity is not essential, the only object of obtaining a decree being to make certain, positive, and record evidence of the nullity of the marriage.

In 1st Greenleaf on evidence, Section 339, it is said that, "On a trial for polygamy, the first marriage being proved and not controverted, the woman with whom the second marriage is had is a competent witness, for the second marriage is void." . . . "It seems, however, that a reputed or supposed wife may be examined on her voir dire, as to facts showing the invalidity of the marriage." * * * "Where the parties had lived together as man and wife, believing themselves lawfully married, but had separated on discovering that a prior husband supposed to be dead, was still living, the woman was held a competent witness against the second husband, even as to facts communicated to her by him during her cohabitation."

In this state, it was decided by Judge Pearson, of the Court of Common Pleas of Dauphin County, that a party to a second marriage is a competent witness to prove its illegality. Shaak's Estate, 4 Brewster, 305.

In the present case. Miss Yoke testified that, after her marriage, the defendant talked with her about his first wife, who lived in Gilmanton, New Hampshire, and told her that he had received word that the woman in Gilmanton was dead. At the argument, the District Attorney produced a certified copy of the record of a proceeding in divorce in Cook County, Illinois, by Herman W. Mudgett against Clara A. Mudgett, and in his petition sworn to December 11th, 1886, the present defendant swore that he was married to Clara A. Mudgett on July 4th, 1878, at Alton, New Hampshire. The case was dismissed by the court on June 4th, 1891, for want of prosecution. As the competency of this witness was a question for the court, the production of this record satisfies me that he was not only married to the lady in Wilmette,

Illinois, but that he had a former wife living in New Hampshire at the time he married Miss Yoke, and consequently the marriage with her was null and void.

Proof of the ceremony of marriage in such cases is not necessary. No better evidence is required than a man's declaration against himself in a question involving the competency of a putative wife to testify against him. This is called direct proof, and is as effective as proof of a ceremony. Heffner vs. Heffner, 23 Penna. 104; Greenawalt vs. McEnelley, 85 Penna. 352; even in criminal cases arising out of marriage; Commonwealth vs. Wyman, 3 Brewster, 338; 2 Greenleaf on Evidence, section 461, and note.

In Forney vs. Hallacher, 8 Sergeant & Rawle, page 159, Judge Gibson decided: —

That, "to support an action for criminal conversation there must be an actual marriage, but it is quite another thing to say that such marriage shall be proved only by the oath of an eyewitness to the marriage ceremony. We at once feel the good sense of the rule that excludes the mere reputation of marriage which always arises from the declarations or ads of the plaintiff himself. But how a defendant's unqualified and positive acknowledgment of the marriage in fact can be excluded on any principle or rule of evidence I am at a loss to discover."

Inasmuch as the defendant had in writing admitted that the lady in Wilmette was his wife, and also written about his marriage to her, I have no doubt whatever that his declaration against himself justified me in considering him a married man at the time he entered into the contract with Miss Yoke, and therefore that she was not his lawful wife. Consequently she was a competent witness against him, and as such she was properly admitted.

Eleven, (b) Allowing evidence of the whereabouts of the children and finding their dead bodies in Toronto. This has been sufficiently answered in the consideration of the seventh, eighth, ninth and tenth reasons.

Eleven, (c) Permitting jurors to enter the box who upon their voir dire stated that they had formed or expressed an opinion regarding the guilt or innocence of the defendant. The question raised by this reason has been so often considered by the Supreme Court of this State, and decided in favor of the competency of such jurors, that it would be a work of supererogation to cite all the authorities in support thereof.

I refer to Commonwealth vs. Crossmire, 156 Penna. 304, as probably the latest decision on the subject. No more can be required of persons called as jurors than their oath that they can decide the case according to the evidence, laying aside any impression they may have or opinions they have formed. That evidence may be required to change their opinion does not militate against them as jurors, for it is manifest that with jurors as well as judges evidence is required to change impressions or opinions. There was no talesman received as a juror who did not come clearly within the rule laid down, and was not entirely competent to serve as a juror according to all the law on that subject. The jury was an uncommonly intelligent jury, selected by the prisoner himself, who seemed disposed to reject all who were untidy and unintelligent in appearance. The defendant certainly had twelve intelligent and thoughtful men to decide his case. They were selected by himself, with discretion and judgment. They were unbiased by fixed immovable opinions, listened attentively to the evidence, and rendered a verdict according to their oaths on the evidence only.

The twelfth reason is that the court erred in charging the jury by giving undue prominence to the evidence given by the Commonwealth, and not sufficient prominence to the evidence favorable to the prisoner.

The statement upon which this reason is based is not true. There was no evidence given by the defense, and, therefore, nothing of that character for the judge to call to the attention of the jury.

In the argument it was alleged that the cross-examination furnished the prisoner's defense. As before said, there was a theory advanced that Pitezel committed suicide; that he arranged a bottle containing chloroform and attached it to a rubber tube with a quill outlet; that he put the bottle on a chair beside him, and that the chloroform ran down through the tube into or upon a cloth on his mouth, and thus produced his death, but there was no evidence that such a bottle or tube was found in the house.

Detective Geyer stated that the defendant told him that the body found at No. 1316 Callowhill Street was a substituted body which he had procured from a medical friend in New York, and brought to Philadelphia in a trunk; that he met Pitezel in Philadelphia and gave him the check for the trunk, and then left for the West, and the next place he saw Pitezel was in Detroit, Michigan. He stated that he told Pitezel how to prepare the substituted body, by laying it on the floor, placing an arm across its breast, pouring a liquid into the stomach and then setting fire to it.

Geyer testified in a subsequent interview, that the defendant told him that the story about there being a substituted body in No. 1316 Callowhill Street was not true, and that the body found there was really the body of Benjamin F. Pitezel. He also told the detective that when he went to the house on Sunday, September 2, 1894, he found Pitezel dead on the third story, lying on the floor, with his arm across his breast, with a bottle of chloroform on a chair with a gum hose and quill attached to it, so arranged that the chloroform would fall on a piece of cloth across Pitezel's mouth; that he found a note which told him to look in a bottle in a closet, that he broke the bottle and found a note in cipher from Pitezel, which told him that Pitezel was tired of life and had committed suicide; that he found the body in the third story and dragged it to the second story back room and placed it in the position in which it was found, taking a bottle of liquid and placing it alongside the head, breaking it, lighting a pipe, throwing the pipe on the floor, lighting matches and throwing them down, to make it appear as though an explosion had taken place there. He told Captain Linden, superintendent of police, the same stories, retracting the first before telling him the second. The testimony of Detective Geyer and of Captain Linden on this subject was read in the charge to the jury.

That the first story, to wit, that there had been a substituted body placed in the house, was false, is proved by the defendant's own admissions. In an affidavit made before the Coroner on September 23, 1894, the defendant swore that he learned of Pitezel's death through the newspapers, and saw and identified the body at the City Burial Ground. He also swore that the last time he saw Pitezel alive was in November, 1893, in Chicago, which was another deliberate falsehood. The truthfulness of the second assertion, to wit, that Pitezel had committed suicide, was submitted to the jury with as much emphasis as any other part of the case. A repetition in detail of these inconsistent stories would only tend to bring out in a stronger light the untruthfulness of the defendant, and his utter unreliability. To dwell on these inconsistent stories would only bear so much the harder upon the defendant. The condition of the body when found, to wit, a discharge of the bowels and the bladder, which the physicians testified generally accompany death, and which takes place at or immediately before dissolution, showed that Pitezel was not killed on the third floor, but on the second floor, where he was found.

There was evidence in the case which proved that the defendant was furnishing money to support Pitezel, that Pitezel was addicted to the use of liquor to excess, and that he had purchased a pint of whiskey the night before the day on which he was killed. It is not a violent presumption to infer that the defendant found Pitezel under the influence of liquor and then resolved upon killing him in order to get rid of the burden of supporting him and to obtain the money from the insurance company. Confirmation of this may be found in a question put by the defendant to Dr. Mattern in which the defendant asked the doctor whether he was prepared to give a professional opinion as to the effect that one-half hour before Pitezel died or at the time of his death, he was not in an insensible condition from the excessive use of alcohol. This suggestive question, like several other questions put by the defendant to witnesses, indicates his knowledge of Pitezel's condition, and justified the inference of the jury that the defendant administered the chloroform to Pitezel.

Under our code of criminal procedure it is not necessary to set forth in the indictment or prove in detail the exact manner in which a murder has been committed. If it were it would be impossible in many cases to furnish such proof, and therefore many guilty persons would escape.

In Twitchell's case, 1 Brewster's Rep., page 551, the defendant was convicted on the theory that he killed his mother-in-law by striking her on the temple with the angle of a poker. After Twitchell's death it became generally known that he had killed his victim with a slung-shot.

In Bell's case, 164 Penna. 517, the defendant was convicted of killing his victim by choking her. This was inferred from well defined thumb and finger marks on the neck of the deceased.

In The Commonwealth vs. Johnson, 162 Pa. 63, the defendant was convicted of killing his own child by drowning it. There were no marks of violence on the body, which was not found until six days after the last day the child was seen alive.

In Crossmire's case, 156 Penna. 305, the defendant was convicted of strangling the deceased, which was the opinion of a medical expert, and there was no direct proof as to the manner of killing.

In Gray vs. The Commonwealth, 101 Pa. 380, the deceased was last seen alive on February 20th, 1877. On April 4th, 1878, or nearly fifteen months thereafter, a human skull and jawbone were found in the river nearby. The skull was identified as the skull of the deceased. There were wounds on it which it was testified were sufficient to produce death. The defendant while in prison for another offence, admitted to a fellow prisoner that he had murdered the deceased with a hatchet. The defendant was convicted and executed, yet there were no eyewitnesses to the murder.

The present case is not singular by any means. There is much similarity between it and Udderzook vs. The Commonwealth, 76 Penna. 340, in which Chief Justice Agnew commenced his opinion with this phrase: "This is indeed a strange case, a combination of two to cheat insurance companies, and a murder of one by the other to reap the fruit of the fraud."

In that case the murdered man was supposed to have been burned in his shop on February 2d, 1872. On July 1st, 1873, which was seventeen months afterwards, the prisoner and the man who was supposed to have been burned were seen together. On July 9th, 1873, a man travelling on the turnpike observed buzzards in the woods, and smelled a very unpleasant odor. Obtaining aid, he uncovered the earth and leaves around the place, and found the body of a man, with the legs and arms cut off, and hidden sixty-five feet away. This body was subsequently identified as the man who was supposed to have been burned. The defendant was indicted, convicted and executed upon circumstantial evidence. There was no proof as to the manner of killing. The deceased, like Pitezel, had an alias name, was in the habit of drinking to excess, and his clothing was found burned in the woods like Pitezel's was in the house.

In the present case, as in the cases above referred to as examples of kindred cases, there was no eyewitness to the crime. The defendant was convicted on what is called circumstantial evidence; that is to say, a succession of circumstances tending irresistibly to the conclusion that the defendant killed and murdered the deceased, as charged in the bill of indictment. That condition of his victim, that is, whether he was asleep or under the influence of liquor, is a matter not only difficult of proof, but entirely unnecessary. The main question was whether Pitezel had been killed, and, if killed, whether by himself or the defendant. The jury found that the defendant killed Pitezel, on evidence which was as convincing as human evidence can be made.

The thirteenth reason is that the Court erred in charging the jury as follows: "You will notice by the testimony which w-as read to you that the doctors who examined him say his death was caused by chloroform poisoning, and that it could not have been self-administered. Now if it was not self-administered who was it administered the poison to him? Who poisoned him and who took his life? "

Exactly what error appears in this reason I confess myself unable to see. It was simply a submission to the jury of the question they were sworn to try, which was whether the defendant killed Pitezel, without in any manner whatever indicating any opinion on the subject.

The fourteenth reason is that the court erred in charging the jury as follows: "If you are not fairly satisfied with the evidence of his guilt he is entitled to the benefit of the doubt."

It has been so often said that it is not necessary to cite authorities to prove it, that a charge is to be considered as a whole and not by selecting sentences and criticising them by themselves. If it is not proper to select sentences apart from the entire context, how much more important is it that parts of sentences should not be separated and alleged as error.

The sentence from which the above is taken is to be found in that part of my charge in which I was treating of the question of doubt, which was fully and emphatically laid before the jury. The entire sentence as found in the charge is as follows:

"If, after considering the testimony, you are unable to come to the conclusion that he is guilty, there is a doubt about it and you hesitate, or, in other words, if you are not fairly satisfied by the evidence, of his guilt, he is entitled to the benefit of the doubt and should be acquitted for that reason."

The counsel for defendant omitted the first, as well as the last and most important part of this sentence, to wit: "That if the jury are not fairly satisfied by the evidence of the guilt, he is entitled to the benefit of the doubt and should be acquitted." The word "fairly," when used in connection with the measure of proof required as a defense has been held by the Supreme Court to be the proper word to use in such cases.

Commonwealth vs. Bezek, 168 Pa. 603, is the last case on this subject. It is true that the word was used in connection with the proof offered by the defendant as to his insanity, and the Supreme Court said that the defendant was bound to satisfy the jury by fairly preponderating evidence, while to hold him to proof by clearly preponderating evidence was to hold him to too strict a burden; in other words, that the rule is that the defendant's proof should, like the Commonwealth's proof, be of a character that will fairly satisfy the jury of the matters attempted to be proved.

The word "fairly" was not the only word used in this connection. In the next sentence, the jury were told that if upon a consideration of the entire evidence, they were firmly convinced of the defendant's guilt, then it is a case of murder as charged; and in answer to defendant's fifth point, the jury were told that unless they were thoroughly satisfied with the evidence that the defendant is guilty, he cannot be convicted.

In Turney vs. The Commonwealth, 86 Pa. 54, it was held that, "A conviction can be had only after the jury have been convinced beyond a reasonable doubt of the defendant's guilt." There no qualifying adverb WHS used. The jury must be convinced or satisfied by the evidence.

Having in view the decisions of the Supreme Court in which this subject has been considered of late years, I used the word "fairly" because it is the proper adverb to be used in that connection.

The fifteenth reason is that the court erred in not affirming points No. 3 and No. 6 submitted by the defendant.

These points were based upon the theory that Pitezel committed suicide, and asked the Judge to decide as a matter of law that the evidence does not establish beyond a reasonable doubt the commission of the crime alleged.

These points were refused, and the question was submitted to the jury upon the evidence to find whether Pitezel had been murdered by the defendant or committed suicide.

As to the question of doubt, that is a condition of the minds of the jurors after they have heard the testimony. It is not for the Judge to say that there cannot be a conviction for murder, because it was possible that Pitezel killed himself. In every case of murder such possibilities may exist. A man who is shot may have died from heart disease caused by the fright of being chased by another with a pistol in his hand. A man who is struck with a club may not receive his death in consequence of that blow, but may strike his head upon a stone and thereby come to his death. But in all cases, and especially in a case like the present, where the evidence tended unmistakably to prove the willful, deliberate, and premeditated killing by the defendant, the mere theory of his counsel that the deceased committed suicide, without any evidence whatever to sustain the theory, does not create a legal doubt, such as to require the Judge to decide the question as one of law. The case is for the jury, and to the jury it was submitted.

If a mere theory without evidence is to prevail over facts alleged by the commonwealth and proved by evidence, tending irresistibly to but one conclusion, then it will be impossible to convict anyone of crime except by the proof of eyewitnesses; and not even then if cunning devices such as were resorted to in this case shall be set up as probable truths and accepted as positive facts, to be declared and enforced by the Judge, to the exclusion of every other possibility.

Upon the whole case, we are convinced that the commonwealth proved such a chain of circumstances as led irresistibly to the conclusion that the defendant did kill and murder Benjamin F. Pitezel on September 2d, 1894, as charged in the bill of indictment; that Pitezel was killed by chloroform poisoning administered by the defendant; and whether Pitezel was asleep or under the influence of liquor at the time the chloroform was administered is not important. The theory advanced by the defendant, and argued by his counsel to the jury, that Pitezel committed suicide, and that the defendant arranged his body in such a manner as to make the death appear to have been the consequence of an explosion, has no substantial evidence upon which it can be based. An act of that kind would require coolness and deliberation, whereas the testimony shows that the defendant, immediately after he had left Pitezel, was excited, nervous and worried, and his underclothing was wet with perspiration. This was the condition of a man who had committed a great crime, rather than one who was trying to conceal the evidence of a suicide. The defendant's flight must not be overlooked in this case. If Pitezel had committed suicide, and the defendant simply tried to conceal the suicide, it is not probable that he would have fled from the city. Flight is the act of a guilty man, and not the act of a cunning man. Being firmly convinced of the guilt of the defendant, we approve the verdict and refuse a new trial.

APPENDIX I.

THE DECISION OF THE SUPREME COURT.

This is a voluminous record. An examination of it shows that the trial of the defendant furnished some unlooked for situations and dramatic incidents, but no one of them seems to have been the result of anything irregular or sensational in the manner or rulings of the learned trial Judge. On the other hand, it is apparent that they were due to the extraordinary character of the circumstances with which the defendant had surrounded himself, and to his interference with the usual methods of trial. Indeed, the assignments of error, although thirteen in number, have been intended to raise no questions except such as may be characterized as general questions of law, and they have been presented in this Court and discussed in the oral argument in a thoroughly lawyer-like manner and with decided ability. We proceed to consider them in their order.

The first, second, third and fourth assignments relate to the admissibility of the testimony of Georgianna Yoke who was called as a witness by the Commonwealth and whom the defendant alleged to be his lawful wife. At the time this witness was called there was evidence before the Court showing that the defendant had an establishment of some sort at Willmette in the State of Illinois which was known, at least to some of his acquaintances, as his home, where as H. H. Holmes he lived with a woman who was understood to be his wife. The evidence further showed that a letter which had been left at this establishment with this woman in his absence by the witness Cass, had been promptly replied to by H. H. Holmes; and that in the answer he referred to this woman as his wife saying, "I am in receipt of a letter from my wife stating that you called on her in regard to Mr. Pitezel. She also enclosed me clipping from paper which I presume you gave her." All this evidence tending to show that the prisoner was a married man, and that his wife lived in Illinois and was known as Mrs. Holmes, was before the Court when Georgiana Yoke was called. There was nothing in the name of the witness and there was nothing in her testimony when she was first on the stand to suggest that she was the wife of the prisoner, or to throw any doubt upon his being, as he appeared to be at that stage of the evidence, the husband of the woman of whom he had written as his wife.

An objection to her competency taken when she was first called and examined would have had nothing on which to rest. At a later stage of the trial she was recalled by the defendant and examined upon this subject. She then stated that she had been married to the prisoner by a clergyman in the city of Denver in January, 1894; that his name was then Howard, and that she was married to him by that name. She stated further that, during much of the time between January and the following November, she had lived with him as his wife supposing that she occupied that position towards him, but that she had learned before his arrest that he had been married some time previously to a woman living in Gilmanton, N. H., whom she understood to be still living. She had heard still earlier of the woman at Willmette, but did not understand that Howard had been lawfully married to her. She had talked with him about the woman at Gilmanton while they were at Boston, not long before his arrest. His sister had told her that the prisoner had accounted for having married her while his wife was living at Gilmanton by telling his father's family that he had been seriously injured in a railroad wreck; that she (Miss Yoke) had nursed him and had been instrumental in saving his mind, but had married him before he knew where he was or what he was doing. This story she told the prisoner. He did not deny or explain the story, but said in his own defence that when he married her he had been told that the woman at Gilmanton was dead. The witness was apparently satisfied that her marriage was not valid, and she had resumed the use of her maiden name.

As she was competent, prime facie, when called and examined, the burden of showing her incompetency was on the prisoner who alleged it. The testimony of Miss Yoke, to which we have just referred, was given for that purpose, and it was all the evidence upon that subject. The fair effect of it was to show that no legal marriage had taken place, that Miss Yoke had been cruelly deceived, and that the legal wife of the prisoner lived at Gilmanton, N. H. Let us grant that if the defendant had been on trial for bigamy the testimony of Miss Yoke might not have been sufficiently definite as to the fact of the first marriage to justify a conviction of the defendant, yet we must remember that, so far as the competency of the witness was concerned, the burden of proof was not on the Commonwealth. She was apparently competent. The burden of establishing her incompetency by proof of a lawful marriage between himself and her was on him who alleged it. The learned Judge would have been justified in doing what the prisoner's counsel complain that he did not, viz: treat this question of competency as a question of law, and overrule the objection to her testimony at once. What he did was more favorable to the prisoner than he had a right to ask. He submitted the question of the legality of the marriage to the jury, instructing them that, if they found it to be valid, they should reject the testimony of the witness altogether. We do not see how the prisoner can expect successfully to complain of a ruling that gave him one more chance for a favorable decision upon the question of the competency of the witness than he had a right to ask.

The fifth and sixth assignments are in effect but a different mode of raising the question we have just considered. They complain of the submission of the testimony of Miss Yoke to the jury. She had been examined very fully as to the movements of the prisoner on that Sunday on which he had stated to Mr. Linden, Superintendent of Police, that he saw and arranged the dead body of Pitezel in the Callowhill Street house. This evidence the learned Judge referred to and submitted to the jury. It is not suggested that her evidence is not fairly repeated, nor that any statement is attributed by the Court to her that she did not make. The burden of the assignment of error must therefore be that the testimony was treated by the learned Judge as competent and as properly before the jury. This was not an error for the reasons given when treating of the question of the competency of the witness, and we do not see that it was inconsistent with the action of the learned Judge in submitting that question to the jury, since it was necessary, at least provisionally, to call their attention to the effect of the testimony and the questions to which it was related. These assignments are therefore overruled.

The thirteenth assignment should be considered in this connection, as it is directed against the action of the Court in submitting to the jury the question of the existence of a legal marriage between the prisoner and Miss Yoke at the time she was called as a witness, and the direction to them to consider, or to exclude from consideration, her testimony as they might find upon that question. We have already said that while the submission of the question might not have been necessary, we cannot see that it did the prisoner any harm. The verdict undoubtedly shows that the jury decided this question against the prisoner, but so we think the learned Judge should have done if he had undertaken to pronounce upon the effect of Miss Yoke's testimony in regard to the legality of her marriage to the prisoner. The prisoner cannot complain that he should be taken at his word upon this question; and the story told by him to his father's family, which Miss Yoke afterwards called to his attention and his excuse made to her for marrying her while he had a wife living at Gilmanton, are enough to discredit the alleged marriage. We do not see how the jury or the Court could have done otherwise than say that the prisoner had not successfully shown the witness to be incompetent; and whether the Court had disposed of the question in the first instance by an instruction, or allowed the jury to dispose of it without any controlling direction upon the subject, the prisoner had no ground for complaint.

The twelfth assignment is to the refusal by the learned Judge to allow an exception to the opening address of the District Attorney, As we understand the situation, the objection to the opening address was not made at the time of its delivery, but several days later, near the close of the trial. The District Attorney had in his opening stated the case of the Commonwealth. He had detailed in their order the incidents connecting the prisoner with Pitezel, with the procurement of the policy of insurance on his life, with his subsequent death, the identification of the body, the absorption of the insurance money by the prisoner and his subsequent movements. He called attention to the part taken by Alice in the identification of her father's body, and to the fact that she was kept thereafter from a meeting with her mother whom the prisoner had led to believe that her husband was still alive. He then spoke of the remarkable journeys upon which Alice and her brother and sister were moved in one group, Mrs. Pitezel and her other children in another, and Georgianna Yoke by herself or in company with the prisoner in a third. He told how they went from place to place, near to each other, were housed at the same time in the same city, but always without meeting, until one by one the three members of one group disappeared. He then spoke of the finding of their remains, and of the powerful array of circumstances connecting the prisoner with their death, and the disposition of their bodies.

The theory of the Commonwealth was that the motive for the killing of Pitezel was to secure the insurance money; and the killing of Alice and the two children who were with him grew out of his desire to prevent Mrs. Pitezel from knowing of the death of her husband, and of her consequent right to the insurance money. The several homicides were thus alleged to be connected, to have a common motive and to form parts of one general plan. In opening his case it was natural for the District Attorney to state, indeed it was his duty towards the prisoner, to state fully what he intended to offer for the consideration of the jury bearing upon his guilt. This he did do, and, so far as we are advised, without objection from the Court or the prisoner.

The trial proceeded upon the lines indicated in the opening, until the subject of the disappearance and murder of the children was reached. An objection was interposed by the prisoner's counsel on the ground that the evidence offered was intended to show the commission of an independent crime not charged in the indictment. After some consideration the objection was sustained by the learned Judge and the evidence excluded.

Then, as we understand the course of the trial, and not until then, the application was made for leave to except to so much of the opening address of the District Attorney as related to the excluded evidence. The learned Judge well said, in answer to this request, that there was no method by which an exception could be sealed by the Court to statements in the address of an attorney, days after they had been made; and that, if any statement made by the District Attorney had been deemed objectionable, the attention of the Court should have been called to it at the time when it was made, and when its correction was possible. To this we are disposed to add another consideration — viz, that such a practice would require the trial Judge to anticipate the course of the trial and decide upon the admissibility of evidence in advance of its being offered.

We have no doubt of the power, nor in a proper case of the duty, of the Court to supervise the addresses of counsel so far as may be necessary to protect prisoners or parties litigant from injurious misrepresentations and unfair attack, and the jury from being misled. When this power should be exercised must be left to the sound discretion of the Judge, and he should not hesitate to act where the fair administration of justice requires him to do so.

But there was nothing in the address of the District Attorney in the opening of the case of the Commonwealth that either the defendant's counsel or the Court seemed at the time to think required the exercise of this discretionary power. The subsequent action of the Court in rejecting a part of the case of the Commonwealth did not have a retroactive effect upon the opening address.

It is probable that the learned Judge entertained some doubt about the admissibility of this evidence and gave, as he should always do, the benefit of his doubt to the prisoner. But if he had admitted it, we are not prepared to say it would have been error. Assuming the correctness of the theory of the Commonwealth, the evidence was admissible under the authority of a line of cases, among which are Turner vs. the Commonwealth, 8G Pa. 54; Kramer vs. the Commonwealth, 87 Pa. 299;

Commonwealth vs. Goerson, 99 Pa. 398, and the Commonwealth vs. Bell, 166 Pa. 405. But the decision of this question is not necessarily involved. It is enough for the purposes of this case to dispose of the question raised by the assignment and hold that there was no error in refusing the request for an exception to the address of the District Attorney made several days after the address had been completed.

The next question, following the natural order of the assignments, is that raised by the eighth. It relates to the admission of the story told by Mrs. Pitezel about the manner in which she saw and recognized the remains of three of her children within a few weeks after the death of her husband. This was part of the general story of her search after her husband, whom she supposed to be still alive, and the three children, who were kept just a little ways ahead of her until, one by one, they had disappeared. The search was made under the control and direction of the prisoner. She followed on where he promised her husband would come and her children would meet her. During all this time he knew her husband was sleeping in the Potter's Field. He knew that first the boy and then Alice and her sister had gone out of sight while under his general care and their bodies had been mutilated or concealed. She saw them, or their remains, at last. When and how she saw them she was allowed to state, and to that extent, at least, it was competent for her to speak of her children regardless of the question raised by the assignment of error last considered. The whole story of Mrs. Pitezel has a unity of character, and its incidents are so affected by the prisoner's acts and declarations in regard to her husband and his whereabouts, that we do not see any reason for rejecting as irrelevant any portion of it. We think also that it had a direct bearing upon the question of motive. At least it was for the jury to say from it whether the persistent concealment of Pitezel's death from his wife and his representations to her that the insurance money had been obtained by fraud were not induced by his desire to escape litigation over the money and to avoid the suspicion of murder being started against him in her mind.

The ninth assignment is directed towards a statement made by the learned Judge in his charge to the jury. Speaking of the death of Pitezel, he said: "You will notice by the testimony which was read to you that the doctors who examined him say his death was caused by chloroform poisoning, and that it could not have been self-administered." This, it is alleged, was wholly unwarranted by the evidence. As to the first part of this statement there could be no complaint, for the fact that the deceased came to his death by chloroform poisoning was practically conceded by the prisoner. The contest was over the question whether the poison from which he died was self-administered and his death was due to suicide, or was feloniously administered by the prisoner and his death due to murder.

In the interview which was testified to by E. J. Linden, Superintendent of Police, the prisoner gave his own account of Pitezel's death. He found him, as he alleged, on the floor of a third-story room in the Callowhill Street house, dead. He said he was led to the third floor by a note left for him on the table in the front room on the first floor, directing him to search for a letter in a bottle in a closet opening off the same room. In the bottle, he says, he found a long letter telling of the purpose of the writer to commit suicide, and that his body would be found on the third floor. Going to that floor he alleges he found Pitezel, dead. A large bottle with the chloroform stood nearby, and leading from it to the dead man's mouth was a tube with a quill inserted in it so as to reduce the aperture for the flow of the fluid.

He says he felt that the appearances of suicide should be removed or a defence might be made to the policy upon that ground. To do this he dragged the body down to the second floor, broke the bottle, scattered some inflammable liquid over the face and beard of the dead man and set it on fire to give to the body and the room the appearance of an explosion and the happening of death by accident.

The theory of the defence included, therefore, the idea that Pitezel's death was due to chloroform poisoning, and the objection must relate, therefore, only to the statement that the doctors had testified that the poison could not have been self-administered. The post mortem examination had disclosed the presence of an ounce and a half of chloroform in the stomach at that time. How did it get there? As the story of the prisoner indicated, by a slow process of self-administration by means of the tube, or in some other manner? Upon this subject medical experts were called. They explained the effects of the drug upon the nerves and brain, and upon the lining of a living stomach. They gave two reasons why the chloroform could not have been self-administered in the manner alleged by the prisoner. In the first the intoxicating quality of the drug would cause such semi-conscious or purely involuntary motions of the muscles, and changes in the position of head and body, as would break the connection between the bottle and the mouth by means of the alleged tube. In the next place the chloroform had not affected the lining of the stomach, in other words, it had been introduced into the stomach after death. This testimony fully justified the statement of the learned Judge now complained of, and the assignment of error is overruled.

The eleventh assignment alleges error in the answer to a point submitted on behalf of the prisoner. The instruction asked by the point was somewhat involved. It was in substance a request for an instruction that, if the jury should believe the deceased died from chloroform poisoning, and that it was possible for him to have administered it to himself, and that this theory was as consistent with the facts in the case, as that it was administered with criminal intent by the prisoner, then the verdict should be not guilty. This was another way of saying that if the theory of suicide was as consistent with the facts as the theory of murder, then the prisoner should be acquitted, and it might have been affirmed without more. The answer, though not categorical, was in effect an affirmance. It was, "If you believe he (the deceased) did it himself, why of course the prisoner is not guilty." When to this is added the general instruction that the burden of proving the guilt of the prisoner beyond a reasonable doubt remains upon the Commonwealth from the beginning to the end of the trial.

If, therefore, the jury adopted the theory of suicide, or if, being unable to adopt it, they were yet unable to accept beyond a reasonable doubt the theory of murder, in either event they were told the verdict should be not guilty. This fully guarded the rights of the prisoner, even if it be conceded that a categorical affirmance of the point would have been in better form.

This brings us naturally to the tenth assignment of error which denies the clearness and adequacy of the exposition by the learned Judge of the doctrine of the reasonable doubt. The passage from the charge embodied in the assignment of error is the least important part of the instruction given to the jury upon this subject, and does not fairly represent the learned Judge. He said in immediate connection with the passage complained of: "In all criminal cases, gentlemen, it is essential that the defendant shall be convicted by evidence which persuades the jury of the guilt of the prisoner beyond a reasonable doubt. By a reasonable doubt I do not mean an obstinacy or a resolution not to consider the testimony of the witnesses carefully. But it is that condition of the mind in which hesitancy arises after having given the evidence a fair consideration, and you find yourself unable to come to a conclusion as to the guilt of the prisoner." This was a full and adequate presentation of the subject. Take the passage embodied in the assignment in connection with that we have just given (and they stand in immediate connection in the charge) and it is apparent that the prisoner has no just ground of complaint because the doctrine of the reasonable doubt was not fully stated and brought into sufficient prominence.

The remaining assignment is to the whole charge, which, it is insisted, was wanting in clearness, was not impartial, but was calculated to prejudice the minds of the jurors against the prisoner by giving undue prominence to such circumstances and considerations as were hurtful to him. It must be borne in mind that the defendant called no witnesses. The evidence before the Court and jury was only that of the Commonwealth, which had been gathered together for the purpose of clearing up the mystery surrounding the death of Pitezel and fixing responsibility for it upon the prisoner. His real reliance was upon the reasonable doubt. The web of circumstantial evidence that had been woven about him consisted of many threads, but the web taken as a whole was strong.

It was impossible for the learned trial Judge to present the case to the jury in an intelligent manner without the strength of the circumstantial evidence being felt. This was not due to the rhetoric of the learned Judge, for he indulged in none. It was due to the convincing character of the facts and circumstances themselves, and to the completeness with which an adroitly arranged and badly executed scheme had been unravelled by the Commonwealth, and its detail laid before the Court and jury.

"We have examined this charge as a whole carefully, and with a view to the question raised by this assignment, and we cannot agree that it is inadequate or that it is wanting in fairness of spirit. The evidence was reviewed, for the benefit of the jury, with reference to its bearing upon the great questions submitted to them for final determination. These were stated in their proper order:

First. Was the body that was found in the Callowhill Street house the body of B. F. Pitezel? This seemed to be quite clear of any difficulty.

Second. If the body was that of Pitezel, did his death result from chloroform poisoning? This was asserted as a fact by the medical witnesses, and was assumed by the prisoner in his statement to Superintendent Linden.

Third. If Pitezel died from chloroform poisoning, was the poison self-administered, with suicidal intent, or was it feloniously administered by the prisoner? This was the only real point of controversy.

Finally, was there upon the whole case a reasonable doubt of the prisoner's guilt of the murder charged in the indictment?

This review was not elaborate, but it was adequate. It presented the questions of fact clearly, and laid down the legal rules by which the jury should be guided in investigating and determining them. "We are satisfied that this assignment is without merit and that it should be overruled.

The defendant had a fair trial, and that is all he has a right to demand. At one stage of the trial he was placed perhaps at a disadvantage for a short time by his own conduct in dismissing his counsel and assuming the responsibility of conducting his own defence; but the Court was in no sense responsible for this. The prisoner and his counsel were; and the learned Judge did all that could reasonably be done to protect him from himself, as well as to secure to him a fair trial, upon evidence restricted to circumstances of the admissibility of which there was no reasonable doubt. In no respect has any just ground of complaint been made to appear, and the judgment must be affirmed.

It may be well before concluding this case to say that the object of a trial before a jury is to ascertain with as much certainty as can be attained in a human tribunal the guilt or innocence of one charged with crime.

When, as the result of such a trial, a verdict has been rendered against the prisoner, it ought not to be set aside by the trial Judge, or by proceedings in a Court of Error, unless in some essential particular the trial has been erroneous. No merely technical or formal objection not affecting the result should be listened to. It is neither for the credit of the Courts, for the interests of society, nor does it tend towards the repression of mob violence or the preservation of good order, that the course of justice should be blocked or turned aside by technical objections which, however valuable they may once have been, are now, and long have been, empty shells; or by verbal distinctions that in this age mark no real differences. The prisoner has been found guilty of murder in the first degree by a jury after a protracted and a fair trial. No substantial error in that trial has been pointed out. The evidence fully sustains the verdict and we are not disposed to disturb it. All the assignments of error are overruled and the judgment appealed from is affirmed.

APPENDIX IV:
from THE NEW YORK TIMES, MAY 8, 1896

HOLMES DIES DENYING HIS GUILT

Before His Hanging He Asserts That He Did Not Murder Any of the Pitezel Family

SPOKE CALMLY FROM THE SCAFFOLD

Leaves Minute Directions, Through Which His Lawyers Believe They Can Prove Him Innocent

HIS BODY BURIED IN CEMENT

The Hanging of H. H. Holmes in Moyamensing Prison Yesterday Morning Was Attended With Few Sensational Features, But the Condemned Man Made a Cool, Straightforward Statement from the Gallows Denying That He Had Ever Committed Murder—The Drop Broke His Neck, But It Was Fifteen Minutes Before His Heart Ceased to Beat—He Was In Good Spirits All Morning and Conversed Freely With His Friends—Leaves No Money, But a Mountain of Manuscript—According to His Own Instructions, His Body is Embedded in a Ton of Cement in a Vault in Holy Cross Cemetery

May 8th, 1896.

Holmes walked up the steps of the gallows in

Moyamensing Prison yesterday morning more steadily than the priests at his side, and made a speech to the men who had been invited to watch him die more calmly than any man in the little party could have made it. He told them in an unshaken voice that he was innocent of the many crimes charged against him, and repeatedly denied the murder of Benjamin F. Pitezel and the three Pitezel children. His nearest approach to murder, he said, was the criminal operation performed by him on Miss Emmeline Cigrand and Mrs. Julia Connor, the two women who had been in his employ in Chicago.

When he had completed his statement he put his arms around lawyer Rotan, who stood beside him, and whispered a few last words of farewell. Then he stepped backwards to the centre of the scaffold, submitted quietly to the shackling of his hands, and when Assistant Superintendent Richardson was adjusting the black cap and noose he said, with a slight smile on his face:

"Take your time, Richardson; you know I am in no hurry."

The fixing of the noose occupied but a few seconds, and in muffled tones from under the somber cap came the words:

"Good-bye—good-bye, everybody."

The murmured responses from the crowd were

drowned in the crash of the falling trap doors, and the body fell swiftly downward until the narrow rope grew taught and stopped it with a fierce jerk. It swayed and moved about for several minutes, the hands opening and closing convulsively and the back and chest heaving. Then, very gradually, the swaying ceased and in fifteen minutes the flock of doctors hovering about the body said that there was no life left in it. The drop fell at 10:12 ½ o'clock, and the fall had dislocated the neck.

No autopsy was performed, and the remains were turned over to Lawyer Rotan, who caused them to be conveyed directly to Holy Cross Cemetery, where a vault had already been secured. In accordance with Holmes' written instructions they were placed in a large box half-full of cement, and on top of them sufficient more of the same material was packed in, so as to completely fill it. In this way the body was incased in a solid block of cement weighing a little over a ton. It will be buried later.

Holmes left no will, but gave explicit instructions to Lawyer Rotan as to the disposition of his small estate. He left very little money but turned over a great may papers and documents, most of them in the form of letters to be mailed after his death.

AS HOLMES CHOSE TO DIE

When the priests left Holmes' Wednesday night

he was very weak and tearful, but in the light of later events it is apparent that his condition was the result of the many excitements of the day, rather than of a general breaking down, as was feared. The only man who remained with him was Keeper George Weaver, the night watch, who asked the condemned man if he proposed to go to sleep, receiving a low-spoken reply in the affirmative. He undressed slowly and almost painfully, saying very little and taking but little interest in the conversation of the guard.

"I don't know where I'll sleep to-morrow night," he said, when he had gone through his brief devotions and stretched himself on the couch. "But nobody knows that."

He turned his back towards the light that was burning just beside the open door of his cell, and almost immediately fell asleep. He moved only once or twice during the next six hours, and did not wake up at any time. The guard looked at his recumbent figure, at the piles of paper folded on the little table, at the picture of a woman on the wall, at the crucifix above the bed, at the folded clothes that were so soon to be a shroud, and at the well word slippers on the floor, which were never to be worn again. He knew Holmes better than anyone else knew him, and he was very heavy-hearted.

Refreshed in the morning

When the prison clock struck 6, Keeper John Henry, the day watch, came down the corridor to relieve Weaver and the two awakened Holmes. They called him twice and then shook him with considerable vigor before his eyes opened and his last night's sleep on earth ended. He sat up and greeted them almost cheerily.

"Good morning," he said, "is it 6 o'clock already?"

"Yes," replied Henry, "how do you feel?"

"First-rate. I was very tired last night and was glad to get to bed. I never slept better in my life."

He made some inquiries about trivial matters, and dressed as unconcernedly as a man might do who had a thousand more toilets to make before he died. The thought that he was now doing everything for the last time did not seem to affect him at all, and he ordered quite a substantial breakfast. Weaver left and Henry took the guard seat at the door, Holmes resuming work at the almost innumerable letters which he felt himself called upon to write just prior to his execution. These letters are to go to all the women he has married, to most of his relatives and even to the friends of some of his victims. He has written out, also, very minute instructions to his lawyers as to the disposition he wants made of his entangled estate.

The minutes passed rapidly. It was just 8 o'clock when a keeper bearing the condemned man's breakfast came in, followed almost immediately by Lawyer Rotan. The young attorney glanced anxiously into Holmes' face, and when he saw it lit up with a smile of welcome his own brightened.

"You're all right," he said, "You look lots better than you did last night."

He Tests His Nerves

In reply, Holmes held out his left arm with the fingers of the hand separated and said:

"See if I tremble."

There was no tremor noticeable, although the guard looked too, and Holms and his lawyer almost immediately fell into a lengthy and earnest conversation. It concerned the padcking of the body after the execution, in dembent, a plan that was thought out by Holmes during the long days that he spent in prison waiting for death. Rotan told him that he had been offered only the day before $5,000 for the remains, and had put the man who made the proposition out of his office.

"Thank you," said Holmes quietly, "I'll see that no one gets my body, either by buying or stealing it."

A little after 9 o'clock Fathers Daily and McPake came into the cell and were warmly greeted by Holmes. He was just finishing his breakfast, and they remarked that his appetite had not failed him. Superintendent Perkins, Assistant Superintendent Richardson, who was to do the hanging, and several other prison officials stopped on their morning round to visit the condemned man, and he chatted with all of them without the slightest nervousness.

When the breakfast dishes were removed Holmes wrote a few words on a piece of paper and handed it to Lawyer Rotan with the remark that he would never touch pen to paper again. The words were a brief sincere tribute of personal affection and gratitude for all that the attorney had done for him. After this last writing Holmes turned himself over entirely to the priests, and from that time on until the drop fell they were always with him. He entered into the ceremonies of the fearful occasion with a solemn face, but did not for a moment show signs of depression.

Gathering of the Witnesses

While Holmes was on his knees in his little cell saying over and over again his final prayers there was a most businesslike activity in the offices and reception room of the prison. The fifty-one people who had been invited by Sheriff Clement to witness the execution had all arrived by 9 o'clock, many of them coming in carriages and leaving in front of the gray building a row of vehicles to help attract a crowd, occasionally having to call in the assistance of a policeman.

On the inside there was a dampness in the air and a smell of a prison. The witnesses moved restlessly about from the stone roadway in the centre of the main entrance to the reception room, which opened from it, asking each other if they had ever seen a hanging before. Most of them had not. The gathering was a very curious mixture of youth and old age, the juvenile newspaper reporter on his first assignment of the sort rubbing elbows with the gray-haired physician who had seem more executions than he had time to talk about just then.

In addition to the fifty-one people in the Sheriff's party it was discovered that some of the Prison Inspectors had taken advantage of their official position bring in between twenty-five and thirty of their personal friends, who mingled freely with the other guests. The Sheriff was very indignant at this, and called public attention to the fact that, while he had done all he could to keep the number of witnesses down, his endeavors had gone for naught. The question of ejecting the outsiders was debated for a few minutes between the Sheriff and his two solicitors, and it was abandoned because of the lateness of the hour.

Swearing in the Jurors

The twelve men who were to constitute the jury were called together in the reception room by the Sheriff and lined up before a long table, where they were addressed by Assistant Solicitor Grew. The latter explained their duties in as few words as he could, and at the conclusion he administered the oath which bound them to report truthfully the cause of the death they were about to witness. They all took the oath and signed the pledge.

The jury was composed of Ex-Sheriff William H. Wright, Dr. Benjamin Pennebaker, Ex-Sheriff John J. Ridgway, Select Councilman R. R. Bringhurst, Samuel Wood, Dr. W. Joseph Hearn, Dr. W. J. Roe, E. B. Detweiler, Dr. M. B. Dwight, Dr. J. C. Guernsey, James Hand and Dr. John L. Phillips. It was a curious coincidence that Samuel Wood, a yarn manufacturer of Germantown, who was a member of the Sheriff's jury, and saw the execution, was also a member of the jury that tried and convicted Holmes.

After the swearing in of the jury there was quite a long wait, during which the nervousness of most of the witnesses perceptibly increased. Superintendent Perkins and his assistants, Dr. Butcher and Inspectors Cullinan and Hill made mysterious visits to the gallows and to Holmes' cell, both of which were in the long corridor running north from the reception room. When the door leading into this corridor opened and closed a glimpse cought be caught of the scaffold.

The March to the Gallows

At 10 o'clock sharp President Perkins asked the

jury to fall in line, and back of them everybody else took up a more or less favorable position. The door was opened and down a short flight of steps and across the asphalt pavement the long procession of men with bared heads and grave faces paced slowly by the endless row of cells. The one in which Holmes stood awaiting his final call and listening to the steady tramp of the men who had come to see him die was closed tight, and in front of it two guards were stationed.

The scaffold reached entirely across the corridor, with a door on one side permitting the witnesses to pass through. When the last man had crossed the threshold of this door it was closed, shutting off all observation. Almost on the instant, the door of Holmes's cell opened and he stepped out between Fathers Dailey and McPake, followed by Assistant Superintendant Richardson and Lawyer Rotan. He had demanded the privilege of the latter's presence on the scaffold, and Sheriff Clement gave his reluctant consent.

Superintendent Perkins and the Sheriff walked arm in arm up the thirteen steps which led to the scaffold, and behind them came the chanting priests, whose white robes made even that gruesome scene look picturesque. Holmes, when he reached the scaffold, held a crucifix in his hand, and continued praying until the priests stopped. Then he opened his eyes, lifted his head and walked to the edge of the scaffold facing the white faces of the crowd below. Between him and this crowd was a semicircle of uniformed guards. The rail reaching to his waist ran around the edge of the scaffold, and on this he rested his hands as comfortably as if he was himself a spectator and the rest of the little party a show.

He Calmly Denies It All

There was nothing pitiable in the picture made by the condemned man as he stood looking calmly down upon his audience. His slender frame was clothed in a loose-fitting suit of black and above the cutaway coat appeared a white handkerchief knotted loosely about his throat. His face was more than pale—it was yellow. His brown moustache and hair had been recently been trimmed, but it cannot be said he presented a good appearance. The prison pallor on his face gave one a chill. He looked dead already.

When he had surveyed the crowd he began to talk, and his tones were as steady and smooth as those of an orator making an after-dinner speech. He made no gestures, but his words were emphasized here and there, and everything he said was plainly audible. No one else in the crowd could have kept as steady a voice.

"Gentlemen," he said, "I have very few words to say. In fact, I would make no remarks at this time were it not for the feeling that if I did not speak it would imply that I acquiesced in my execution. I only wish to say that the extent of the wrongdoing I am guilty of in taking human life is the killing of two women. They died by my hands as the results of criminal operations.

"I wish also to state, so that no chance of misunderstanding may exist hereafter, that I am not guilty of taking the lives of any of the Pitezel family, either the three children or their father, Benjamin F. Pitezel, for whose death I am now to be hanged. I have never committed murder. That is all I have to say."

The Fall of the Drop

As he spoke the last sentence he turned half around and put his right hand on Lawyer Rotan's broad shoulder. He smiled as he said:

"Good-bye, Sam. You have done all you could."

He whispered a few other words and then hugged the young attorney, who almost ran down the scaffold steps when he was released. The priests motioned to the condemned man to kneel, and he did so, still grasping the little crucifix in his hands. For two minutes his lips moved in silent prayer, and he arose steadily to his feet when he had finished. He shook hands with the greatest heartiness with Fathers Dailey and McPake, turning again and for the last time to face the audience as the priests resumed their chant.

Richardson now stepped forward, and drawing Holmes' hands behind him dexterously handcuffed him. The man stood as straight and steady as one of the black beams beside him, looking quietly upon the last human faces he was ever to see. Sheriff Clement and Superintendent Perkins left the scaffold and Richardson drew the black cap down over Holmes' face, the latter remarking as he did so:

"Take your time about it. You know I am in no hurry."

His advice was not needed. Richardson unwound the rope from about the beam, ran out the noose, and slipped it over Holmes' head. As he drew it tight about he neck there came in muffled but steady tones:

"Good-bye—Good-bye, everybody."

Richardson stepped back and dropped a handkerchief. The black boards on which Holmes stood parted in the middle, and down through the opening his body fell, stopping with a jerk that knocked his head to one side and sent his legs swinging far out towards the spectators. The horrible contortions lasted for a minute, the body turning round and round and the legs swaying backwards and forwards as if the man were struggling to break the merciless rope. The back and chest heaved, the fingers opened and closed repeatedly, and there were twitchings around the exposed neck.

Dead in Fifteen Minutes

From this ghastly spectacle most of the spectators turned to look at the whitewashed walls. Two of them fainted and one fell, but was quickly brought to his feet. The dangling body slowly but surely settled at the end of the rope, and gradually all movement ceased. Drs. Butcher and Sharp felt the pulse and put their ears over the heart. For fifteen minutes they were unable to discern heart beats, and at the end of that time they pronounced him dead. All the other doctors present did and said the same thing.

The crowd of spectators took to wandering about the corridor, and most of them were relieved to know that the body would not be lowered until it had hung for another quarter of an hour. After life was extinct Lieutenant Tomlinson was permitted to bring his sergeants and patrolmen and they marched in line by the scaffold, each one critically surveying the corpse. It was about the strangest reception that a man could imagine, and it made one shudder to hear the comments. The policemen seemed to enjoy the spectacle.

When the delay began to seem intolerably long Dr. Butcher gave permission to lower the body, and it was let down onto a truck very much like a bag of meal is sprung from a truss. The officials had a very hard time with the rope. The noose had sunk deep into the flesh and did not easily become unloosened, and Superintendent Perkins refused to have it cut off, although Lawyer Rotan begged him to do so. After several minutes of struggling the job was accomplished and the black cap taken off.

To Prove His Innocence

The dead man's face was a thing too ghastly for description, and even the doctors turned from it. An examination of the neck showed that the axis had been separated from the atlas by the fall, in other words that the neck had been broken. No autopsy was performed on it, and Lawyer Rotan stood by the truck on which it lay to see that Holmes' wishes in this respect were obeyed. While standing there he was asked what the contents of the papers were that Holmes had turned over to him. He replied:

"I have not gone over them yet, but I understand they are mostly directions to his attorneys to keep up the effort to prove his innocence of murder."

"Does he want that effort kept up?"

"He does and he believes it will one day be successful. So do I."

"Did he leave any money with which to prosecute a search?"

"He did not leave any with me—not one cent."

The arrival of the undertaker's wagon at this point attracted Mr. Rotan's attention in that direction. He superintended the handling of the corpse, and saw that it was well taken care of. As the wagon drove out through the tremendous crowd awaiting it at the west gate the young attorney followed it into the street. He did not return to the prison and it will be a very long time before he goes there again.

It was not very long after the lowering of the body that the crowd of spectators began to thin out. They left he prison one by one, facing all manner of questions when they passed through the mob waiting at the gate, and giving thanks for the privilege of breathing the free air and seeing the good old sun shine once again. Assistant Superintendent Richardson was frequently congratulated on the success of the execution and he said just as frequently that Holmes was the nerviest of the sixty-seven men he had seen die. Superintendent Perkins said the same, and so did the physicians.

Some of those who witnessed the execution were: Dr. J. Howard Taylor, Chief Medical Inspector of this city; L. G. Fouse, president, and Solicitor Campbell, of the Fidelity Mutual Life Association; Colonel J. Lewis Good, of the Board of Health; Hoxie Godwin, of the Sheriff's office' R. R. Mason,

Sheriff of Baltimore, who said that it would soon be his duty to hang five men; A. S. Eisenhower, Chief of the Bureau of City Property; Assistant District Attorney Samuel A. Boyle. William E. Peterson, of the Board of Health; Detective Captain Peter Miller, Detective Frank Geyer, Ex-Sheriff Horatio P. Connell, Coroner Samuel H. Ashbridge, Police Lieutenant Benjamin Tomlinson, Deputy Sheriff John Ertel, Dr. William J. Scott, one of the witnesses at the trial; Dr. S. J. Ottinger, Dr. J. C. DaCosta, Dr. Joseph Hearn, Deputy Sheriff Williamson, Frank A. Monaghan, Deputy Sheriff John B. Meyers, Major Ralph F. Culinan, Inspector Hill and Prison Agent Camp.

BODY BURIED IN CEMENT

Unique Method of Interment Devised by the Murderer to Protect His Body From Ghouls

The body of H. H. Holmes reposed last night in the vault of the Holy Cross Cemetery. All that is mortal of the celebrated criminal is now firmly incased in a box of cement, hard as granite, and weighing more than a ton.

Attorney Rotan arranged for the interment and followed the express wish of Holmes in every detail. Having a horror of the dissecting room and knowing that medical men would like to examine his brain, the cunning criminal evolved the scheme of being buried in a solid ball of cement which would resist all ordinary agencies of attack and insure his body immunity from ghouls, who were not armed with dynamite and allowed plenty of time for the task of securing the coveted cadaver. Unique in life, Holmes will be unique in the grave. When the interment takes place, which will probably be to-day, the incidents of the usual burial will be absent. The undertaker will simply have the task of rolling a dead mass of impenetrable cement, weighing two thousand pounds, in a hole large enough to contain it. There will be no empty coffin for the clods to rattle against.

It was a few minutes before noon when Undertaker J. J. O'Rourke, whose office is at the corner of Tenth and Tasker streets, drove to the Moyamensing Prison with an undertaker's wagon. In this wagon was an ordinary pine box in which the body was placed. The wagon was then driven out of the Reed street entrance to the prison and hurried to the yard back of the residence of Mr. O'Rourke. Here was the larger box and five barrels of cement and sand. The mortar was hurriedly mixed and a layer perhaps ten inches deep was placed in the box, which was first put in the wagon on which it was to be hauled to the cemetery. On the top of this was placed the body of the felon, attired as he was when he dropped through the trap.

Packing in the body.

A silk handkerchief was placed over his face and then more mortar was piled into the box. It was packed tightly around the lifeless form and soon covered the still features. After the wondering eyes of the two Pinkerton detectives engaged to watch the body had taken the last look that will ever be had of Holmes' body more mortar was thrown into the box until it was full. The lid was then nailed down and the wagon started away for Delaware county, where Holy Cross Cemetery is located.

It was nearly 2 o'clock when the undertaker's wagon reached the cemetery. There an unexpected delay was encountered. The superintendent R. B. Campbell, refused to allow the body to be placed in the vault without special instructions from Joseph F. Haley, a clerk in the Cathedral, at Eighteenth and Race streets. In vain Mr. O'Rourke pleaded and exhibited the stub of the burial permit which had been issued by the Board of Health in this city, and the permit from the borough of Yeadon, secured in exchange for the one issued in Philadelphia. Mr. O'Rourke also had a document signed by Father Dailey and know as "Lines for a Christian Burial," a necessary step to secure interment in a Catholic cemetery. Superintendent Campbell was obdurate and said that he had to obey orders.

There was nothing to do but dispatch a man to secure the permit from Mr. Haley. After a tedious wait of three hours the messenger returned and then preparations were made for removing the box and its heavy contents to the vault. To pull the box out of the wagon and let it drop onto the ground was a comparatively easy matter. To move it after it was on terra firma was different. Mr. O'Rourke, his two assistants, the two detectives and a couple of attaches of the cemetery took hold and lifted, but the box did not move. Again they heaved and strained and succeeded in breaking the handles, but the hardened cement refused to budge. The men were in a quandary. They had never had such a task before and they regretted that they did not have a block and tackle, such as is used for moving safes.

Trouble at the Cemetery.

Finally the group of reporters who had been watching the proceedings came to assistance of the men. Thirteen pairs of stout arms seized the corners of the box, and by dint of shoving and pulling moved it inch by inch into the vault. Once there the vault was closed and the group of tired and perspiring workers all left the cemetery, except the detectives. They remained all night, keeping a lonely vigil over the vault in which was the oblong box of cement, which serves as a shroud for the man whose name will be mentioned more frequently today than that of any other mortal, living or dead.

Undertaker O'Rourke does not know when the burial will take place. Under the customs of the Catholic church there need be no more religious ceremonies connected with Holmes, and it is unlikely there will be any. It is probably that Mr. O'Rourke will delegate the matter of interment to the cemetery authorities, in which case the burial can be made quietly and without attracting undue notice. Certain it is that it will be done at a time when few people will be around and without any fuss or display. No more men will be there than will be necessary to move the cumbrous box in which the body is imbedded as firmly as if in a cast iron mold.

Before a body can be deposited in the Holy Cross Cemetery it is necessary that the fee of $4 for digging the grave and $1 for the use of the vault by paid. This amount, $5 was sent to the Cathedral office Wednesday night by the undertaker. Father Dailey also called the Cathedral and explained the matter so that there need be no hitch.

The lot or grave in which Holmes will be buried has not yet been bought. This will have to be attended to soon as it is against the law to keep a body more than three days in the vault. Mr. Rotan will either select the lot or else will delegate the choice to Mr. O'Rourke.

As soon as he was notified that the execution had taken place, Undertaker O'Rourke filed a return of death with the Board of Health. This was recorded by Registry Clerk Theodore M. Carr, and in deference to the notoriety of the deceased, he made the record with red ink. The certificate of death, which was signed by Benjamin F. Buther, M.D., gave the nae of the deceased as Herman W. Mudgett, alias H. H. Holmes, and further described him as white, male, 35 years old, married.

The cause of death was stated as "Hanging according to the law." Undertaker O'Rourke in his certificate did not give any occupation for the deceased, and gave the broadly indefinite location, United States, as the place of birth, and named the Holy Cross Cemetery as the place of burial.

Was Holmes Hung?

CHICAGO, January 20 —The Inter-Ocean has this remarkable story this morning: "H. H. Holmes was never hanged in Philadelphia on May 7, 1896, as the newspapers reported and as the people who witnessed the alleged execution believed. On the contrary, as he always declared, he cheated the gallows. He is today alive, well and growing coffee in San Parinarimbo, Paraguay, South America." This is the substance of a long story. A dummy was used for hanging.

from the EL PASO DAILY HERALD, JANUARY 20, 1898

2017 APPENDIX

H.H. HOLMES' BURIAL SITE

SATURDAY MAY 6, 2017

On the eve of the 121st anniversary of his execution...
four hours after the exhumation hole had been filled in.

H.H. HOLMES RISES FROM THE GRAVE, 2017

By Matt Lake

If H.H. Holmes were your average common-or-garden serial killer, his story would end with the bad guy getting buried, and everyone thinking justice had been served. But there's nothing normal about the story of H.H. Holmes. His arrest and incarceration had been a boom time for newspapers covering the lurid details of his death. And why should an execution get in the way of that?

It wasn't long before newspapers started to speculate about the unusual circumstances of his execution, and what they might have concealed. Holmes had made a lot of money selling his story, the rumors went, what might he have spend it all on? Maybe he bribed the hangman and witnesses and doctors to fake the hanging. And that weird cement coffin—couldn't that have been used to conceal the body of somebody who wasn't H.H. Holmes at all? What if he faked his own execution, and escaped?

This was exactly the story that circulated in the fake news sites of their time—the yellow journalism of the gutter press. One of them went so far as to suggest that Holmes had absconded to an obscure town in a South American country, and was living out his life with the proceeds of his crimes and the sales of his book. And that story circulated through the nation's newspapers as fast as 19th century re-Tweeting could.

It's a story that Holmes's own descendants have held onto for more than a century. And in the spring of 2017, the culmination of this particular strand of family lore came to the public attention once again. Several of Holmes's direct descendants—his great-grandchildre John and Richard Mudgett and Cynthia Mudgett Soriano—petitioned the Delaware County court for permission to exhume his ancestor's grave and conduct DNA tests on the remains. The Mudgett family provided DNA samples for comparison purposes. This would finally set the story to rest, reasoned Mudgett, and enable the family to close that chapter of family history.

Under the supervision of Judge Chad Kenney, the courts granted permission for the exhumation to take place, and a lot was excavated in Section 15 of Holy Cross Cemetery. Despite the insistence of the courts that a carnival atmosphere be avoided, at least one helicopter circled overhead during the big dig, with NBC10's reporter George Spencer in the passenger seat providing commentary with cameras trained on him and the scene below.

Shortly afterwards, a van from Petrosh's Big Top, a local party supply rental store, delivered a tent to cover the excavation. The only cameras present were affiliated with the History Channel, and were capturing footage for a documentary featuring another of Holmes's descendents, Jeff Mudgett, as he uncovers the story of his notorious ancestor.

A week later, the hole was filled in, and the site went back to normal. And until Jeff Mudgett appears on the History Channel in his documentary, nobody except for Mudgett, his documentary crew, and the DNA labs at the Anthropology Department of the University of Pennsylvania will know exactly what they uncovered.

"SAVE ME FROM ETERNAL DAMNATION"

The really exciting news to come out of the media circus surrounding Holmes's exhumation came from an unlikely source: A family safe deposit box in New Jersey. A retired company executive Larry Fannelle and his wife Claire caught one of the news segments on NBC 10 out of Philadelphia. The name H.H. Holmes had been bandied around the family after Claire's aunt had passed away and she had sorted through some books in a box.

What she found there was almost as explosive as the nitroglycerine Holmes had tried to use to kill Ben Pitezel's widow: A note written and autographed by Holmes in a family Bible.

Better than that, the Bible belonged to one of the two priests who was present at Holmes's execution. And even better than that, the note was dated 7th May, 1896, the day of Holmes' execution.

The Bible belonged to a cousin of Claire Fanelle's great grandfather. The cousin, Father Patrick J. Dailey, was a Catholic priest at the Annunciation of the Blessed Virgin Mary, right next to Moyamensing prison. Contemporary news reports mention Father Dailey repeatedly. He and Father McPake were the two priests who met Holmes at 9 o'clock on the morning of his execution, accompanied him to the gallows with their chanting, waited for him to make his final address to the crowd, and prayed with him for two minutes before he ascended the gallows.

The Fannelles found the Bible in a box of family books in the early 2000s, and were curious about the value of the book itself. It was in pretty poor condition, with yellowed and loose pages and, strangely, newspaper articles tucked in it. As they examined the newspaper articles, they began to learn the story of the famous case that their relative had been connected to. But what surprised them most was the fly leaf to the Bible, which had Father Dailey's name in pencil, and an inked inscription in another hand.

The inscription is shaky in places and part of it is pretty much illegible. But the signature and handwriting look very similar to the many examples of Holmes's handwriting that are in the public record. The inscription itself reads as follows:

Dear Father Dailey,

I must write and make you know the kind feelings I have for you [*a few illegible words follow*]. I know that you by God's Grace have done much to save my soul from Eternal Damnation. I need your prayers after my death. With all my heart,

H. H. Holmes

May 7th, 1896

The flaky century-old paper it was written on was kept inside a plastic sleeve for protection—it had years ago come loose from the binding of the Bible and had been tucked back between the pages alongside newspaper clippings of the Holmes case, some of them as much as forty years after the execution, showing that the family had at one point actively kept track of the story. But as the story faded from the news, the family passed the book around from family member to family member, without really knowing its significance.

The Fannelles believe that Holmes's inscription conveys a sense of remorse at the eleventh hour. He's appealing to a man of the cloth to pray for his soul after he dies. He's thanking the priest for doing what he could to save his soul from Eternal Damnation (with capital letters, no less).

From anyone else, it could sound like genuine contrition. But we suspect that if Frank Geyer had read this inscription—and he may have done, since he witnessed the execution—he would have another interpretation: This reads like a charming con man telling a priest the kind of thing that would make him feel good about himself—an interpretation that's far more in keeping with Holmes's character.

Of course, in this case, Holmes could not have profited from charming a potential mark—there's no profit to be made if you're twenty minutes away from death—but for a practiced people-pleaser like Holmes, winning people over must be a hard habit to break, even when he was minutes from having a noose placed around his neck.

Made in the USA
Columbia, SC
30 April 2018